SEXUALITIES
& SOCIETY

For my mum, Cyn, whose wit, advice and humanity are much missed

MEGAN TODD

SEXUALITIES & SOCIETY

An Introduction

Los Angeles | London | New Delhi
Singapore | Washington DC | Melbourne

Los Angeles | London | New Delhi
Singapore | Washington DC | Melbourne

SAGE Publications Ltd
1 Oliver's Yard
55 City Road
London EC1Y 1SP

SAGE Publications Inc.
2455 Teller Road
Thousand Oaks, California 91320

SAGE Publications India Pvt Ltd
B 1/I 1 Mohan Cooperative Industrial Area
Mathura Road
New Delhi 110 044

SAGE Publications Asia-Pacific Pte Ltd
3 Church Street
#10-04 Samsung Hub
Singapore 049483

Editor: Natalie Aguilera
Assistant editor: Eve Williams
Production editor: Katherine Haw
Copyeditor: Audrey Scriven
Proofreader: Jill Birch
Indexer: Megan Todd
Marketing manager: George Kimble
Cover design: Francis Kenney
Typeset by: C&M Digitals (P) Ltd, Chennai, India
Printed in the UK

Library of Congress Control Number: 2020935621

British Library Cataloguing in Publication data

A catalogue record for this book is available from the British Library

ISBN 978-1-4462-7428-6
ISBN 978-1-4462-7429-3 (pbk)

CONTENTS

CONTENTS

ABOUT THE AUTHOR

Megan Todd is Senior Lecturer and Course Leader in Sociology at the University of Central Lancashire. Her research focuses on sexualities, gender and violence; she has published on issues relating to intimate partner violence, ageing, health, feminisms and homophobic and misogynist abuse online. Megan has been involved in a range of research projects, including LGBT+ domestic abuse service users in Lancashire. More recently, she is developing work on universities' management of their LGBT+ heritage. She has been teaching sociology in Higher Education for nearly two decades, prior to which she taught English literature at secondary school.

LIST OF TABLES

ACKNOWLEDGEMENTS

This book was completed whilst at the University of Central Lancashire and I would like to extend my gratitude to my understanding colleagues there. Thanks too, to all my undergraduate and postgraduate students, who have been consistently inspiring. The initial idea for the book came from Chris Rojek at SAGE. Anyone who knows me will be aware that this book has taken a long time to come together – a series of moves and losses are part of the story – thus I would like to thank Natalie Aguilera, John Nightingale, Delayna Spencer, Eve Williams and Katherine Haw (an embarrassment of riches) for their patience, advice and encouragement. I am also grateful to the anonymous reviewers, who provided incisive feedback on early drafts.

Special thanks to those family and friends who have been patient (Ness!) and generous enough to discuss many of the themes in the book. Crow, in particular, for her sharp mind and enthusiasm. My biggest debt is to my dad, Allan, and my partner, Cat, for their continued support, sympathy and help, and who under my anxious gaze, read the entire manuscript and still managed to find positive things to say.

Chapter 6 was originally published in 'Intimacies' with S. Hothershall, in C. Yuill and A. Gibson's *Sociology for Social Work* (Sage, 2010) though it has been significantly revised. Similarly, aspects of Chapter 12 appeared in 'Sexuality and Health' in A. Barry and C. Yuill's *Understanding the Sociology of Health* (Sage, 2011). I am grateful to the publishers for permission to revisit the material.

INTRODUCTION

A quick glance through the magazines for sale in supermarkets, or a scroll though the many 'confessional' reality shows on television, such as *Sex Tape* or *Sex on the Couch*, is a timely reminder of the proliferation of cultural products which are attempting to tell us something about sexuality. Sex, it would seem, sells. Sexuality can be exciting, embarrassing or frightening. It can also be divisive, provoking fierce debate and strong emotions. Issues about marriage, adoption and contraception, for instance, still prompt heated discussions. Sexuality, as we shall see, is everywhere. It is written in laws, reproduced in medicine, plastered over billboards and floats through the air on the radio waves. All of these arenas, and more, have been used to invoke ideas of normality. But, look closely enough and we will also find challenges to those constructions of the norm.

As we progress through the book, we will be asking a series of questions of both ourselves and society. For instance, we will interrogate what, if any, differences there are between **sex**, **gender** and **sexuality**. We will reflect on what assumptions dominate our thinking about sexuality and where these come from. There will be time spent looking at the ways in which ideas about sexuality have been forged through history, conflict and politics. Global differences in relation to understandings of sexuality will also be acknowledged, though this text is written in the **west** and arguably brings with it a perspective which comes as a result of that.

In order to approach these issues, and more, we will be looking at a range of theories and examples from research into sexualities. I will tell my own, brief, sexual story at this point and 'come out' as a feminist, lesbian and sociologist. These subject positions, as well as others I hold, have shaped the questions I ask, the examples I use and the thoughts I share with you. You need to bear that in mind as you read on; you may agree with me, you may disagree, but that is part of the joy of academic research into something as diverse as sexuality.

Given the widespread presence of sexuality and sexual images in modern popular culture, it is arguably more necessary than ever to attempt to study and explain the origins and social construction of this aspect of human society. The study of sexuality is, however, in many ways, a relatively new discipline within sociology. In part, as we shall see in the forthcoming chapter, this is the result of the relative lack of 'presence' of both women and those of diverse sexualities within the academic world. This lack of 'presence' applies to sociology itself, as well as to other academic disciplines. Perhaps significantly, sociology is seen as having 'founding fathers', with many women thinkers being excluded from the official list – this is still a problem in academia, with various school curricula in the UK being accused of continuing to erase the contributions of female academics. Even more significantly as regards the study of sexuality, these male classical theorists assumed, to a greater or lesser extent, that gender differences between men and women were the result of 'natural' divisions based on biology. Ideas concerning the issue of sexuality were entirely absent from their works which, at bottom, were 'essentialist' works.

Fast-forward to the twenty-first century, however, and we find that interest in sexuality and its related topics is rapidly expanding. This has led to a relative explosion of theory and research on sexuality and how it intersects with other social categories, such as gender, social class, ethnicity, age, (dis)ability and religion. Hopefully, by the end of this book, you will have a better understanding of the theory–research connection and can position yourself on the intersection of sexuality with the other social categories you occupy, as you reflect on the impact of sexuality in your everyday life.

What's in a name?

At this point, it might be useful to think a little bit about language. Language is powerful and reveals much about its historical and social contexts. Terminology matters and has been the cause of many an argument, and no doubt some of the vocabulary I use in this book will offend some (and if it does, I apologize, no offence was meant) whilst pleasing others. One reason why it is difficult to write about sexuality is that the available terminology can be difficult to negotiate and is often inadequate. Social, cultural and political events impact on words which are deemed appropriate or otherwise. Language reveals one's political allegiances, it marks the 'tribe' to which we belong and can so easily offend. Before we begin unpacking sexuality, therefore, it may be useful to have a brief discussion about the language in this book. 'Sexuality' or 'sexualities' refers to sexual identity (or orientation, though I tend to avoid this term), rather than simply sexual activity; sexualities, of course, indicates that there are multiple expressions of any given sexual identity. It also references the point that sexuality is fluid, fragmentary and fragile. Many texts on sexuality tend to focus on the minority, those who differ from the norm. That is not my intention in this book, as whilst there will be many examples from **LGBT+** lives, because arguably that is where most research has been done, it is important to interrogate that unmarked norm, heterosexuality. I have chosen, where possible, not to use the term '**homosexual**', it being derived, as we shall see, from nineteenth-century sexology and having many negative connotations associated with medicalization. Instead, where possible I use 'LGBT+' (**lesbian**, **gay**, **bisexual** and **trans** – the '+' indicates that it is inclusive of other identities, such as **queer**), currently the favoured reference in the UK (LGBTQI is perhaps more common in the US) or 'lesbian' and 'gay man', because these are the terms more usually used by the lesbian and gay community. Also used often is the phrase '**coming out**' to refer to those (LGBT+) people who acknowledge their sexuality openly and the related 'closeted' (someone who has not come out of the closet). It is also important to recognize, too, that coming out is not a one-off event as decisions about when and where to disclose one's sexuality can be a daily experience. None of these terms are adequate to express the range of experiences and expressions of sexuality, no one label fully captures the experiences of those to whom it refers. This language, as we shall see, also places the text very firmly in the west. But we must use the best words we have to hand, as best we can, whilst acknowledging that many labels were forged through a bitter or violent history, and thus are painful.

A brief guide to the book

This is an introductory textbook, and as such it doesn't include all that could possibly be written about sexualities. Instead, it reflects both my own interests, topics I've taught, and stories and issues which are particularly pertinent or illustrative more generally. If you are studying sexuality, or gender, media, politics, families, religion, health or the **life course**, hopefully you will find aspects of the book useful. It is divided into three parts: the first explores the history of sexuality before moving on to look at theories of sexuality, and finally it considers how research into sexualities has been, and could be, conducted. The second part focuses on sexuality and culture. Within, are chapters on some key social institutions and their relationship to sexuality: the media, religion, our intimate relationships, the political sphere, and finally the impact of living in a global world. The third and final part deals with a few 'issues' pertinent to sexualities. We begin with a focus on identities, before moving on to consider how youth relates to sexuality, and then older age. The penultimate chapter turns attention to the ways in which health impacts on understandings of sexuality, and finally we examine how sexualities can be framed by violence.

Although it is absolutely fine to read this book by going straight to a particular chapter, you may find it more useful if you start by reading the first two chapters before moving on to your favourite topics. Whilst the individual chapters make sense in their own right, they are interlinked, and in order to avoid repetition, certain issues may only be mentioned briefly in one place if they are more developed elsewhere. Each chapter will have some 'discussion points' where you may be asked to reflect on a question or engage in a little research of your own, and there will also be suggested readings if you wish to study a topic in a little more depth. Some words may appear in bold within a chapter and this indicates that there is a definition within the glossary, should you wish to check it.

What *is* sexuality?

What is 'sex'? Sex today 'serves a multiplicity of purposes, including pleasure, the establishing and defining of relationships, the communication of messages concerning attitudes and lifestyles, and the provision of a major mechanism for subjection, abuse, and violence'. It 'assumes many forms' and 'is bound up with more things' than ever before. (Plummer, 2003: 19)

In advance of starting proper, perhaps we had better start thinking about the subject of this book – sexuality. Sexuality, typically, is constructed as being located in the private sphere (a sphere and association feminists have problematized). In contemporary societies of the west, sexualities and sexual identities are considered central to a meaningful life, and on a fundamental level, constitute one of our basic human needs and rights. Indeed, it is so important that the World Health Organization (WHO) has gone to the length of providing a definition of sexuality as the integration of 'somatic, emotional, intellectual and social aspects of sexual being, in ways that are positive, enriching and that enhance personality, community and love' (WHO, 2006). This is a radical take on sexuality and a marked shift from how it was seen only a few decades ago. As we go through this book, we will start to look at the ways in which sexuality is related to emotion, identity, politics and culture. We have seen, in a relatively short time, a transformation from seeing sexuality as rooted in nature, as a universal experience, to **social constructionist** approaches, to the (reformist?) framing of sexuality as a 'right', such as the right to form committed relationships.

In order to think usefully about sexuality, we first need to consider the ways in which gender, sex and sexuality are inextricably linked. *Gender* is often understood as a system which divides society into two categories – masculine and feminine – and is relational, in that one cannot understand what is meant by 'masculinity' without having some notion of what it is to be 'feminine' and vice versa. Gender is something which organizes virtually every aspect of our lives without us thinking about it. Sometimes it is difficult for us to see it in operation precisely because it is everywhere; we are called upon to declare our gender when we walk into public toilets or changing rooms, it's stated on our birth certificate, driving licence and passport. Because of this, gender can seem natural. However, much research (for example anthropologist Margaret Mead's observations in Papua New Guinea) highlights the fact that gender is not expressed in the same way across the globe or over time. Many people reject the gender binary system, identifying as **non-binary**. We can therefore argue that gender is socially constructed; it is often conceptualized as the social and cultural expression of sex. The **binary** system, crucially for feminist thinkers, operates as a set of hierarchies, in that we tend to privilege the masculine over the feminine. It is a system of power therefore and not just about observable differences (or similarities). Understanding that gender is socially constructed, however, means that there is potential for change; the system has not always operated in this way and need not continue to do so.

When gender is used in feminist analysis, it is frequently defined in relation to *sex*. Feminist thinkers were the first to separate gender from sex. In our society we tend to recognize only two sexes – male and female – but it is important to state that this is not a universal approach to, or experience of, sex, as we shall see in later chapters. Sex is often conceptualized as the natural, or biological, differences between men and women. This binary system may not be as stable as we might think; if we were to take a cross-sample of society and test their chromosomes, hormones, genes, physiology and so on, very few of us would fit neatly into the 'ideal' male or female categories. Many sociologists would argue that how we categorize sex is also influenced by culture.

Ideas about *sexuality* are intimately tied up with gender and sex. Heterosexuality is viewed, in contemporary western society, as the appropriate or proper expression of gender. A stereotypical 'masculine' man is assumed to be **heterosexual**. Within western society, it is argued that we privilege men; active male sexuality is acceptable and expected, appropriate female sexuality is passive and synonymous with the reproductive role – motherhood is the only acceptable expression of female sexuality. Penetrative heterosexual sex (penetration of a vagina by a penis) in our society is deemed to be 'real' sex or natural sex. This is reflected in our legal codes; it is only relatively recently, for example, that UK law has broadened the definition of rape to include the penetration of an anus (so men can now be legitimate victims of rape). Heterosexuality is a powerful conceptual tool in society; Adrienne Rich (1980) refers to 'compulsory heterosexuality', the idea that heterosexuality is the default or obligatory sexuality. Sexuality, therefore, only really makes sense in relation to those other categories of sex and gender.

Before you progress to the first chapter, I would like you to pause for a moment and write down a few thoughts on sexuality – what is it, where does it come from? Pop these notes into the back of the book, and I will encourage you to revisit these at the end ...

TIMELINE

1835 – Last two men – James Pratt and John Smith – are hanged in the UK for 'homosexual' acts

1880s – Mortimer Granville invents an electric device to massage muscle aches (the vibrator)

1882 – Dr Wilhelm Mensinga invents the diaphragm, which has to be prescribed by gynaecologists

1895 – The trial of Oscar Wilde takes place

1896 – The earliest known pornographic film, *Le Coucher de la Mariée*, is screened in Paris: it features a 'striptease'

1901 – Havelock Ellis asserts that women can enjoy sex and that same-sex desire is an inborn trait

1916 – Margaret Sanger opens the first birth control clinic in Bookyln, New York: it is shut ten days later and Sanger is imprisoned

1919 – Magnus Hirschfeld founds the Institute for Sexology in Berlin: it is destroyed by the Nazis as 'ungerman' in 1933

1919 – Latex condoms are invented

1920s – Japanese and Australian scientists devise the 'rhythm method' of pregnancy prevention based on the menstruation cycle

1921 – Three MPs attempt to make sexual acts between women illegal in UK: it is unsuccessful on the basis that legislation would draw attention to lesbians and encourage more women to try it!

1921 – Margaret Sanger founds the American Birth Control League

1930 – Hollywood Production Code bans references to 'homosexuality' in US films

1938 – Birth control is decriminalised in the US

1947 – Institute for Sex Research (Kinsey) is founded

1948 – Adoption of the Universal Declaration of Human Rights

1950 – Ernst Grafenberg publishes a study of the role of the urethra in female orgasm and is eventually recognized as having discovered the 'G-spot'

1953 – First issue of *Playboy* magazine is published by Hugh Hefner

1961 – The UK launches the contraceptive pill, available only to married women

1967 – The contraceptive pill is made more widely available in the UK

1967 – The Sexual Offences Act decriminalizes sex between two men over 21 'in private'

1967 – The Abortion Act UK legalizes abortion for women up to 24 weeks pregnant

2

1969 Police raid the Stonewall Inn in New York, prompting riots which mobilize the LGBT+ community across the world

1969 – Gay Liberation Front is founded in New York

1969 – Canada legalizes contraceptives and abortion is no longer illegal, though it remains heavily restricted

1970 – London Gay Liberation Front (GLF) is established

1972 – The Pill is made available countrywide to unmarried women in the US

1973 – First issue of *Playgirl* is published

1973 – First UK Rape Crisis Centre is established

1974 – 'Homosexuality' is removed from the *Diagnostic and Statistical Manual of Mental Disorders* (DSM), and no longer categorized as a disease

1979 – The UN General Assembly adopts the Convention of All Forms of Discrimination Against Women

1981 – AIDS is first reported in *The New York Times*

1988 – UK Prime Minister Margaret Thatcher passes Section 28 of Local Government Act: local authorities cannot 'promote' homosexuality and teachers must not promote homosexuality as acceptable as a 'pretended family relationship'

1988 – Canada overturns abortion restrictions, making abortion accessible to all Canadians

1990 – The World Health Organization declassifies homosexuality as a mental disorder

1991 – Rape in marriage becomes a crime in England and Wales (Scotland had recognized this in 1982)

1994 – Age of consent between two men lowered from 21 to 18 in the UK

1998 – The FDA clears Viagra for sale to treat impotence

2001 – Age of consent between two men is lowered from 18 to 16 in UK

2000 – The Netherlands becomes the first country to legalize same-sex marriage

2003 – UK Labour Government repeals Section 28

2003 – UK Communications Act makes it illegal to send images that are 'grossly offensive' of an 'indecent or obscene' nature, though whether 'dick pics' themselves are illegal between adults is unclear

2004 – UK Gender Recognition Act

2005 – Canada legalizes same-sex marriage

2005 – UK Civil Partnerships laws

2008 – UN Security Council Resolution 1820 is adopted, recognizing that sexual violence can be categorized as a war crime and calling for protection from violence in refugee and displaced persons camps

2009 – Grindr, a dating app aimed at LGBT+ people is first released

2010 – Hungary replaces its gender equality unit with a board of just two people

2012 – Tinder, a heterosexual dating app, is first released

2013 – Russia passes legislation which forbids 'propaganda' promoting 'non-traditional sexual relations'

2013 – India criminalizes 'homosexual' acts

2012 – United Nations pass resolution outlawing Female Genital Mutilation

2013 – Uganda passes an act which states that the promotion and practice of 'homosexual' acts could result in life imprisonment

2014 – Same-sex marriage becomes legal in England and Wales on 29 March and Scotland on 14 March

2016 – Turkish Government publishes a parliamentary report to tackle the rising rate of divorce that recommends couples should seek marriage counsellors, many of whom are religious imams or clerics: the number of feminicides nearly quadruples between 2011 and 2018

2016 – China, whilst enacting a new law on domestic violence, also closes groups advocating women, especially those with a particular focus on domestic violence: it is still very rare for a woman to get a restraining order against a perpetrator

2016 – The Armed Forces Act 2016 removes 'homosexual acts' as grounds for discharge

2017 – Russia partially decriminalizes domestic violence

2018 – Lord Ivar Mountbatten becomes the first member of the extended British Royal family to have a same-sex wedding

2019 – *Statutory Guidance on Keeping Children Safe in Education 2019* includes advice on sexting

2019 – Voyeurism (Offences) Act 2019 is extended to include 'upskirting'

2020 – Preventative HIV drug PrEP to be made available in England from April

2020 – Same-sex marriage is legalized in Northern Ireland

PART I

THEORIES AND METHODS

1

HISTORIES OF SEXUALITY

─────────── **Learning outcomes** ───────────

By the end of this chapter you should be able to:

- Recognize the ways in which meanings of sexuality are historically constructed
- Reflect on the relationship between historical context and the formation of sexual cultural norms and concepts
- Explore your own attitudes to, and understandings of, sexuality and consider how they are shaped by history

Introduction

To write a history of sexuality is perhaps a surprisingly challenging task; despite the fact that it often seems like sex is something everyone else is doing, or at least talking about, historically, desire often went unrecorded. The record of desire that we do have was, for the most part, not written by women either – little wonder then, that the histories we have as given to us by poets, playwrights, historians and medics, have largely ignored women's sexuality or presented it in particular and restricted ways. It is also an undertaking made more difficult when we have to remember that we must try not to view what our forebears were up to through a contemporary, or present-minded, lens. Yet, such a history of sexuality is necessary if we are to chart the ways in which, as British historian Jeffrey Weeks (2004) suggests, sexuality is to be understand as an ideologically determined social construct, rather than something rooted in biology. Though this textbook looks at global sexualities, a global history of sexuality would need a book all of its own, thus this chapter will predominantly focus on a western history of sexuality, as that is what has had the largest impact on the theories we will be exploring later on. In order to do this, we look at ideas of sexuality which have come from the Classical World, i.e. the Ancient Greeks and Romans. We then briefly turn to the increasingly important role (Christian) religion began to play in defining and circumscribing sexualities and sexual behaviours (see Chapter 5 for more on this). Finally, we consider the continuities in thought introduced by the new 'science' of sexuality.

FACT FILE

The earliest recorded chat-up line?

One poem from Ancient Egypt, dating from around 1800 BCE, has one male god attempting to seduce another by saying 'What a lovely backside you have!'. This shows that same-sex desire is not a recent invention, and studies of a large number of cultures and societies show that this was not 'imported' from one culture to another.

Ancient Greece and sexuality

Sexual relations in Ancient Greece

It has been the civilizations of Ancient Greece which have perhaps had most relevance for later ideas about sexuality in Europe. Much of our language of sexuality is derived from the language of ancient Greek – nymphomania, aphrodisiac, narcissism – which starts to tell us something about the society. Their written culture was often concerned with sex, with heroes such as Hercules 'ravishing' virgins. Particularly important is the widespread belief that the Ancient Greeks were tolerant of 'homosexuality'. So persistent was this belief that Victorian and early twentieth-century writers often referred to male same-sex relations as 'Greek love'. To an extent, this has arisen because, as Wilton (2000: 37) has noted, 'many of the most important historical figures from ancient Greece seem to fit a contemporary definition of homosexuality'. Figures who openly and 'unashamedly' had same-sex lovers include such philosophers as Plato and Aristotle, military conquerors like Alexander the Great, and writers such as Sappho. Sappho, for instance, was a poet who lived from about 630–570 BCE on the island of Lesbos. Although only fragments of her poems survive, many suggest that, in addition to clear sexual desires for other women, she also had sexual relations with women. It was the name of her island which, in the nineteenth century, gave us the terms 'lesbian' and 'sapphism' to describe same-sex love and sexual relations between women.

Hupperts (2010: 29) asserts that the fact that Ancient Greeks had stories about their gods that sometimes involved them having same-sex relations is significant. This is because the Greeks imagined their gods anthropomorphically; they had passions and sexual desires which were the same as those experienced by humans. Thus the mythologies of Ancient Greece are a reliable indicator of sexualities and sexual behaviours in their societies. For instance, a 4th-century BCE historian reported the custom of 'kidnapping' of youths by older men, as part of the ritual of initiating the younger males. This involved the youths being given presents and spending two months in the countryside with their older lovers. On their return, the youths became part of an elite group. In Sparta, same-sex relations between adult males and youths were part of the military training process. This included penetration of the youth by his older lover and the term used to describe this was *lakonizein* – 'to do it the Spartan way'.

The problem of 'concepts'

However, historians have pointed out that it is not correct to see Ancient Greece as being tolerant of same-sex relations in any modern sense. In part, this is because the idea of a specific type of person who was gay was unknown in the culture of classical Greece. Ancient Greece lacked the concepts and words of 'heterosexual' and 'homosexual', and thus didn't divide people into clearly-defined groups consisting of specific *types* of persons, such as heterosexuals, gay men or lesbians. In fact, such concepts are relatively new ones.

Few Greeks took the view that a man who loved a boy had a different identity to a 'heterosexual' man (Hupperts, 2010). In the course of an Athenian man's life, both forms of sexuality could appear together or in succession. This is in marked contrast to modern times, when the social construction of such types has led to an assumption that you are either one or the other, and has prompted doomed attempts to discover what 'causes' non-heterosexual behaviours. For the Ancient Greeks, what today is referred to as '**sexual orientation**' was essentially a matter of personal taste as opposed to a permanently-defining characteristic of personal identity. This, in turn, raises three important questions:

- Why, since the nineteenth century, have modern societies come to see a person as either 'gay' or 'straight'?
- Why has the existence of different sexualities come to be seen as being so important?
- Why have some sexualities been – and still are – punished by social exclusion, imprisonment or even death?

Discussion point

'The past is another country: they do things differently there.'

Do you think this quotation from the prologue of L.P. Hartley's novel *The Go-Between* (1958: 7) shows that sociological attempts to understand modern-day sexuality by looking into the past are bound to fail?

Power relationships and sexuality

Ancient Greek society was extremely hierarchical, and the main social division was between free adult male Greek citizens and everyone else (women, youths, slaves, foreigners). Thus, as in most societies – past and present – the **power** relationships of political life shaped wider cultural relationships, including those of sexualities and gender relations. The various communities in Ancient Greece were extremely patriarchal. As a result, artistic and written depictions of sex, whether gay or straight, are almost exclusively by men, about the actions of men, for other men.

An adult male Greek citizen could have sexual relations with anyone who was not also an adult male Greek citizen. In addition, in such relationships, the adult man was expected to be the 'active' partner, i.e. to be the one who penetrated. The sexual preferences of such men did not really matter, although there might be some teasing if someone exhibited a very strong preference for male partners. However, although any kind of penetration by adult male Greek citizens was acceptable, it was considered shameful for such men to be penetrated themselves. Men who played the passive role were considered to have 'made a woman' of themselves – yet, apart from social opprobrium, such relationships were not punished.

These attitudes are significant in that, arguably, they have had a lasting impact on contemporary ideas about what constitutes 'sex' and how we view sexuality in gendered terms, serving to galvanize ideas about men and women. US legal academic Catherine MacKinnon argues in 'Does Sexuality have a History?' that the 'sexualization of aggression or the eroticization of power and the fusion of that with gender such that the one who is the target or object of sexuality is the subordinate, is a female, effeminized if a man, is relatively constant' (1992: 122–3).

The significance of pederasty

Therefore, it was entirely acceptable for an adult man to take a non-adult male partner, in fact, this was encouraged as a way of training youths in all aspects of Ancient Greek culture, including military training. Plato's *The Symposium* (written about 380 BCE) refers to the desirability of a society being built on the love between adult men – according to one of the characters in the dialogue, it would be impossible to have a better state or army than one consisting entirely of lovers and loved: '… a handful of such men, fighting side by side, would defeat practically the whole world' (1951: 43).

Such cultural practices have led to a long and intense debate about the nature of the relationship between Achilles and Patroclus as depicted in Homer's Ancient Greek epic poem (dating from about 750 BCE), the *Iliad*. The term used to describe the sexual relationships between youths and adult men was *pederasty* ('boy love'), with the youth known as the *eromenos* ('the beloved'), and the man as the *erastes* ('the lover'). Most scholars have seen the Achilles–Patroclus relationship as a literary example of pederasty.

This alternative form of sexuality was highly regarded in Athens: there were no laws forbidding it, and it seems to have not been unusual for a man to have a 'boyfriend' even after marriage. In fact, according to Hupperts (2010: 35), it sometimes happened that boyfriends were brought into the family circle. He also argues that, because sexual desire and pleasure were central to pederasty, promiscuity was common, with men who had had many partners gaining an enhanced reputation. Pederasty is an example of a sexual practice which, if viewed from a contempaory perspective, is troubling. It is often confused, in modern society, with paedophilia but from an Ancient Greek perspective was not considered exploitative but rather an important social custom and an essential part of growing up. This was also a society with a different understanding of childhood. It is also interesting to note that many who view the practice as abusive do not get so angered about the fact that this was a culture where girls as young twelve were often married off to older men (Cavanaugh, 2017).

However, pederasty was not the only form of same-sex behaviour in Ancient Greece: there are several black-figure vases which show adult men courting other men. Such depictions are particularly common in the work of a painter known as the 'Affecter', who operated between about 550 and 520 BCE, while Athenian red-figure vases, which date from about 530 BCE onwards, often show seductions between youths of a similar age.

Sappho and same-sex relations between women

The only explicit mention of lesbian sexuality in Classical Greek literature occurs in Plato's *Symposium*, in the speech by Aristophanes, but he is somewhat reluctant to label such women as 'women who love women exclusively' (1951: 47). Moreover, instead of using the term *eros* (used by him to describe male sexualities) to describe the erotic feelings that women have for one another, he uses the more neutral term *trepesthai* ('to be focused on'). Given the patriarchal structure of Ancient Greek society at the time, it is perhaps not surprising that same-sex relations between women were received slightly less enthusiastically, as such a relationship was perhaps viewed as one which was rejecting the dominant, 'natural' order of things.

Yet, as Sappho's poetry shows, there existed in many early Ancient Greek communities a 'system' of adult women educating girls which was very similar to the adult man–youth system of pederasty. As well as woman–girl same-sex relationships, Sappho's writings also make it clear that love affairs between adult women also took place. However, as the city states evolved, greater emphasis was placed on marriage for girls, who remained increasingly within the home. As a result, female same-sex love was increasingly marginalized.

Discussion point

Hidden from history?

Consider why the mapping of a history of women's sexuality has perhaps, at best, been a history of *terra incognita* (an unknown land). A land, we might add, which has at times been thought of as dangerous, intemperate and wild.

Roman culture and sexuality

Galen, a prominent Roman physician of the second century CE, believed that the differences between men and women were the result of heat. Men are fully developed due to sufficient body heat. Women, on the other hand, are underdeveloped because of coldness – they are damp, leaky and imperfect. From this grew beliefs that masculinity is synonymous with heat, action, reason and courageousness, with femininity their opposite; femininity is read as putrefying, unstable and threatening. It becomes possible, from this perspective, for men to become 'feminized' if they adopt supposedly 'feminine' characteristics such as passivity or emotionality. Such a model privileges 'man' with respect to 'woman'; masculinity is the yardstick against which all else is measured.

Power to the penis

Like Ancient Greece, Rome was a hierarchical and patriarchal society, and women in Rome were generally the property of the men of the family. Masculinity was understood not only in terms of self-government and the control of those from lower social orders, but also with regard to dominance in sexual relations. Ancient Rome was a **phallocentric** culture and many of the words that we still use for the penis come from the Romans. Often these words denote violence and aggression, such as 'sword', 'dagger' and 'tool'. Sharing an ideal of masculinity with the Greeks, where sexual relations mirrored social relations, Roman masculinity was based on physical penetration of social inferiors, whether that was women or slaves. Men were constructed as sexually active and women were understood as their sexual opposites, i.e. passive and there to be penetrated. Whilst it was assumed that men would be sexually interested in both women and men, sex needed to reflect social status. Thus, Julius Caesar's alleged relationship with Nicomedes was widely derided, not because he was in a relationship with a man but because it was believed that he assumed the 'feminine' role of being penetrated. Self-control was important too. Larson (2012) shows that moderation in matters sexual was advised because it reflected a man's ability to exercise political power.

Regulation of women

Control of women, their bodies and sexuality, was closely connected to regulation of the state, e.g. a husband had the right to kill his wife on the spot if she was found guilty of adultery, whereas attitudes to male fidelity were, surprise, surprise, somewhat more relaxed. It was expected that he may have sex with servants of the house or prostitutes as long as he was the penetrator and they were of lower status: only sex with another man's wife constituted adultery for men (Larson, 2012). He also had the right to divorce his wife if he felt she was drinking excessively. It was allowed that women could express their sexuality within marriage and, at various moments, women who had several children were rewarded with special privileges.

Also, as with Ancient Greece, prostitution was a part of social life which was often organized by the state. Whereas in Greece, higher status prostitutes could wield a degree of power, in Rome, prostitution was viewed as a more degrading role but a necessary one all the same. One sex act which was felt to be unsavoury was oral sex of any kind. Cunnilingus was considered disgusting, which tells us something about the importance of female pleasure, and Pompeian brothel graffiti such as 'Theodosia sucks cock well' (Keegan, 2014: 257) reflects the fact that fellatio was also considered a degrading act, only really fit for prostitutes to perform.

Roman attitudes to female same-sex desire were also rather dismissive, which again was not surprising given the general outlook on women. Those who formed sexual relationships with other women were known as *tribas*, meaning 'to rub', and the term was often used as an insult. Society wasn't outraged by such relationships, but they were considered 'not quite right', perhaps because they were seen to be excluding men and it was presumed that such women were assuming a 'male' role in sex. Indeed, some thought that *tribas* had enlarged clitorises which they used to penetrate their partners, such was the phallocentric understanding of 'sex'.

Like a Virgin? Early Christianity and the Middle Ages

The cultures of the Mediterranean world – Greek, Roman and Jewish – had a huge impact on medieval society in Europe, with many of their ideas being passed down and filtered through Christian teachings. Saint Augustine of Hippo was perhaps the most influential writer, famous for ranking women according to how much sexual activity they engaged in (virgins, widows, wives) from best to worst! As we have seen, sexual renunciation had begun to be viewed as an ideal form of masculinity by Late Antiquity, a belief which continued with the new religion of Christianity. Sexuality has been, and still is, strongly affected by religious (or other supernatural) beliefs, as we shall further explore in Chapter 5, but it is useful to reflect a little on the ways in which modern-day ideas about sexuality have their origins in this period, where we see a growing discomfort and anxiety in relation to the sexual body.

Early Christianity was somewhat conflicted about sex. On the one hand, it idealized chastity; lust was associated with Adam and Eve's original sin and ascetics (people who were celibate) were considered to be closer to heaven. However, it also realized that in order to survive sex was necessary. Marriage became a key way for the Church to control sexuality and people were judged for what they did, with whom and how. Sex should only happen in marriage, and it should only happen for the purposes of reproduction and definitely without a hint of passion. Second wave feminists have pointed to the ways in which patriarchal attitudes have enabled capitalism to thrive and such an argument might explain some of the attitudes during this time. By the later Middle Ages especially, society had become more mercantile and many families had sizeable inheritances to pass on to their children. Thus, regulation of marriage and the idea of no sex outside of marriage became more important to preserve a family's status. People's sexuality and sexual behaviours began to be judged according to what were perceived to be the 'rules' of nature: for instance, would those acts result in reproduction? Potentially non-procreative forms of heterosexual sex become frowned upon, such as anal sex, sex standing up or women on top. We also see the Church beginning to regulate when sex could and could not take place, e.g. not on Sundays, feast or fast days, at night-time only and when virtually fully clothed. Those who had same-sex relations were grouped together with others, including those who used contraception, whose sexual acts would not result in procreation, so masturbation, oral sex and bestiality were a no-no. Laws around prostitution, adultery and sodomy in particular were heavily enforced. In 1533, for instance, Henry VIII introduced the 'Buggery' law, where 'sodomy' – the insertion of a penis into any anus, male, female or animal – resulted in hanging.

Eve was framed and shamed

Women's sexuality in particular, though, was under scrutiny. As Helena Kennedy (1993) has argued, Eve was framed (and shamed) as the original seducer, and female sexuality was seen as an unnatural instrument of the devil. Hartnell (2018) asserts that during the Middle Ages women's bodies were believed to be biologically inferior to men's. As with the Ancient Greeks and Romans, in the medieval period it was believed that men's bodies were hotter, more vital. Women were colder, slower to grow, weaker and more fragile. Such misogynistic assumptions based on no scientific evidence, were used as a tool against women. The Catholic Church saw childbirth as women's punishment for Original Sin, and other religious discourses, such as Judaism and Islam, which equated blood with uncleanliness, used this as an excuse for demonizing women. Menstrual blood was believed to perish crops and drive animals mad; a sideways glance from a woman was thought to put a spell on men. Wombs were believed to give off deadly fumes if not 'purged' regularly. Having an 'inferior' and 'dangerous' anatomy became an excuse for barring women from virtually every key social institution; formal education was male-only (women's brains, it was argued, were too small and hence too much learning might cause their wombs to wander), and women were denied significant positions within the clergy.

As will be seen in the following section, the moral and sexual 'standards' drawn up by the various Christian religions were, in several ways, buttressed during the nineteenth century by developments in medicine, psychology and 'sexology'. Even though religion-based **essentialism** declined as a social influence, the following section will show how nineteenth-century scientific and psychological theories about the centrality of biological reproduction and what was 'normal/ abnormal', ensured a considerable continuity in the ways in which society thought about sexuality.

Modernity and sexuality

Although, from the late nineteenth century, science came to challenge and eventually to displace religion as the dominant way of explaining human behaviour and society, most of these forms of science had something in common with the religions: both were essentialist as far as understanding sexuality and gender issues. Most nineteenth-century science disciplines, including medicine and psychology, developed biological rationalizations of human sexuality and gender divisions.

The Enlightenment

From the 1680s to the start of the nineteenth century, what became known as **the Enlightenment** saw the emergence of ideas about sexuality which were in several ways the start of modernist conceptions of self and identity. At this time, the influence of the Church waned. There were some challenges to the patriarchal order (look at the work of John Locke, for instance) and a rise in pornography in novels such as the Marquis de Sade's.

There was a more rational approach to attempts to understand society and human behaviours which, according to Jackson and Scott, provided 'the origins of the modern self' (2010: 57). These rational approaches examined 'the laws of nature' – and tried to understand, and shape, the self. Ultimately, one of the main thrusts of the Enlightenment was to understand (in order to control) nature.

This emergence of a more rational approach began the slow process of secularization which undermined the influence of religious beliefs and the power of the Church. This process also affected the ways in which society reacted to same-sex relations. As noted by Sibalis (in Aldrich, 2010: 103), intellectuals in the eighteenth century began to discuss sodomy in secular rather than religious terms. The criminal law codes in many countries were eventually changed – and generally improved – as regards the legal status of 'sodomites'. In addition, distinct gay subcultures began to appear in the major urban centres of western Europe, and during the eighteenth century, despite continued persecution, ideas began to emerge that saw sexual acts between men as signs of a distinctive, and even exclusive, identity.

For Kant and the philosophers of the Enlightenment, the key was 'nature'. For them, sexual pleasure was nature's incentive for men and women to procreate and perpetuate the human species. Accordingly, same-sex desire was 'anti-physical' or 'unnatural'. The fact that it nonetheless existed was explained by them as arising from social or psychological causes, but not from nature itself. Thus, while they argued against harsh persecution and punishment as being both cruel and unnecessary (they believed social and moral reform would eliminate it), they continued to condemn it as contrary to 'nature'. As a result, from the Industrial Revolution and especially the late eighteenth century onwards, the Enlightenment's traditionalist 'scientific understanding' of the 'natural' division between men and women, and the 'unnatural' deviation of non-heterosexuals, became culturally dominant across the western world.

Urbanization and sexuality

From the late 1800s, as urban cities and populations grew as a result of the Industrial Revolution, the Church and government sought new ways to regulate people's bodies. People were working in closer proximity to one another and more anonymously than ever before and this raised the potential for a range of undesirable 'problems', such as the spread of sexual diseases and unwanted pregnancies. Foucault (1979) highlights the ways in which sexual acts gained new social significance, depending on who was doing what and where. Within marriage, for the purposes of reproduction, sex was fine – anything else was deemed 'immoral'. Based on middle-class values, the ideal woman emerged as one who was sexually passive, pure and innocent – 'the angel in the house'. As the gynaecologist William Acton (2013 [1871]: 162) said, 'the majority of women (happily for them) are not very much troubled by sexual feeling of any kind. What men are habitually, women are only exceptionally.'

Women in particular experienced a range of social and legal controls over their actions and bodies. For instance, the Poor Law Amendment Act of 1834 had a Bastardy Clause, in which unmarried woman with children were seen as not deserving of welfare – in other words, they were made responsible for their children whilst the fathers were not. Effectively, this reinforced the idea that poverty and immorality were negative aspects of women's sexuality which must be judged harshly and punished. Christian beliefs that women's sexuality was potentially disruptive and dangerous were linked to recent scientific enquiries into the transmission of sexual diseases. We see the old virgin/whore dichotomy at play again with the introduction of the Contagious Diseases Act of 1864. Rather than challenging the men who paid for the use of their bodies, or doing something about the social conditions which forced women to earn money this way, the new law resulted in the brutal 'treatment' of prostitutes, who were subjected to invasive and painful examinations. Again, this shows us how constructions of normality, such as female sexual passivity, rely on social institutions.

This period also saw an increase in the policing of acts such as masturbation – no longer was your right hand your best friend. 'Self-abuse', 'onanism' or 'the solitary vice' was believed to be the cause of various physical and mental disorders. 'Science' told teachers and parents that excess masturbation could lead to weakening of the muscles, blindness, and in excessive cases perhaps even death. One 'expert' on such matters stated 'that insanity arises from masturbation is now beyond a doubt' (Acton, 2013 [1871]: 109). Schools were encouraged to introduce plain diets and cold showers to avoid overly exciting and raising the temperatures of their boarders. Reprehensible as masturbation was for males, for girls it was an even graver situation. Extreme measures were sometimes undertaken to prevent girls from masturbation. Whilst we often think of FGM being a practice associated with 'other' cultures, clitoridectomy was, on occasion, used to prevent this practice.

Sexology

'Essentialist'/biological beliefs about sexualities and sexual behaviours were, from the late nineteenth century onwards, apparently supported scientifically by the emerging academic study of the 'science of desire': this tradition became known as sexology. The most important of these proponents were Richard von Krafft-Ebing, Havelock Ellis, Auguste Forel and Magnus Hirschfeld. In addition, Sigmund Freud – possibly the most well-known sexologist – and others, also studied and attempted to explain sexualities, including the existence of sexual 'perversions'. On one level, sexology helped undermine certain religion-based myths and assumptions about sexuality.

Whilst they made important contributions to extending our knowledge of sexual behaviours, they also attempted to classify and codify sexual behaviours, 'perversities' and 'traditions'. As a result, their coherent body of assumptions, beliefs and even prejudices contributed to the creation of a 'sexual tradition' which shaped, and to an extent still shapes, the ways in which individuals lived their sexualities. These attempts by sexologists to understand sexual difference, and especially to categorize sexual 'perversities', contributed to what Weeks has described as 'the codification of a "sexual tradition", a more or less coherent body of assumptions, beliefs, prejudices, rules, methods of investigation and forms of moral regulation, which still shape the way we live our sexualities' (Weeks, 2011: 6).

Arguably, there are certain similarities between the beliefs arising from sexology and those from the Christian tradition. This is the result of an 'essentialist' or naturalistic assumption that human sexuality is based on 'Nature', and that sexology provides the best way of understanding all its facets – and of classifying those different facets into clear and separate categories. In addition, these sexologists often disagreed with each other and, eventually, many were forced to admit that their attempts at classification had not been completely successful.

The underlying assumption of the science of 'sexology' was that, as with other animals, human sexual organs were primarily intended for reproduction. Such a traditionalist view seemed to be strongly supported by the evolutionary theories put forward by Charles Darwin and others. These theories and explanations effectively replaced the idea of some 'divine creation' with that of an on-going process of 'natural selection' which, like religion, placed sexual reproduction at the core of human development. They also seemed to provide a scientific 'naturalist' explanation of gender differences, which led to the view that non-procreative sexualities were hence perversions of the 'natural' process.

Yet this new sexological 'science', though it claimed to have established a new scientific body of knowledge around questions of sexuality and gender, to a large extent actually reproduced and legitimized existing patriarchal and heteronormative ideologies and values. Even those undertaking sexological studies who considered themselves to be reforming liberals, such as Havelock Ellis, were greatly influenced by pre-existing cultural assumptions (many of them religious-based) about 'natural' sexuality and sexual behaviour, ideas about the 'natural' differences between genders, and definitions of masculinity and femininity. As a consequence, any departures from these 'natural' behaviours came to be seen as 'abnormal inversions' or 'perversions'. Krafft-Ebing (1998 [1886]), for instance, distinguished four main 'perversions': sadism, masochism, fetishism, and 'contrary sexual feeling' ('inversion'). As a result of drawing on the moral culture of their time, their theories reduced sexuality and gender to the biological function of reproduction. This, in turn, merely reconfirmed existing social 'understandings' of sexuality and gender.

Kinsey

In the mid-twentieth century, sexology's attempt to catalogue human sexuality and sexual behaviour was taken a step further by the work of Alfred Kinsey and his colleagues. Although his background was in biology rather than in social science, his studies were in many ways sociological in approach. The importance of his work for an understanding of sexuality was that he revealed the diversity of sexual practices, and argued that much of what was defined as 'abnormal' was in fact quite common and therefore not 'deviant' according to scientific rules. In particular, the 'Kinsey Scale' suggested that, instead of there being a rigid opposition between two sexualities, most people's sexuality was located somewhere along a continuum.

Discussion point

Kinsey's categories

Kinsey's findings include evidence that at least thirty-seven percent of men had had a same-sex experience, culminating in orgasm, since the onset of adolescence. This clearly challenged the belief that those engaging in same-sex relations were a discrete identifiable category, clearly marked off from 'normal' sexuality.

- What are the implications of such a finding for the use of such terms as 'gay', 'deviant' and 'abnormal'?

Yet Kinsey had one aspect in common with earlier sexologists, in that he too tended to see sexuality as 'natural'. According to John Gagnon, this bias was linked to Kinsey's desire to 'justify' disapproved sexualities and sexual behaviour by arguing that all sexuality was biological in its origins and therefore 'natural'. Also, in his earlier studies, he tended to make assertions about the 'natural' differences between female and male sexuality. However, he recognized these earlier biases in his later work and, instead, placed more importance on social factors as shaping aspects of sexuality. For instance, he stated that 'the very techniques which have been suggested in marriage manuals, both ancient and modern, have given rise to some of the differences that we have thought were inherent in females and males' (Kinsey et al., 1953, quoted in Gagnon, 2004: 93).

Thus, Kinsey's later work, according to Liz Stanley (1995: 37), was 'located within a framework in which sexual behaviour and sexual convention are treated as malleable, as the products of culture and history and circumstance'. Although Kinsey believed that, ultimately, sexuality was 'natural', most of the work done by his contemporaries in the 1950s and 1960s was even less rooted in a social constructionist perspective and, instead, continued to endorse a biological and/or psychological approach. In fact, according to Stanley, such studies were based on a series of assumptions about sexuality – even when the evidence seemed to suggest those assumptions were, at best, inadequate. These assumptions included the following:

- 'Sex' was vaginal penetration; all other sexual practices being defined as 'petting'.
- 'Sex' was defined as heterosexual.
- Sex was entirely 'natural'; men and women were 'naturally' different as regards sexual desires and capacities, with men being treated as the norm.
- Sex was a biological and innate need or drive (although it could be shaped by social factors).

The medicalization of sexuality

The new science of sexology was a way of examining sexuality which was closely linked to the medical and psychological **paradigms** of the late nineteenth century. Many doctors and psychologists during the nineteenth century shared the religious values of the various Christian churches concerning sexuality, and even when they did not, they nonetheless attempted to apply and enforce their categories, 'standards' and 'understandings' on those they dealt with. This included the development and use of the term homosexual.

'Homosexual' was a Greco-Latin neologism, invented by a Hungarian doctor in the late 1860s, which rapidly became adopted to describe same-sex behaviours. According to Parkinson (2013: 9) '"homosexual" is a term coined in the nineteenth century as part of the medicalization of human sexuality, and it can sound as if it is reducing people to scientific curiosities'. Foucault saw this act of naming as helping to create a social category and sexual identity: 'sodomites' committed acts of sodomy, but 'homosexuals' were understood as being in possession of an inborn identity. The term was thus the product of nineteenth-century scientism, the medicalization of sexuality, and the idea of psychological make-up, and made a distinction between 'homosexuality', on the one hand, and the practice of non-heterosexual acts, on the other. As with all binary pairings, homosexuality as a concept makes no sense without its opposite, and thus the label 'heterosexuality' also began to be used at this time.

The culture of Victorian Britain was very much based on earlier Christian values and beliefs. This was especially evident when it came to government, religious and general public concern over some of the issues arising from rapid industrialization and urbanization. Middle-class Victorians were especially concerned with aspects of 'vice', such as prostitution, and as shown by the trial of Oscar Wilde, same-sex relations.

FACT FILE

The trial of Oscar Wilde, 1895

Oscar Wilde, an extremely successful and popular playwright, novelist, poet and essayist, became passionately involved with Lord Alfred Douglas (known as Bosie) towards the end of the nineteenth century. Wilde began a court case of libel against Alfred's father, the Marquess of Queensberry, but the trial revealed Wilde's 'sodomy'. Though advised by his friends and lawyer to flee the country, Wilde decided to stay, and was eventually arrested and tried for 'gross indecency' in 1895. He was convicted and punished for his sexuality by being sentenced to two years' hard labour. After serving his sentence (in Reading Gaol), he immediately went into exile in France where, following the French Revolution, sodomy had been decriminalized in 1791 – making France the first West European state to decriminalize same-sex relations between consenting adults. In 1900, his health broken by his time in prison, Wilde died at the young age of 46. Known for wearing a green carnation in his buttonhole, Wilde's conviction led many of London's bohemian circles – whether gay or not – to stop wearing them and to dive for cover in face of the public hysteria whipped up by the media and some politicians.

The expansion and institutionalization of natural science which followed on from Darwin's work influenced not just the emerging discipline of sexology, but also medicine and psychology in general, giving their views considerable legitimacy. The assumption was that science was simply a neutral, value-free, process of inquiry and investigation to establish 'true' facts. This ignored the fact that, when applied to sexuality, such investigations were carried out by scientists educated in a specific historical and cultural context in which the influence of religious ideas, if not of organized religion, was considerable. Furthermore, the specific context of the nineteenth century was that there was significant social concern surrounding sexuality and gender issues.

This markedly impacted on the direction of their investigations and the conclusions they came to. Hence, for instance, as we saw earlier, Acton, in an influential medical textbook, pronounced that 'want of sexual feeling' was a common condition among women (though he went on to add that most men, himself included, were fairly ignorant about the female 'condition'). Active sexual desires in women thus soon came to be explained, and treated, as physiological or psychological disorders. Even the sexual desires of men were seen as needing to be controlled by the civilized mind. Such attempts to control the 'lusts' of both men and women had much in common with traditional religious moral codes.

As Jackson (1996) has argued, these ideas did not emerge in a vacuum. At the time, feminists were protesting about an array of issues surrounding sexuality – prostitution, rape in marriage, the sexual abuse of children, domestic violence. These women were challenging the prevailing belief that men were victims of their sexuality, unable to control their urges, instead arguing that men's sexuality was used as a way of maintaining gendered social inequality (such arguments will be examined more closely in subsequent chapters). By placing sexuality within the sphere of the 'natural', in effect, these sexologists can be seen as protecting sexuality from a feminist critique.

Psychology

In some ways, Freud's psychoanalytic approach was an extension of the work done by sexologists such as Krafft-Ebing and Havelock Ellis. Freud's ideas and work became the basis of clinical intervention and therapy – as ways of treating/'curing' various sexual 'disorders' such as non-hetero sexuality. This should not come as a surprise, as his cultural milieu was the same as that of religious thinkers and the sexologists. Yet Freud did not regard same-sex sexuality as an illness or pathology, whether mental or physical. In addition, he also considered attempts to limit sexuality to heterosexuality as repressive and therefore psychologically damaging. In part, this was because he believed that human sexuality was neither absolutely masculine or feminine – instead, he saw a continuum between what were considered 'normal' and 'perverse' behaviours. To some extent, his work therefore challenged both the prevailing scientific approaches which, whether focusing on biology or psychology, were essentialist, and the moral norms of the late nineteenth century.

As many have argued, in Freud's ideas about sexuality and gender we can see a distinct tension between culture and biology as influences on human sexuality. As well as arguing that sexuality was the result of innate sexual drives and the anatomical differences between males and females, Freud also showed that sexual development and sexuality had a social context, and for him this was essentially the family rather than the wider society. Some of his terms, such as 'repression' or 'inhibition', refer both to internal drives which were inbuilt in the human psyche, and to external social influences which shaped human sexuality and behaviour. Additionally, rather than seeing sexuality as orientated towards procreation, he believed it was driven by '**polymorphous**' desire.

He also made reference to the tension between, on the one hand, pre-social sexuality, and on the other, cultural requirements and expectations designed to control and channel sexual drives in order to ensure the continuation of civilization. It was this tension which Freud believed led to neurosis. Although many aspects of his work were challenged and re-interpreted in the 1970s by Lacan (1977) and post-Lacanians, it is important to note that their work was to a large extent based on Freud's earlier writings. His work was also developed by radical writers such as Reich (1951) and Marcuse (1956, 1964), both of whom extended sexual repression from the family and located it firmly within wider society – specifically, the capitalist economic system. According to them, sexual repression was a way of tying humans to the 'work ethic' in the service of capitalist exploitation, though like Freud they still tended to locate sexual drives in 'nature', thereby offering little by way of a challenge to this influential framework.

Many have argued that we should view Freud's work as part of the emerging scientific essentialism regarding sexuality. In large part this is because, at base, he argued that, after infancy, we move into a heterosexual gendered and sexual identity which results from the anatomical distinction between the sexes. In this sense, his ideas are similar to those of biological sexology, i.e. that anatomical differences explain the social concepts of masculinity and femininity and, even more significantly, by equating these concepts with orientation towards the opposite sex/gender. Thus, he reduced sexuality to gender which, in turn, is reduced to anatomical sex. Heterosexuality becomes a force of nature where 'the strongest force working against a permanent inversion of the sexual object is the attraction which the opposing sexual characters exercise upon one another' (Freud, quoted in Gay, 1995: 292). In this sense Freud is also an essentialist, despite his ideas about an assumed polymorphous sexuality during infancy. Like earlier sexologists, he assumed, without any scientific basis for this conclusion, that there was some innate/biological and pre-social physical source of sexual desire.

Like anyone else, Freud was a product of his time, a time dominated by men. He has come under fire for failing to adequately address female sexuality, instead producing theory which was orientated towards men; for him, women were essentially an unknowable 'dark continent' (Freud, 1959 [1926]: 212). Perhaps most famously, he asserted that women suffer from penis envy, that little girls 'notice the penis of a brother or playmate, strikingly visible and of large proportions, at once recognize it as the superior counterpart of their own small and inconspicuous organ, and from that time forward fall a victim to envy for the penis' (Freud, quoted in Millett, 1999: 181). Though many of us may find such an assumption laughable, this belief has been a powerful shaping force. The penis and the act of penetration continue, in other words, to be central to ideas of masculinity and femininity – penetration is viewed as the only act which is truly 'sex'. Such a belief continues to hold sway, as we shall see in later chapters, shaping, for instance, understandings of what counts as rape or sexual assault. This takes us back to the Ancient Greeks, where if a person was penetrated, it was a sign of low status and potentially shameful (Wilton, 2000). Freud belied that women needed to submit to their inferior role and yield to penetration; pregnancy and childbirth were the only way to experience their own, substitute, penis.

Thus, where earlier sexologists began, Freud's work continued to give shape to the heterosexual. To become heterosexual was to become a fully gendered, social and moral actor. His work paved the way for viewing heterosexuality as the superior sexual identity. This understanding was also highly gendered – the Oedipal struggle was not so demanding for girls, thus, he concluded, they are less evolved and less formed as moral agents (Smart, 1998: 173). Smart argues that, once achieved, male heterosexuality need never be questioned, whereas female sexuality, including heterosexuality, remained dubious at best. Indeed, it was perhaps from this moment that heterosexuality effectively became invisible as a socially constructed sexual identity for many decades: as with all dominant categories, such as 'whiteness', their hegemonic position renders them absent from scrutiny. Towards the end of his life, Freud was still asking 'what does a woman want?' (Jones, 1955: 421). The question is a significant one because it assumes that all women want the same thing and that their wants are fundamentally different to men's.

Within psychology, many practitioners to an extent shared an outlook about the dualist split between mind and body which had much in common with religious beliefs. Hence many 'immoral' or 'abnormal' behaviours came to be seen as psychological 'pathologies' or 'disorders', or as the result of a lack of control over 'lustful' urges. Although the research methods were often based on theories and influences (and value judgements) rather than on systematic research and the gathering of adequate data, pronouncements by the early psychologists were usually taken fully on board by the sexologists. As a result, 'deviant' sexualities and sexual behaviours (such as heterosexual women's sexual desires, and same-sex desires and behaviours) were increasingly seen as 'abnormalities' arising from 'pathological' conditions (such as mental disorders). All this shows just how powerful pre-existing cultural definitions of the 'norm' and the 'deviant' are in shaping the views of scientists and researchers, especially those working in potentially controversial fields connected to sexuality. The idea that sex and sexuality were primarily designed for reproduction and the survival of the species clearly remained – and still remains – strong.

Self-identification

An important aspect regarding the social classification of sexualities is that connected with self-identification. Non-heterosexual identities clearly challenge traditionalist views of gender relations. However, such challenges have wide-ranging implications, as they are not just a question of personal/private choice: they have implications for most aspects of social life, such as politics and power, cultural beliefs and values, and social structures. Thus, as we shall consider in the following chapter, sociology has moved from the study of biological 'sex' to consideration of the social construction of gender and sexuality. Particularly significant have been attempts to understand how such aspects are organized hierarchically, and which social groups benefit most from such social inequalities regarding gender relations.

In fact, it is important to realize that most of the scientific and psychological investigations into sexuality and gender were not only undertaken by male members of the bourgeoisie, but were also largely funded by the rapidly emerging, and increasingly wealthy, capitalist class. Marx suggested that the dominant culture supports the needs of the dominant class. In this view, we could see the newly emerging science of sexuality as serving both the needs of capitalists and capitalism and hence also the needs of **patriarchy**. The consolidation of a specific domestic **ideology** within the dominant bourgeois class, supported by both the emerging sciences and reformed religious doctrines, can be seen as a method of social control. Essentialist and moral constructions of masculinity and femininity, and the creation of a family ideal, reinforced the belief that heterosexual relations were both natural and moral. Consequently, anything lying outside of this 'norm' is stigmatized and punished in a variety of ways.

Summary: 'The past is never dead'

According to the American writer William Faulkner (1897–1962), *'The past is never dead. It's not even past.'* If Faulkner is correct, it should not be too surprising that, over a century after the work of the early sexologists and psychologists, never mind lingering aspects of religion-based morality, essentialist ideas about sexuality still affect how people are allowed to live and behave in the twenty-first century. Huge sums of money continue to be thrown at essentialist research which attempts, but fails, to assert clear differences between male and female brains, or gay and straight genes.

Sociological attempts to develop an historical understanding of sexuality, on the other hand, are based on the willingness to question the 'naturalness' and 'inevitability' of sexual categories and assumptions. Instead, these are seen as being largely inherited from the past and reproduced in the present. Foucault went as far as to query the concept of 'sexuality' itself: 'Sexuality must not be thought of as a kind of natural given which power tries to hold in check, or as an obscure domain which knowledge tries gradually to uncover. It is the name that can be given to a historical construct' (1979: 105).

In many ways, Foucault's work grew out of developments in sociology, anthropology and radical social history. To such attempts to understand what formed sexual beliefs and behaviours, Foucault added the idea that the history of the idea of sexuality itself was an important area of study. For him, sexuality in modern western societies was a social relationship of beliefs and practices which had its roots in the past. As a result, sexuality could be seen as related to other social phenomena, such as politics and economics, with power relations (gender, class, ethnicity, disability, religion, age) being at the heart of it all. The historical stigmatizing of 'other' sexualities, and the promotion of heterosexuality, have regulated and policed intimate lives in a number of ways which will be examined in later chapters.

So, sexuality can be said to have a history: the meanings we give to it, the way we relate to it as a society, differ greatly across time, though as we have seen there are also some significant continuities. Of course, if the conclusion is that sexuality is a social construct arising from varying degrees of human **agency**, we can also extend this argument by thinking about the history of sexuality in a similar way. No doubt the dominant histories of sexuality presented in this chapter will shift and come to be viewed quite differently in decades to come. They tell us as much about the society in which they are produced as they do about the 'nature' of sexuality.

Key questions

- In what ways might the history of sexuality and sexualities change?
- Why is history and chronology an effective way to learn about sexualities?

FURTHER READING

An excellent resource for attitudes to sex in the Antiquities is Jennifer Larson's *Greek and Roman Sexualities: A Sourcebook* (Bloomsbury, 2012).

For an exploration of medieval and early modern understandings of sexuality, Phillips and Reay's *Sex before Sexuality: A Premodern History* (Polity, 2011) is useful.

To bring things slightly more up-to-date, look at Houlbrook and Cocks' *The Modern History of Sexuality* (Palgrave Macmillan, 2006).

2

THEORIES OF SEXUALITY

Learning outcomes

By the end of this chapter you should be able to:

- Identify the two broad approaches to thinking about sexuality – essentialist and social constructionist
- Understand the development of theoretical approaches to sexuality
- Recognize the contribution of feminism and lesbian and gay studies to the study of sexuality
- Understand debates about the future for theories of sexuality

Introduction

Theory can sometimes have a bit of a reputation as being dry, difficult or boring and so you may be tempted to skip this chapter. But fear not! Read on and you will see that theory can actually be interesting, perhaps even thrilling, and is often not that far removed from your everyday thinking. Think of it as a tool to crack open a tough nut, in this case, ideas about sexuality. Yes, sometimes theory is written in difficult language, but this chapter will help you to not only understand that language but also recognize that the ideas themselves are not always as complex as you might first think. Engaging with the theory helps you to see how thought has developed, and how theories not only differ from one another but also, often, overlap in their approach or ideas. Crucially, it will help you to see its relevance to your own life and perhaps offer you a way of thinking about yourself and others in a new way. It will help give you the strength and confidence to form your own arguments about sexuality, either in academic essays or in your personal conversations. By helping us to understand what we observe and experience, theory also has the capacity to help us bring about change. Thus, theory has the potential to be enlightening, empowering and radical.

As we have already seen in Chapter 1, many of these theories centre around the nature or nurture debate, i.e. is sexuality an innate part of us or something which is shaped through social interaction? These differing views are often referred to as essentialist or social constructionist theories (though many incorporate both aspects). Social theory, as we shall see, is closely mapped onto processes of social change. The 1960s, in particular, was a time of great social and political upheaval. New social movements, such as the civil rights and women's movements, challenged traditional ways of thinking about identity. These movements, in turn, influenced ways of thinking about sexuality – crystalized by the Stonewall riots of 1969 (see Chapter 7). In this chapter we will look broadly at some of the key theories from each camp – essentialist and social constructionist. We will begin with a brief consideration of essentialist theories, before moving on to look at sociological theories of sexuality. From here, we will explore the ways in which feminist studies, which in turn have helped shape and been shaped by Foucauldian analyses of sexuality, map onto **queer theory**.

Essentialist accounts

Jeffrey Weeks (1986) has shown that an essentialist, sometimes described as determinist or naturalist, approach sees sexuality as biologically determined, where sexual traits are fixed and social structure has minimal, if any, influence. Sexuality is seen as an inborn essence – stable across the lifespan and historically and culturally universal. As we saw in Chapter 1, until recently, Victorian sexologists such as Richard von Krafft-Ebing (1886) and Henry Havelock Ellis (1897), the psychoanalyst Sigmund Freud (1905), psychologists and most of the medical profession in Europe and the US believed sex was built into the body via genetics and hormones, and that humans were born sexual. Progressives, such as Havelock Ellis, Magnus Hirschfeld, Karl Ulrichs and Edward Carpenter, adopted this stance in an attempt to gain social sympathy and acceptance for those whose sexual self was considered 'deviant', though when taken up by legal, religious and medical institutions often these theories served to further pathologize them, rendering them 'mad, bad or dangerous to know'. In particular, it was believed that nature programmed humans for sex, driven by a procreative gene or maternal instincts to reproduce and rear children.

Anatomical differences between men and women, it was believed, led to biological differences in sexuality. Presumed gender traits such as male dominance and aggression and female submissiveness and nurturing are assumed to be expressed via sexuality. In this view, male sexuality is a natural, strong and often uncontrollable urge. Female sexuality, by contrast, is understood as passive. Heterosexuality, in such a context, is understood as being the normal and natural expression of sexuality.

Later, in the 1950s, Functionalist theorists like Talcott Parsons and George Murdock, who saw women as the expressive 'heart' of families and men as their rational 'head', whilst arguing that we learn our gender through adoption of social roles, drew on essentialist ideas about gender, sex and sexuality to explain such role differentiation within the family. As we shall see later on in this chapter, this is an influential perspective on sexuality and often frames 'commonsense' views of sexuality seen in popular culture and pop-science.

Discussion point

The shoring up of heterosexuality

If heterosexuality is so natural, many theorists have asked why it is something which has had to rely on so many laws and ideologies to encourage or 'enforce' it. Marriage has long been a key institution to normalize heterosexuality (Coontz, 2006), which is one of the reasons why same-sex marriage has caused so much controversy in recent years.

- In what other ways is heterosexuality normalized and supported in society? Think of laws, rituals, advertising etc.

Let's talk about sex: scripts, discourse and language

Sociology: sex roles and sexual scripts

Many have critiqued an essentialist view of sexuality, arguing instead that it is something shaped by social and historical forces. Law, religion, popular culture and medicine are just a few of the ways in which the meanings of sexuality are forged. Such theories do not necessarily reject the body entirely but would argue that it does not directly determine what we do with our bodies and the meanings we attach to this. Some began to view sexuality as a social role, an approach taken by British sociologist Mary McIntosh. In a significant essay,

'The Homosexual Role' (1968), where she draws on labelling theory, she argues that same-sex desire should not be seen as a condition that some people have and others don't. Instead, we should start to consider the ways in which ideas about sexuality are used as a form of social control, segregating the 'deviants' from those who are presumed normal. Seeing 'homosexuality' as a 'role' rather than a medical or psychiatric condition, she posits, allows sociologists to begin to ask the right questions about sexuality.

Taking such ideas even further, symbolic interactionists John Gagnon and William Simon's (1973) rejection of essentialist ideas about sexuality was sweeping. They argued that sexuality is not innate but rather it is a matter of sexual scripts. By this, they meant social meanings and norms which we learn in various social situations and in our interaction with others. Society teaches us, during the course of our growing up, what feelings and desires count as sexual and what the appropriate 'scripts' for sexual behaviour are. These sexual scripts tell us with whom we're supposed to have sex (based on factors such as age, ethnicity or class), where and when we can have sex, and what it means when we do. Scripts will vary across time and between cultures, with each culture having its own ideas for appropriate sexual relations. They suggested that we learn to *want* to have sex. Thus, Gagnon and Simon argue that sexuality is not an inborn element, but a product of social labelling. The British sociologist Ken Plummer (1975) also developed a labelling perspective on sex, arguing that through interaction in the gay and straight world, rather than being born gay, people learn to be gay by recognizing that certain feelings or attraction to people of the same sex indicate a gay identity. For Gagnon and Simon, sexuality becomes a way to exert non-sexual desires too. For instance, men learn to use sex in order to feel like a 'manly' man. Their work on sexual scripts has influenced some feminist thinkers, who have used some of their ideas to think more specifically about gendered inequality and the ways in which sexuality is used to maintain women's oppression. Jackson and Scott (2000), for instance, have considered how sexuality is scripted in terms of the gender assumptions mentioned previously – male competition and drive versus female passivity.

Feminist theories of sexualities

Feminism has a long and diverse history and reading more widely on this would certainly bolster the understanding of a student of sexualities (see Evans, 1995; Humm, 2014; Tong, 2009). However, it is possible to say that it is a political movement which seeks to challenge sexual and gender inequalities. First wave feminists of the nineteenth century had attacked the 'double standard' of morality which stigmatized and repressed prostitutes but not their male clients. In effect, this was a recognition, several generations before second wave feminism, of how sexuality had been central to women's subordination for a very long time.

Sex, gender and sexuality

When Simone de Beauvoir stated, in 1949, that 'one is not born, but rather becomes, a woman', she was paving the way for second wave feminist theorists of gender. Women are not born women but 'become' as a result of history and culture. Such a view applies not just to gender differences and inequalities, but also to those relating to sexuality. These inequalities result from cultural assumptions, and in social policies and practices which can often be traced back to earlier historical periods. These essentialist assumptions about sexuality, based on beliefs about biology, have shaped not just social structures and cultures, but also identities and everyday behaviours; they have resulted in explanations/justifications for the inequalities between men and women, and between heterosexual and non-heterosexual groups.

A key aspect of second wave feminist thought is the conceptual division of sex from gender and sexuality (Woodward, 2016). Sex was understood as the biological foundation and gender referring to the social constructions and expectations based on sex (as we shall see later, increasingly, feminists have 'troubled' this distinction, arguing that both are social and cultural categories in many respects, helping to shape one another). Such a separation, allowed for the possibility of change, a challenge to the imposition of unequal identities. From this, the ways in which different feminists have explored the relationship between gender and sexuality are various. Many view gender as intertwined with sexuality (see Cranny-Francis et al., 2003: 7), with some seeing gender (sexed identities and practices) as the foundation of sexual identities and practices. These views, which tend to assert that gender comes first, and that sexuality is subsequently shaped by gender, are not shared by all feminist writers (Jackson, 1995). Catherine Mackinnon (1982), for instance, sees sexuality as key for the formation of gender, and Gayle Rubin (1984), who influenced queer theorist Eve Kosofsky Sedgwick (1990), theorizes gender and sexuality as two analytically separate domains.

Essentialist ideas did find their way into some feminist work. Firestone asserted that women are oppressed because of their biological capacity to reproduce, and thus in order to be liberated, they also need to be liberated, through reproductive technologies, from childbirth: ' ... the end goal of feminist revolution must be, unlike that of the first feminist movement, not just the elimination of male privilege but of the sex distinction itself: genital difference between human beings would no longer matter culturally' (1970: 19).

Some cultural feminists, such as Mary Daly (1978), have also been accused of essentialism in seeing femaleness as essentially superior to maleness. Nevertheless, building on the work of McIntosh, Gagnon and Simon and Plummer, many feminists continued to challenge the idea of sexuality as an innate, 'natural' part of human nature, arguing that it was a public and political issue. A key concept for second wave feminists of the 1960s and 70s was that of patriarchy (see Millet, 1970), a 'system of social structures and practices in which men dominate, oppress and exploit women' (Walby, 1990: 214).

FACT FILE

The problem with patriarchy?

There has been intense debate over the concept of patriarchy. Some have argued that, as defined by feminists such as Millett, it is too simplistic and restrictive a concept, e.g. it has been argued that it doesn't adequately explain relations between men and other men, or women and women. Whilst many responded to these criticisms by expanding on and refining the theory (for instance Walby, who argued that she addressed problems such as reductionism, ahistoricism and universalism by identifying six key structures that oppress women – housework, paid work, male violence, culture, sexuality, and the state), many feminists increasingly shied away from using the word, though seemingly still discussing the phenomena. Concepts such as 'gender regime' or 'male hegemony' (using Gramsci's term 'hegemony' from his analysis of class politics) were often used in its stead. Anthias and Yuval-Davis (1992) argued that despite refining the concept, Walby does not adequately deal with racism, patriarchy and capitalism, instead treating them as additions or layers of oppression rather than analyzing the impact of their intersections. In recent years, however, it seems to be enjoying a resurgence in popularity.

One of the keyways in which women are oppressed, it is argued, is through constructions of sexuality. For instance, Millett (1970) argued that sexuality was integral to the patriarchal order, and that sexual violence and the sexual **objectification** of women were central to patriarchal domination. Even litera-ture, she maintained, perpetuated this dynamic, especially in novels written by the likes of D.H. Lawrence and Norman Mailer. The difficulty lies in the fact that this political issue is a hidden one; patriarchal systems like marriage, reli-gion and education present this relationship between the sexes as 'natural' and 'inevitable'. This is a concept related to the well-known feminist slogan 'the personal is political', as Millett points out that motherhood, childcare and contraceptive rights, amongst other issues, are central to maintaining women's oppression. Radical feminism, in particular, focused on sexuality as a key to patriarchy (see MacKinnon, 1987). Much like exploitation is central to class relations, she saw sexual exploitation as a key feature of what she termed the 'sex class system'.

Heterosexuality was critiqued, as an institution which served to oppress women in a variety of ways (see Jackson, 1996). An answer to this for some, was to reject heterosexuality as an institution. In 1979 the British Leeds Revolutionary Feminist Group coined the term 'political lesbianism'. Their argument was that women don't need to have sexual relationships with other women but they should remove themselves from social and sexual connections with men. These ideas were theorized by American feminist poet Adrienne Rich in an influential essay 'Compulsory Heterosexuality and Lesbian Existence' (1980). The concept 'compulsory heterosexuality', explained the ways in which society is organized around heterosexuality. Rich argued that heterosexuality had to be seen as a political institution with coercive power. There are 'inducements' to heterosexuality, such as financial rewards for married couples, or cultures created to romanticize heterosexuality (think boy meets girl narratives in Hollywood films), and there are also punishments for those who do not conform (ridicule or violence) which operate as mechanisms of exclusion.

Discussion point

Is heterosexuality still compulsory?

Rich's theory is nearly forty years old, and there have undoubtedly been some significant social changes in many countries with regards to sexuality. This doesn't mean that the concept is redundant however, and it might be interesting to reflect on the ways in which it may still have some salience. You could think about the following:

- Are there any laws which differentiate between heterosexual couples and same-sex or **transgender** couples?
- Do contemporary 'romantic' films and television programmes include regular representations of LGBT+ intimacies, and crucially are these representations which reject stereotypes?

Heterosexuality, for Rich, has material consequences for women, in the form of reduced legal and economic rights. However, by rejecting the 'naturalness' of sexuality, radical feminists raised the possibility that it can be transformed by cultural and historical change.

In challenging ideas that gender and indeed sexuality are fixed, universal categories, second wave feminist thinkers were among the first to consider transgender practices theoretically. However, the story of feminism's relationship with transgender scholarship has often been presented as if they are 'pitted against one another in mortal battle' (Halberstam, 2006: 98). Certainly, in very recent years, the relationship between feminism and trans issues has been a contentious one, and you might want to consider some of the heightened debates in the public sphere, once you have engaged with some of the theory, in order to assess the validity of arguments from both camps.

Some feminist scholars, such as Janice Raymond (1979) and Bernice Hausman (1995), read transgenderism as reifying gender essentialism. Many, however, have adopted what might be considered as more progressive approaches to transgender. Conceptualizations of the ways in which trans identities and practices disrupt notions of gender binaries as fixed and natural have emerged, which troubles some of the feminist accounts that have been accused of being essentialist themselves (see Fausto-Sterling, 2000). In addition, through the growing body of literature on trans phenomena a new and contested binary opposition has emerged, that of **cisgender** and trans (Enke, 2012). The term 'cisgender' (shorthand 'cis') comes from the Latin *cis*, meaning on the same side or remaining with the same orientation. It is used to distinguish between trans people and 'non-trans' people (those whose gender is considered congruent with that assigned at birth) (Enke, 2012).

At a crossroads?

It is over thirty years since the term '**intersectionality**' was used theoretically (Crenshaw, 1989). Using the metaphor of an intersection, or crossroads, Kimberlé Crenshaw maintained that to resist the violence in black women's lives, intersectional thinking was a necessity to explore how 'race' and gender affect the lives of women in different ways. Crenshaw, working around the issue of domestic violence, contended that feminist work often missed out the experiences of black women, and the black community often ignored the gendered nature of the abuse; intersectional thinking allowed academics to map the convergence of racism and patriarchy. The theory emerged as part of a critique of studies of inequality which considered social divisions using an additive approach, with ethnicity or sexuality, for instance, being tagged onto analysis. The traditional feminist approach, it is argued, has been to see gender as the primary source of women's oppression, the notion of intersectionality, however, starts from the acknowledgement that we exist in social contexts created by the intersections of systems of power (i.e. 'race', class, gender and sexuality) and oppression (**prejudice**, class stratification, gender inequality and heterosexist bias). Since then, considerable scholarly attention has focused on the potentials and limitations of using an intersectional lens to analyze a variety of social divisions (Berger and Guidroz, 2010).

Whilst there has perhaps been a relative under-development of sexuality in the application of intersectionality, it remains a useful tool for scholars of sexuality. Academics have variously explored the ways in which sexuality is tied in with other social identities, looking at, for instance, sexuality and age (Cronin and King, 2010; Todd, 2013), sexuality and class (Taylor, 2009), and sexuality and gender (Jackson, 2006). It has also proved fruitful for developing analysis of the intersections between sexuality and transgender issues (Hines, 2010).

A turn to Foucault

Whilst Gagnon and Simon did not necessarily consider power, it was certainly something at the heart of the work of much feminist theory and also that of Michel Foucault. In turn, despite the fact that Foucault did not produce a gendered understanding of power, his ideas had a considerable impact on feminism and studies of sexuality from the 1980s. A key question Foucault asks is why modern people talk so much about sex? In *The History of Sexuality: An Introduction* he claims there is an important relationship between confession, truth and sex. Foucault argues that in order to understand sexuality in the west, it is important to consider how knowledge operates and how particular forms of knowledge, such as the science of sexuality (*scientia sexualis*) and psychology (see Chapter 1), have dominated our ways of thinking about gender and sexuality.

Sex Talk...

These knowledges are a form of discourse – ways of thinking about and constructing knowledge about the world. Incitement to discourse, Foucault argues, began in the seventeenth century and culminated in the nineteenth-century science of sex. Each discourse creates its own set of 'truths' which it then endlessly confirms. Victorian 'knowledge' about sex effectively brought sexuality into being, including much of our terminology about sex. Christian confession, the ritual of admitting to sins and seeking a means of penance from a priest who hears the confession, became reconstructed in the increasingly revered scientific form of psychiatry and psychology. Revealing sexual habits, desires and obsessions was seen as providing a way to unearth the authentic self, in the interests of science or the health of the individual. As we saw in Chapter 1, Foucault saw the naming of sexual acts and types as bringing sexual identities into being. Sexual identity, in other words, is a relatively recent cultural construct, produced through particular ways of talking and thinking about sex.

Thus, sex was treated as an object of knowledge and the confession, he suggests, has become one of the most valued ways to uncover 'truth' in our society. From being a ritual, it has become widespread and is part of family life, work relationships, medicine and policing. As sociologist Frank Furedi (2003) posits, confession now dominates personal, social and cultural life – reality television programmes like *Sex on the Couch*, *Love Island* and the controversial *Jeremy Kyle Show*, and social media platforms such as *Facebook* and *Twitter*, revolve around confessions. Healthy sexual relationships, it is insisted, require truth-telling which enables an expert, like a therapist, to reveal our 'authentic self'. The proliferation of talking about sex in this way, Foucault argues, is one of the reasons why sexuality is seen as such a fundamentally important aspect of our identities.

Discussion point

Sexy stories

List some of the contemporary spaces and places where we are encouraged to 'confess' all about our sexuality:

- Who is the audience? Who are the experts?
- What is the message given about healthy or 'normal' sex?

Liberation or domination?

The persuasive promise of such confession is that the more detailed and frequent it is, the more we will learn about ourselves, and hence the more we will be liberated. But this will to knowledge and truth is a tactic of power, according to Foucault, becoming a form of surveillance and regulation. Confession doesn't reveal the truth, it produces it. Sexual identities were named and explained but also, crucially, placed on a sliding scale of acceptability. By confessing everything, we give power to experts – a doctor or therapist for instance, to judge, punish or correct us, based on invented standards of normality, thereby condemning the confessor to an endless cycle of shame, guilt and yet more confession. Foucault's other key work, *Discipline and Punish* (1979b), shows the mechanisms by which, in key social spaces, we are watched and monitored. Using the example of prisons and Jeremy Bentham's idea of the Panopticon, Foucault argues that we internalize these sexual norms and regulate, or 'discipline', our bodies and behaviours accordingly.

FACT FILE

The Panopticon

An English social theorist of the Enlightenment, Jeremy Bentham designed an ideal prison, the Panopticon (meaning 'all-seeing'), i.e. a simple premise, whereby inmates are positioned around a guards' watch tower, in such a way as to never know when they are being observed. The theory was that feeling the constant presence of authority, never knowing when they were actually under surveillance, would mean prisoners internalized social norms and 'behaved' themselves. Foucault argued that this principle has become foundational for everyday life, with other social institutions such as schools and hospitals following this design.

Power is productive

A key point Foucault is making is that power is not simply repressive, it is also creative. Power has, through discourses, produced new forms of sexuality. Dominant, or hegemonic, normative discourses, may well have the power to repress particular identities but such power also produces resistances. With the invention of the 'homosexual', we saw moves to label such men and women as abnormal, insane or dangerous and punish them for it. However, for the first time, by being given an identity, or label, such individuals were able to mobilize and come together to speak for themselves. In such a way, they have a choice – to accept the label as given, or to resist and reject it, challenging the dominant regimes and producing a counter-discourse.

A queer eye

If you look in various dictionaries, queer can mean odd, to spoil something or to feel ill. As a consequence, it has also been used as a derogatory, offensive way to refer to the emerging 'homosexuals' of the nineteenth century. By the 1990s, however, political groups such as ACT UP in the US and OutRage! in the UK, re-appropriated the term, to celebrate difference and challenge growing right-wing neoliberal politics (see Chapter 7). Queer politics was about querying or challenging normative and restrictive identities. In part, queer politics and theory emerged in the wake of homophobic health campaigns during the **AIDS** crisis of the 1980s which wrongly positioned the disease as a gay disease. Queer, like some feminists, was also critical of the lesbian and gay communities of the time which it saw as being assimilationist by seeking to enter the mainstream in campaigning for things such as marriage rights.

Drawing on Foucault's ideas, as well as feminist and lesbian and gay theory, queer theorists like Steven Seidman (1997) argue that identity is not innate or stable, but is culturally mutable and lacking coherence. Foucault had already challenged the idea that sex was biological and natural: it was the idea or discourse of sexuality that created what we know as sex. In other words, we are not born sexual, but learn to be sexual beings – and this only happens in societies that have created the idea of 'sexuality'. A core text for queer theory came from the feminist philosopher Judith Butler. In *Gender Trouble: Feminism and the Subversion of Identity*, Butler (1990) drew on Foucault's ideas to advocate a new social point of view on sex, gender and sexuality. She argued that societies that believe in a natural gender order are also organized around the privileged norm of heterosexuality. Butler posited that, as we conform to gender norms, others will likely interpret our behaviour as expressing a core gender identity. However, she argued that there is no such core gender identity driving our behaviour. Instead, these behaviours are modelled on images of what it means to be a woman or man that we take over from our families and our culture. Sex, just like gender, is produced through practices and discourses. Through her concept of *gender performativity*, she states that the everyday, repeated activities that we think of as social expressions of our gender, and which give a semblance of stability, are in actual fact actions which create gender. Her way of illustrating this, is to refer to **drag**. Drag, she suggests, reveals that there is no original, or innate, gender to be imitated or performed. This has important consequences for our understandings of sexuality. Heterosexuality, she argues, requires an apparently stable, natural gender binary, in order to seem 'natural' itself. It requires the 'masculine' man to be attracted to his polar opposite, the feminine woman, and this is achieved through a regulatory system that Butler refers to as the 'heterosexual matrix'. Butler's ideas explain how we project a sexual identity by our actions, but her performative approach does not claim that sex identities are not real because they are produced through a performance. They are quite real as we experience them and in terms of their personal and social consequences. However, as Diane Richardson points out, in attempting to conceptualize gender and sexuality as 'performative' there is the danger of 'losing sight of the ways in which gender and heterosexuality are structurally deeply embedded in the social order, with important material consequences for our lives' (2000: 39).

Nonetheless, the aim of queer theory is to reframe sexuality within a postmodern framework, and in particular, to disrupt the hetero/homo binary, revealing it as a cultural binary, and denaturalize heterosexuality. Queer theory sees 'homosexuality' as central to heterosexual culture, in that the hetero/homosexual binary serves to define heterosexuality at the centre, with homosexuality positioned as the marginalized 'other' (see Halperin, 1995). It depends on lesbians, gay men, bisexuals to be identified as 'outsiders' (Fuss, 1991). Thus, heterosexuality depends for its meaning and coherence on 'homosexuality' as its 'opposite': heterosexuality appears to be 'natural' and 'normal' because it constructs same-sex attraction as un-natural, and not the norm.

By attempting to disrupt the (hetero) centre, queer theory also disrupts the notion of sexual difference: with no accepted 'centre', who or what can one be defined as different from? Therefore, as with feminist perspectives, heterosexuality itself is problematized, and queer theory aims to develop existing ideas about, and a radical critique of, categories of identity associated with sexuality and gender. Distinctions between woman/man, male/female, heterosexual/homosexual become meaningless. Queer theory also claims that sexuality and gender can be separated analytically, and that sexuality is the main focus for analysis – especially of the hetero/homo binary. Queer theory thus examines how the construction of heterosexuality privileges some women and men and disempowers others.

In his seminal text *The Trouble with Normal*, Michael Warner (1999) argues that queer is not just about resisting the norm but also challenging the very idea of normal behaviour. Because queer is about attitude or positionality, rather than identity, anyone who challenges the norm or expected can be queer, e.g. married couples without children. Similarly, Seidman (1997) argues for what he calls a social postmodernism where queer becomes a verb rather than a noun, the intention being to 'queer society'. In this context, his aim is to challenge all norms by recognizing difference. He insists that queer theorists must take into account other forms of social theory and continue in the critique of key social institutions and the analysis of the material conditions which impact on people's lives – something which many other queer theorists neglect. As a theory, it is not restricted to challenging sex, gender and sexuality, it is also used to destabilize other identities, such as 'race' and class.

Queer theory, therefore, in pointing to the fluidity of sex, gender and sexuality challenges long-held dichotomies, including sex/gender, and has perhaps been particularly important for creating a space where it is possible to develop theories of sexuality which go beyond a binary framework of gay or straight. The extent to which this has been done, however, is debatable. Studies of bisexuality are arguably still limited (see Callis, 2009), asexuality is only just emerging as a field for interrogation (see Cerankowski and Milks, 2010), and we have already seen that considerations of trans identities and sexuality are underdeveloped, perhaps because of the ways in which sex, sexuality and gender have been theorized (Hines, 2006). Bockting et al. (2009) have traced the emergence of trans sexuality which is positively based on the erotic appeal of trans identity, trans experience, bodily aesthetics and sexual behaviour. There is growth in literature and media platforms which explore and celebrate trans sexuality, looking at issues connected to sex after trans surgery (see Bartolucci et al., 2015) or the role of pornography in developing trans subjectivities (see Davy and Steinbock, 2011). There is, however, scope and need for much more research which interrogates the relationship between trans and sexuality (Pfeffer, 2014).

In some ways, queer theory's approach to sexuality is similar to questions raised by earlier feminist debates (see Rubin, 1984). However, feminist perspectives have tended to focus on gender – the 'woman'/'man' binary – and have generally dealt with sexuality as constitutive of, as well as determined by, gendered power relations (Richardson, 1997). Despite these differences, you may have noted significant areas of overlap, in that both perspectives see sexuality as a mechanism of power, and that it is encoded in a wide range of social institutions and practices. Indeed, it has been said that queer theory 'owes much to radical feminism in terms of the development of a deconstructive model of gender and sexuality' (Richardson, 2000: 50).

Essentialism revisited

Despite the compelling theories put forward by social constructionists, in recent years we have seen a (worrying to many) resurgence in the popularity of essentialist ideas about sexuality.

One particularly influential approach is that held by evolutionary psychology (EP). It claims its origins in Darwin's theory of evolution. Unlike his painstaking and detailed approach to study, however, EP is based on observations about sexualities and sexual behaviours. It assumes that what people do today is 'evidence' of how sexuality has 'evolved', and is therefore an expression of our natural evolutionary heritage which is fixed in 'human nature'. In other words, we act in particular ways now as a consequence of the ways our genetic make-up has developed through natural selection and other evolutionary processes. EP was heavily criticized at the time for its lack of academic rigour. Indeed, many social theorists have highlighted the conceptual hazards in seeking to reconstruct the past from observing the present.

However, some academics have attempted to use EP to explain criminal behaviour. One worrying example of how this has been used is in relation to rape. Essentialist ideas of gender and sexuality, with women being sexually passive and men being sexually active, competitive and aggressive, are employed to suggest that rape is a reproductive advantage. Thornhill and Palmer (2000), whilst not justifying rape, argue that men with 'pushy' genes are more successful at reproduction, and at times this pushiness becomes force. Not surprisingly, evolutionary psychologists have been challenged with sociological and feminist explanations which stress the influence of historical and cultural constructions on sexualities and gender, including behaviours such as rape. Experts disagree, for example, about the levels of coercive sex in other animals, particularly primates. It is also difficult to see how such a theory explains the rape of a child who cannot physically reproduce.

Despite the weakness of the EP approach and the failure of medicine, to date, to find evidence of 'gay' brains or convincing genes for sexuality (and it should be noted that it is rarely a search for the straight brain, or lesbian for that matter, or gene), essentialist explanations for sexuality which claim we are 'born that way' remain very popular (Richardson, 2018). In part, this has been part of a process of normalizing politics (see Chapter 7), but it is more important to interrogate further the reasons for, and consequences of, this re-essentializing. Is it because it is comforting to know 'it' can't be helped, or is it so that we can find a 'cure' for 'deviant' identities (Brexit Party MEP Ann Widdecombe's recent comments about 'gay cures' might point to the latter)?

Summary: 'Time and Tide'

As society has undergone changes, sometimes very rapidly, theoretical frames of reference for understanding sexualities have also shifted. Essentialist and social constructionist approaches often run alongside one another and, as we have seen, there is no unitary social constructionsist view, they have 'arguments with each other, as well as with essentialists' (Vance, 1989: 19). Social constructionist theories range from those which focus on sexuality at the micro level of indivudal social actors, to those more macro approaches which consider sexuality through an interrogation of discourse and power but perhaps missing the element of the lived experience. More recently, intersectional analyses allow us to understand the ways that sexuality is embedded in other sociocultural and political contexts. To borrow Richardson's (2007) metaphor of the shoreline, we have only dipped our toes into the, sometimes murky, theoretical waters here, but hopefully it is possible to see how the overlapping, ebbing and flowing approaches by sociologists, feminists, lesbian and gay and queer theorists have charted the waters. Theorists have politicized sexuality and established it as very much a public issue. In doing so, they have challenged traditional views on sexuality and provided a variety of new ways to conceptualize sexual relations. In the next chapter, we will consider how these understandings of sexuality have impacted on the ways in which it is researched.

Key questions

- Which of the theories briefly outlined above makes most sense to you? Outline some of the reasons for this.

- What do you think are the most popular explanations for sexuality in contemporary culture? Why do you think this is the case?

FURTHER READING

For a readable introduction to some of Foucault's key ideas, try Barry Smart's *Michel Foucault* (Routledge, 2002).

Diane Richardson's (2007) 'Patterned fluidities: (re)imagining the relationship between gender and sexuality', *Sociology*, 41 (3): 457–74, provides a more detailed exploration of the theories on how gender and sexuality are related.

For a humorous as well as a scholarly and scientific take on some of the problems of an essentialist approach to sexuality and gender, have a look at *Testosterone Rex* by Cordelia Fine (Icon, 2017).

3

RESEARCHING SEXUALITY

―――――――――― **Learning outcomes** ――――――――――

By the end of this chapter you should be able to:

* Identify the two broad approaches to researching sexuality – qualitative and quantitative research methods
* Understand the development of approaches to researching sexualities
* Recognize some of the key ethical concerns regarding researching sexuality
* Understand debates about the future for researching sexualities

Introduction

As you will no doubt have realized, sexuality is a complex, fluid and sensitive concept. How therefore, do we go about researching it? To attempt to do so raises a number of methodological and ethical questions. How best do we explore people's experiences, practices and perceptions of sex and sexualities? What are the best methods to employ in order to achieve this? In what ways does theory intersect with research methods?

As we have seen in the previous chapters, early sexologists of the nineteenth and early twentieth centuries were interested in understanding and categorizing sexuality, but their approach was often positivist, or they saw certain types of sexuality as pathological. The methods they employed to enquire into sexuality were frequently dubious, whilst claiming to be 'scientific' and clinical.

Psychoanalysis, too, had its problems, relying on heavily stereotyped assumptions about gender and sex and drawing from a fairly rigid, binary view of the world. Most 'evidence' came in the form of case histories, presenting a very partial picture of, arguably, upper middle-class (male) sexuality. Kinsey argued that Freud's approaches, and the approach of psychoanalysis more generally, lacked proper scientific rigour. Kinsey came from a background in evolutionary theory, based on observing the morphology of gall wasps. His sample survey of 20,000 respondents, relied on volunteers, rather than being a random sample (Brecher, 1969). Whilst Kinsey's scale of sexuality has been influential, for instance, in terms of bringing a quantitative approach to studying sexuality, many have also criticized his approach for its reliance on, and reproduction of, essentialist understandings of sexuality (see King et al., 2019).

Second wave feminist theories and research, which often critiqued the work of Freud and others for their 'malestream' view of sexuality, had a lasting impact on sexualities research. Many, such as Kate Millett (1970), provided useful critiques of psychoanalytic approaches. They argued that the majority of studies privileged male sexuality. Feminist theorizing of the sex/gender distinction allowed for an understanding of the ways in which much research into sexuality had reinforced false binary notions of gender and sexuality. By challenging traditional views of sexuality, they were able to argue that women's sexual oppression both played a part in reproducing, and was a consequence of, patriarchy (Walby, 1989). Second wave feminism, therefore, was a significant influence on social scientific enquiry into sexuality. One key legacy, is that feminism brought with it thoughtful debate about research methods, on matters such as whether there are certain methods that can be considered feminist, what the relationship between the researcher and the researched is, and whether there are methods which might be considered harmful and so forth (Kelly, 1988; Stanley and Wise, 1993). Much of the research into masculinities added to this growing interest in the relationship between power, sexuality and gender and the importance of appropriate research methods (Connell and Dowsett, 1992). Another key aspect of feminist enquiry has been a sustained critique of heterosexuality as an institution and its role in sustaining patriarchy (Richardson, 1996). Such a focus then enabled interrogations of the notion of **citizenship** in relation to sexuality (Weeks, 2007). Queer theory, which as we saw in Chapter 2, grew out of both feminist theorization and Foucauldian analysis, maintained the feminist concern with methods and the relationship between theory and practice. The majority of studies into sexualities, as we shall see, employ **qualitative methods**, but increasingly, the binary distinction between qualitative and **quantitative methods** is being blurred.

We cannot, in this chapter, cover all forms of social scientific enquiry, nor offer a step-by-step guide to research design (and there are plenty of textbooks which do this brilliantly). Instead, we will explore some of the approaches taken by researchers into sexualities and the related issues, including the ethics of researching potentially sensitive topics and hidden communities, and the challenge of managing and negotiating the role of researcher. Along the way, we will look at a variety of notable studies. We begin with a brief introduction to the relationship between methods and methodology, moving on to consider the role of qualitative and quantitative research methods. You will be encouraged to think critically about research methods and design.

Methods and methodology – what's the difference?

Methodology and methods are terms that are sometimes used interchangeably, however they have slightly different meanings. Methodology, according to Ramazanoglu and Holland (2002), is about a rather complex relationship between theory (ideas about the way society works, such as feminism or queer theory), **epistemology** (what we know and the relationship between knowledge and reality) and **ontology** (the set of categories and concepts in a particular subject area, such as sociology or sexualities studies, and how these ideas all fit together). For example, there were some very interesting discussions in the 1990s about whether there is such a thing as a 'feminist methodology' (Stanley and Wise, 1993). Whilst the conclusion was that there is perhaps no definite feminist methodology, there was some agreement on there being key principles associated with such research. Feminist research challenged the notion of the 'objective researcher' who uncovers the 'truth'. Other central values are, arguably, that it focuses on gender and inequality, it rejects 'scientific' divisions between researcher and researched and takes care to do no harm to either, it encourages **emancipatory research**, it is **reflexive**, and it opens a space for the voices of the marginalized to be heard. It could be argued that many of these values or principles are also true of sexualities research, so perhaps we can talk about a sexualities methodological approach. Oakley (2000) argued that there are two broad methodological 'camps', i.e. the 'scientific' quantitative approach and the interpretivist qualitative approach. Some have argued that, given their methodological aims, feminist research should take the latter approach. However, this distinction, as we shall see, is not one that is generally invested in today.

Methods, on the other hand, are simply the specific tools, or ways in which you conduct your research, e.g. interviews or surveys. However, your methodological framework for research, is likely to influence the tools you choose, and it may become the justification for your choice of research methods. If you are a feminist or LGBT+ researcher, for instance, looking at sexualities – something which you believe to be fluid and fragmentary, as experienced by either a dominant or normative group or those more marginalized – you have to decide what the best tools are to use to not just 'capture' their experience or voices but also represent their voice in a fair way. In this sense, theory, data and method are all related.

Getting the measure: qualitative and quantitative methods for studying sexualities

The questions we ask and the ways in which we ask them have a significant effect on the answers we get, and therefore selecting the right method to help us arrive at answers to those questions is vital. Traditionally, the tools to hand for the social scientific researcher have been broadly divided into two camps – quantitative and qualitative – which are often positioned as being binary opposites and even gendered.

There's no 'I' in science? Impartial observer or subjective researcher?

As we have seen above, some feminists have argued that quantitative methods (which include statistical surveys, big data analysis, questionnaires, online polls) which were considered positivist, 'hard' or 'scientific' were not suitable for a feminist project because they were also associated with the masculine (Oakley, 1998) – not that an ability to work with numbers is an essential masculine trait, an advantage of the so-called 'male brain' (see Fine, 2011, 2017, for an amusing and informative discussion of this), but that the history of quantitative methods can be linked to a patriarchal academy more generally and the privileging of a male perspective on the world. As we began to see in Chapter 2, knowledge has, arguably, been judged by how objective it has been; the more it appears to be unbiased, the better or more rigorous it was deemed to be. Foucault (2000) and others have, however, successfully undermined the view that anything can be objective, and have also challenged the notion that it is something desirable. Instead, many have argued that viewing quantitative methods in this way has been 'an excuse for a power relationship' (Stanley and Wise, 1993: 167).

Qualitative methods (which include focus groups, ethnographic research, unstructured interviews and participant observation), on the other hand, have often been read as subjective, 'soft', non-scientific, and associated with femininity. Viewed as such, they arguably became the 'gold standard' of feminist research. As some have argued, 'it is more logical to accept our subjectivity, our emotions and our socially grounded positions than to assume some of us can rise above them' (Ramazanoglu, 1992: 211). Given that women's lives had been left largely unexplored by the academy for centuries, arguably qualitative methods were a useful approach for mapping uncharted territory.

More recently, many have argued that such a dichotomous view of research methods is not helpful or necessary (Westmarland, 2001); neither method is hard or soft, masculine or feminine. Many research projects will employ a mixed-methods approach, using both quantitative and qualitative methods. Surely any research tool can be more or less feminist, or queer, or emancipatory – it all depends on what you do with it! However, others have argued that there are particular methods which lend themselves to studying sexualities. Certainly, in a society where non-normative sexual identities are still stigmatized, counting that group may well prove difficult. Studies which attempt to do this often end up with unrepresentative samples of people living in specific areas (Fish, 2008). If we take the stance that sexuality is fluid and contested, then qualitative research methods might seem a better fit (Plummer, 2005). For instance, Valocchi (2005) has suggested that ethnography is suitably 'queer' because it enables flexibility and openness.

Whatever approach we take, the messiness of social life means we can only ever hope to capture a partial representation of events (Law, 2004).

Table 3.1 Summary of quantitative and qualitative methods

	Quantitative	**Qualitative**
Purpose	To map the extent of an issue/ generalize results/make predictions	Generate rich, new data, often on an under-researched area
Sample	Often large-scale, representative	Can be small-scale, non-random/self-selected or purposive samples
Data	Verbal, visual, unstructured	Statistical, structured, numerical, frequencies
Generalizability	Large-scale random findings could be generalizable	Tend to be not generalizable but provide useful case studies and insight into experiences
Examples	Statistical surveys, closed interviews, structured questionnaires	Response survey, semi/open-structured interviews, focus groups

The gold standard? Interviews

Interviews arguably remain one of the most popular forms of social scientific enquiry, especially in relation to sexuality. In part, this is because sexuality research is often concerned with the marginalized and under-researched, thus, interviews offer the opportunity to generate rich, new data. One example of this is Linwood Lewis's (2007) research in black young men's negotiation of sexuality. He interviewed a number of black and Latino young men aged between fourteen and eighteen. Over time, Lewis was able to establish a good enough relationship with the young men to afford some sensitive reflections on being a young, black man in a society where stereotypes about black sexuality abound. Such (post)colonial racism serves to construct young black men and women as the sexualized 'other'; figures of both anxiety and an object of fetishized sexuality (Hook, 2005). Young black men are framed as predatory and over-sexualized and a particular threat to white femininity (Makoni, 2016). The findings from the interviews challenge a range of these racist, and sexist, tropes. For instance, many only had their first sexual encounter if a girl took control. The emotional ties from relationships with girls were considered more important than the physical aspects of a sexual relationship, and far from being misogynist these young men resisted what they saw as sexual double standards for boys and girls. They were also very well versed in the stereotypes about black hypermasculinity/sexuality which proliferated in the media.

Using mixed methods

Many pieces of research into sexuality will use more than one method, in an attempt to provide a more nuanced understanding of their research group. Bacchus et al. (2016), for instance, used both quantitative and qualitative methods in their research into gay and bisexual men's experiences of domestic abuse. The research used anonymous health and relationships surveys conducted at sexual health clinics and semi-structured interviews with some of the men who responded to the survey. As a result of the mix of methods, the researchers were able to conclude that many men minimize and normalize the violence they experience, concealing its impact in order to maintain a particular notion of masculinity. They also found that whilst many of these men thought a sexual health clinic would be a suitable place to talk about their experiences, many had never been asked about domestic abuse by a sexual health practitioner.

Robinson et al. (2011) used two methods when looking at the ways in which heterosexual male hairdressers subvert dominant understandings of masculinity. The study used a combination of interviews and participant observation. The observations conducted in hair salons, they argued, enabled them to see gender as performed by these men (Butler, 1990). The **embodiment** of sexual and gender identity was a central focus. The interviews provided a different perspective when looking at how men negotiated their gender and sexual identity in a feminized space.

Ethical issues in researching sexualities

Social scientists are often involved in research because, not only do they want to study society, but often they are also dedicated to improving social conditions for the many (Bauman, 2013). Therefore, it is no surprise that ethics have become an important part of research design. Any social research looking at the lives of people, or groups of people, needs to be designed carefully, so as to ensure no harm is done to anyone, researched or researcher, either during the research, or as a result of that research at a later date. However, given that sexuality is often experienced as something innately private and has also, frequently, been the source of stigma and punishment, research into sexualities needs to be undertaken in a particularly sensitive manner (Frank, 2016).

Ethics and ethnography: Tearoom Trade: Impersonal Sex in Public Places (1970)

Many researchers use ethnographic methods in order to better understand sexualities. Ethnography is about understanding social groups or phenomena from the 'inside'. By immersing themselves in communities or social groups, often for prolonged periods of time, they gain a more nuanced and rich understanding of the social dynamics at play (O'Reilly, 2005).

Laud Humphreys was a PhD student researching what may now be described as 'men who have sex with men'. 'Tearooms' was an American euphemism for the public lavatories where men went to have anonymous sex with other men (the British term is 'cottaging'). Many of these tearooms were in public parks. He was of the belief that American society and the criminal justice system had very simplistic and stereotyped beliefs about the men who engaged in these practices and he wanted to find out more. Keen to know more about the kinds of men who used tearooms and why they did so, he used the ethnographic method of covert observation.

In order to conduct the research, Humphreys pretended to be gay and acted as a scout, or 'watchqueen', for the lavatory users – someone who being a voyeur, would watch sex and in return would give a signal if the police came. At that time in the US gay sex was illegal, as it was in the UK, and the police would deliberately target tearooms as a form of harassment. Because he performed this duty well, and had watched the men's activities for some time, he was able to gain the confidence of some of the men he observed. He disclosed his role as a scientist and persuaded some of them to tell him about the rest of their lives and also their motives. Other men who were less forthcoming he followed, and made a note of their car number plates, with a view to finding out their names and addresses. A year later and heavily disguised, Humphreys went to those men's homes and posed as a health scientist, and then proceeded to interview them about their marital status and job, with a view to finding out more about their attitudes to same-sex relationships.

The results of this research were of great importance in that they exploded the myths and stereotypes surrounding men who had sex with men. Only fourteen percent of the men identified as gay and had sought primarily gay relationships; fifty-four percent were married but a significant proportion had tensions in their marriage. For example, many men expressed the need for quick anonymous sex – something less lonely than masturbation but didn't involve a relationship – because that aspect of their marriage was 'no longer working', the birth of a child often being cited as a reason.

There is also evidence that these findings altered police attitudes to such men. Convictions subsequently fell.

However, this research came under much criticism and is now notorious.

Discussion point

The ethics of covert observation

- What might be some of the criticisms of Humphrey's research?
- Does the end justify the means?

Some researchers are averse to any form of covert research because the people being observed have not been able to give their consent to taking part in the study. However, arguably, the key consideration is whether or not there is any risk of harm to either the researched or the researcher. After all, we are all under more or less constant observation by the State and through our online activities. Arguably, had Humphreys sought informed consent, given the social climate of the time, many of the men may have been likely to refuse. However, in his attempt to find out more about some of the men he had observed, he perhaps put them at risk of being identified.

Researching disability and sexuality: enabling voyeurism?

Tom Shakespeare (1997) provides a useful reflection on ground-breaking research he conducted with others into disabled people's experiences of their sexuality. He argues that sexuality was missing from the literature on disability and that, if present in academic research, disabled people were presented as degendered and **asexual**. In an attempt to redress this paucity of research, Shakespeare et al. (1996) set about qualitative research. Adverts were placed in community magazines such as *Disability Now* and *The Pink Paper*. In all, the research involved 44 disabled people, who identified as heterosexual, lesbian, gay and bisexual, with a greater proportion of LGB people than found in the wider population. In part, this was because they found that LGB people were more likely to be willing to take part in sexualities research. Very few participants were BAME and many were active members of the disability movement. As such, the study could not, and did not, claim to be representative of all disabled people. In an attempt to be inclusive they used a range of methods, including letters from contacts or tapes people had made for them. Although specific questions were not asked about abuse, they found that some respondents talked about episodes of abuse nonetheless. Some participants felt comfortable talking about their personal experiences of sex, and these tended to be women and/or people from the LGB community. A few participants, all men, recounted behaviours which the researchers felt were examples of inappropriate sexual relations, such as the use of pornography, prostitution or other exploitative behaviours. Shakespeare also argues that such research runs the risk of providing erotic material for those who fantasize about disabled sex.

Discussion point

Sexuality and disability

If you were to attempt to redo Shakespeare et al.'s research today, how would you go about it?

- How could you attempt to reach a wider group?
- In particular, how could you try to include more members of the BAME or trans community?
- How would you prepare for the fact that participants might reveal instances of abuse? What strategies could you put in place to protect your participants?
- Why do you think it tended to be women and/or LGB people who were more willing to share their sexual experiences?
- Arguably, any research into sexual behaviours and practices brings with it the risk that it might be read voyeuristically. From an ethical perspective, why might this be a concern? In what ways could academic researchers limit this?

Risk and the researcher

By the late 1980s, researchers started to write reflexively on the impact of studying difficult topics. For example, Alexander et al.'s (1989) analysis of rape prompted them to reflect on its emotional impact. The methodology they employed might be considered relatively 'impartial' or distant, in that they looked at the case review files from rape crisis centres. However, they described experiencing a 'parallel reaction' akin, or parallel to, the impact on victims. They reported feelings of anger, anxiety, and one researcher experienced vivid and terrifying nightmares. Liz Kelly (1988) had a similar, traumatic response to her research into violence against women – it prompted flashbacks and feelings of sadness, and fear for her personal safety. Stanko (1997) and others have reflected that such responses are important and provide an opportunity for academics to acknowledge the role of emotions in research and see it as a resource for adding insights.

Hammond and Kingston (2014) have highlighted the ways that being actively engaged in research on sex work can have a negative impact on the researcher. Using Goffman's (1968) notion of stigma by association, they argue that just as sex work can be considered a stigmatized activity in contemporary society, the stigma of sex work, in effect, rubbed off onto them as sex work researchers. Selling sex is considered a deviant practice and this extends to those who do the research. Kingston has argued that what happens can sometimes be a sexualization of the researcher, who is seen as somehow more 'liberal'. For instance, she received this message from a male senior police officer after an interview: 'Yeah was cool to meet one so chilled and open minded – don't let the gay thing put u off if you fancy a bit of casual sex (just don't tell the bf!) Defo give me a shout though I'll settle for coffee x' (Hammond and Kingston, 2014: 335).

Academics who research sexuality sometimes find that they can experience marginalization and **discrimination** within academia as well (Attwood, 2010). Pioneers of sexualities research in the academy, who were among the first to focus on this in the social sciences, often found colleagues or managers viewing the subject as a 'joke' and 'unworthy' of academic research, e.g. Masters and Johnson had their laboratory vandalized once their work went public. It may well be the case that those who continue to research new areas will still receive such responses. Irvine (2014) has suggested that sexualities research is both necessary (it has informed health practices, social policy and is fundamental to addressing inequalities) and sadly still often stigmatized.

Discussion point

What's 'dirty' now?

Based on Irvine and Alexander's arguments about institutional responses to sexualities research, what areas of research do you think might be viewed as unnecessary/inappropriate today?

- Why do you think these issues might invoke such a response?

In part, it may be that sexualities research somehow challenges traditional divisions between public and private. It could also be a gendered response, in that often it is women who recount negative responses to the sex research; perhaps the rigid binary assumption of appropriate femininity being sexually passive is somehow muddied by women conducting research on sexuality (Braun, 1999).

Trends and new directions

No stranger to controversial research topics himself, Plummer (2005) has recently turned his attention to the methods we use, arguing that in a time of rapid and extensive change, research techniques should similarly adapt. As such, much recent social scientific research into sexualities doesn't strictly adhere to traditional 'scientific' structures of knowledge production. Approaches may include use of art and visual forms or autoethnographies.

Visual methods

One such example is ethnofiction. Using this method, Johannes Sjöberg (2008) explored the lives of Brazilian **transsexuals** (who identified as women) and travestis (who don't identify as men or women) living in São Paulo. In it, local transactivists scripted, then acted out their personal and social experiences, which Sjöberg filmed, to produce an ethnofiction called *Transfiction* (2007). Often working as prostitutes, they were able to narrate their experiences, which frequently involved abuse and violence, and they charted their attempts to leave sex work. Arguably, such an approach, which allows the researched to effectively write their own script, is a useful method for sexualities research conducted in cultures different from that of the researcher. Whilst the trans community working as prostitutes were fairly visible on the streets of São Paulo, they were difficult to access, and as a heterosexual, male foreigner, Sjöberg was likely to have been perceived as a customer. The method was collaborative and demanded a reflexivity from the researcher. In this way, Sjöberg was able to include local knowledge, challenging hegemonic western knowledge production (Haraway, 1988). The piece of ethnofiction asks bigger questions of social scientific research – is fiction, albeit improvised narrative based on lived experiences, a valid form of research, and to what extent does it differ from the narratives we may tell in semi-structured interviews, e.g. can we say that either one are any more 'real' or valid?

Barker et al. (2012) have also argued that visual methods can be useful for researching marginal identities and those whose practices have been stigmatized. Their research focused on trans, bisexual and polyamorous identities (see Chapter 9 for more on these identities). Arguing that more conventional methods of focus groups or interviews are constraining in terms of being able to convey their experiences, Barker et al. argue that visual methods enable more nuanced possibilities. In their research, participants were asked to create visual representations of their experiences or identities using, for example, photographs, collage or models from clay. They were then asked to explain the visual art either to the researcher or to a small group. The researchers then interpret the narrative, rather than the visual artefacts themselves, using participants' own words and drawing together common themes from discussions. The researchers argue that such an approach enables the research community to 'hear' stories which challenge the dominant or prevailing sexual story relating to any group, which can in effect become a rehearsed script (Plummer, 1995). They also argue that the method is one which complements the interests of the communities they were researching; many events for bisexuals, for instance, had craft areas. Such methods might also be useful in researching **BDSM** or kink communities.

Sexualities research online

As technology has become more woven into everyday life, it has also become an increasingly useful tool for sexualities research (Griffiths et al., 2013). Online research brings with it some clear advantages, from access to sensitive or hidden populations to a global reach, and of course for researchers it is arguably a cheaper way to conduct research in a time of funding cuts. As with offline research, research using the internet can include a range of methods such as surveys, interviews, ethnographies, focus groups and emails.

Discussion point

Switched on?

Much has been made of the importance of the internet in transforming research, particularly in relation to sexualities:

- Make a list of some of the methodological and ethical benefits and disadvantages of conducting sexualities research over the internet.
- When you have made your list, you could read Rosewarne (2019) for a detailed discussion of this.

Often, research into sexualities focuses on members of minority groups. As such, especially if they are cautious about revealing their identity, they may well be difficult to recruit offline. However, conducting research online, which perhaps affords more anonymity, may well mean academics have greater access to such populations (Buchanan and Ess, 2008). The cloak of anonymity afforded by the internet has been cited as a bonus by some researchers into sexualities. For instance, Harvey et al. (2007) surveyed emailed messages sent to a sexual health information site aimed at young people. They argued that the online discussions were much more open and frank than the data they received from offline methods. Other research has suggested that members of minority, or stigmatized, groups are more likely to be technology-literate, as a result of conducting a significant portion of their social life online. The ability to reach out across the globe, using the internet, is another important factor involved in the growth of online research (Griffiths, 2012). Though it is important to remember there are considerable differences between the numbers of people with access to the internet in the global north and south; age of participants may also impact on internet usage, as can class and gender.

Hammond (2018) was able to use the internet in order to examine the commercial and non-commercial sexual and relationship experiences of men who pay for sex. Using online platforms, Hammond was able to gain access to men who might have remained hidden otherwise. However, she urged a word of caution – whilst there are some gains to research online, there are also some losses. She notes that the 'physical immersion' in the field of research, which so many social scientists relish, is diminished somewhat with online methods.

Summary

Perhaps unsurprisingly, research into sexualities is both fascinating and not without its controversies. Given its sensitive and often hidden nature, sexualities research is both practically and ethically challenging. Gradually, we have seen a shift from biological and psychiatric-based research to methods which have placed an importance on context, the lived experience of sexuality (Lock and Farquhar, 2007). Much research into sexualities is driven not just by a will to 'know' but also by a desire to improve. Interpreting sexualities carries with it a burden of responsibility. Thankfully, reflexive practice has grown in social scientific research, whereby there has been a move from 'scientific' observation to research which places the researcher very much within the research. This is a direct result of the work of feminist methodologists who asserted that knowledge is contextually specific, and the researcher's social location impacts on what they find out and thus what we come to 'know' (Stanley and Wise, 1993). Increasingly, researchers are expected to scrutinize their own actions and their role in the research design and process (Blaikie, 2000). The idea of the detached, impartial, objective researcher is mostly a thing of the past.

Some of the examples we have looked at reveal the complex relationships between researcher and researched, emphasizing even further the fact that our social selves are unstable. Researchers are also increasingly aware of the power relationships involved in conducting research with people from different cultures, especially those regarded as somehow less 'developed'. It is also clear that, certainly in the not so distant past, such research sometimes came with discrediting attributes. It may have been viewed as frivolous or 'dirty work' (Irvine, 2014), or overlooked for funding because it was deemed too risky. Thankfully, pioneering researchers continue to explore sexualities despite such attitudes, and as a result have allowed us to explore a range of areas which we shall consider in the next section.

Key questions

- Can you identify areas of sexual lives, behaviours or identities that you think need further research? Or can you predict new, emerging areas which will require social scientific enquiry?

- What are some of the current difficulties in regard to research into sexualities?

- As a potential researcher of sexualities, what are your responsibilities towards those you may be researching?

FURTHER READING

For more general information on conducting social scientific research, Alan Bryman's *Social Research Methods* is a great starting point (Oxford University Press, 2016), and in order to look more closely at qualitative methods, David Silverman's *Qualitative Research: Theory, Methods and Practice* (Sage, 2004) is worth looking at.

See Morris, C., Boyce, B., Cornwall, A., Frith, H. Laura, L. and Huang, Y. (eds) *Researching Sex and Sexualities* (Zed, 2018), which provides a range of examples of research methods used to looked at various issues relating to sexualities, including sex work and pornography.

Andrew King et al.'s (eds) *Sexualities Research: Critical Interjections, Diverse Methodologies and Practical Applications* (Routledge, 2019) is a really interesting collection, showcasing various methodological approaches used by sexualities researchers.

PART II

SEXUALITY AND CULTURE

4

THE MEDIA AND SEXUALITY

Learning outcomes

By the end of this chapter you should be able to:

- Consider the relationship between the media and constructions of sexualities
- Analyze the ways in which sexuality can become a commodity
- Identify key areas for study in contemporary society in relation the media and sexualities

---

Introduction

The media, mass media, mass culture, popular culture – the labels proliferate – but whatever identifier you use, there is little doubt that we live in a mediated society and increasingly, we experience our sexual selves through and with these. The media is a diverse realm, involving a range of forms of communication including newspapers and magazines, film, music, television, video games, the internet and social media. It surrounds our public and 'private' lives, making it one of the key social institutions involved in shaping both how we see the world and how we come to understand our place within it. The media is ever-present in modern society, leading many sociologists and cultural commentators to suggest that modern life is 'media saturated'. Academics are generally in agreement that this is an important area for analyzing social lives, not least because of the global reach of many forms of the media. Not only does it communicate messages to a wide audience, increasingly it also offers a space for consumers to produce texts and contribute to discourses about sexuality – in other words, it becomes a process between text, consumer and producer (Hall, 1980).

This chapter considers some of the key debates surrounding the media and sexuality; the material presented is necessarily selective because the media is such a vast area. We will begin by considering why the media is so important with regard to sexuality, examining a range of related theories before moving on to examine a few broad areas of the media industry. First, we look at the entertainment industry, with a focus on film, in relation to sexuality, before moving on to explore the role of advertising. Finally, we consider the impact of social media and new technologies and sexualities.

The power of the media

Much has been written about the importance and power of the media. Marxist theorists have long argued that capitalist groups own not just the means of production but also the media industries which advertise them, thus they can simultaneously manufacture and fulfil our desires. The goal of capitalism is to make a profit, and so mass-produced, cheap products which we are 'encouraged' to think we need are a way to achieve this. The media, it is argued, is not exempt from this; in competing for viewing figures and securing advertising revenues, it conveys ideological messages about society to ensure we continue to perform efficiently as workers and consumers.

Some cultural commentators such as Theodor Adorno and Max Horkheimer identified popular culture as conservative, serving the needs of those in power and helping to maintain the status quo by mollifying the masses and shoring up capitalism. The conservatism of the mass media can be seen in how ideas about sexuality are produced, represented and disseminated. Curran (2005), for instance, draw attention to how the media contributes to processes of control in society, and in particular, how the media can act as ideological agencies. Some of the central issues they identify are how the media represents sections of society in such a way as to reflect and reproduce the disposition of power in society. Such sociological theories also see the mass media as reflecting the views and interests of dominant social groups – not just certain social classes but also, arguably, (heterosexual) men. Various feminist sociologists have offered a critique and re-evaluation of the ways in which society, and its culture, should be examined and understood. In particular, as seen in Chapters 1 and 2, if sexuality is seen as is a product of society and not of nature, the mass media, alongside families and religions, plays a significant role in establishing and re-enforcing 'normal' notions of sexuality. Woodward (1997), for instance, has suggested that modern western culture uses the 'myths of motherhood' to socialize and control the activities and sexuality of women by defining what and who women are and should be. Women, it is argued, are often portrayed in a limited number of roles, based along the familiar virgin/whore binary (wife and mother, or sex object) and this is especially, but not exclusively, true of the various forms of pornography. Much feminist research into representations of femininity has centred on magazines for teenage girls and for women, e.g. Ferguson (1983) and McRobbie (1983) have argued that an ideology of femininity was to be found in such products through narratives of romantic love and 'how to keep your man'.

Foucault (1979) argued that traditional discourses of sexuality, often determined by religion, were part of the rise of what he called a 'disciplinary society'. As well as religion, medical institutions and schools, the media and culture played significant roles. According to him, such disciplinary control relies less on censorship and repression than on the power of normalizing ideas in order to shape individuals' sexual identities and practices. Seidman (2010) sees Foucault's perspective as useful in explaining why many Europeans and North Americans are preoccupied not only with their sexuality and that of their friends and neighbours, but also of public figures and celebrities. The media plays an important role in the creation of the illusion that there are core feminine and masculine gender identities, helping to propagate and reinforce the idea of heterosexual dominance, or a compulsory heterosexuality (Rich, 1980).

Seidman points to how, during the 1950s and early 1960s, US popular culture and mass media promoted a view of gay men as a threat to children, families, and national security. Newspapers, for instance, frequently published the names of those arrested by the police in efforts to close down gay-friendly businesses and to make gay men and lesbians reluctant to frequent known public meeting places. However, he suggests that as the lesbian and gay rights movements developed in the 1960s and 1970s, with their own magazines and journals, and positive gay role models began to appear on television, in films and in the news, many young people came to be both aware and accepting of their sexuality at a younger age than previous generations.

One aspect of how the mass media has altered their treatment of sexuality is provided by the popular US television show, *Queer Eye for a Straight Guy* (currently *Queer Eye*). This is a show that reflects the metrosexual identity, by depicting straight 'masculine' men as being motivated and embarrassed by learning how to be more attractive, and becoming skilled in fashion, cooking and home decoration. According to Seidman, the straight male has literally undergone a gay makeover on prime-time television. Whilst the metrosexual 'phenomenon' is largely motivated by a neoliberal push to sell more products to a wider audience, he does suggest there has been a subtle cultural shift in representations of sexuality in the media (Seidman, 2010: 85).

In order to think this through a little more, you could complete Table 4.1.

Table 4.1   Representation of sexuality in the media

Complete the table below to record the main types of media you experience during just one week. As well as recording how much time you are exposed to these different forms, make a note of (a) how many of these dealt with aspects of sexuality and (b) how many presented positive images of different sexualities

	What did you watch/read/ listen to?	For how long?	How many of these media dealt with sexuality?	Were these representations positive or negative?
Monday				
Tuesday				
Wednesday				
Thursday				
Friday				
Saturday				
Sunday				

Entertainment industry and sexuality

To be born a woman has been to be born … into the keeping of men … Men look at women. Women watch themselves being looked at. This determines not only most relations between men and women but also the relation of women to themselves. The surveyor of woman in herself is male. (John Berger, 1972: 46)

Laura Mulvey's (1975) male gaze theory has been significant for critics interested in the relationship between sexuality and the media. It refers to the male point of view, or way of looking and seeing, that is privileged in patriarchal culture, and which assigns to women the position of sexualized object. She argued that in cinema, women were rarely shown in their entirety; instead the camera focuses on, and fetishizes, parts of women's bodies, feet, breasts, lips – in effect, cutting them up. Through these processes they become fragmented, commodified and alienated from their own bodies and sexuality. She went on to suggest that viewers of film, male or female, gay or straight, are positioned as a heterosexual male, and so we see the world through the lens of hegemonic masculinity. The woman becomes an object, not a subject, of the male gaze.

Carol Adams (1990) makes a similar point about the parallels between how women's bodies, like those of other animals, are effectively consumed, objectified and dismembered.

FACT FILE

Angry girls

Much of western art consists of paintings or sculptures of naked women. This was made explicit in 1989 by the Guerrilla Girls (http://guerrillagirls. com/), a collective of women artists formed in New York to combat discrimination in art, film, pop culture and politics. They presented an artwork to the Metropolitan Museum of Art in New York comparing the number of female artists represented in the museum's collection to the number of paintings of female nudes.

You could do a similar count in your local gallery. Is there a balance of male and female nudity or artists?

Slasher films

Karen Boyle (2005) draws attention to popular US genres which give representations of sexualized violence against women in mainstream media entertainment genres – such as so-called 'slasher' films, which have led some feminists to coin the phrase 'gorenography', to link such filmic representations to pornography in general. Mulvey's work can be used to examine how such films seek to position and gender their spectators. According to Boyle, 'the male spectator also takes voyeuristic pleasure in using another person (woman) as an object of sexual stimulation through sight – his gaze is both controlling and curious. The peeping tom is the extreme expression of this instinct, his victim (and Mulvey uses this word) both unknowing and unwilling' (2005: 125). Feminists in other fields have seen this kind of voyeurism as a form of violence against women as it is a reminder of women's object status, sexualization and lack of power, as well as a violation.

In slasher films, such as *The Texas Chainsaw Massacre* or *Nightmare on Elm Street*, Carol Clover (1992) has argued that terror 'is gendered feminine', and that norms of sexuality are promoted in such films. For instance, both young men and women who have sex in such films are usually killed off, though it is only women's deaths which are sexualized. Clover focuses on the trope of the 'Final Girl', which has inspired a film of the same name – she is the one who survives to the end. Clover argues that her success is partly because she is more resourceful and arguably 'masculine', but also because she is a 'good girl'.

Another genre of film explored by Boyle (2005) is the 'rape revenge' horror film. These have generated considerable controversy and concern for the way they portray sexual violence against women. She gives the example of film critic Roger Ebert who, whilst watching the film *I Spit on Your Grave* (1978), was aware that many of the male audience audibly approved the rape scenes:

> ... the audience seemed to be taking all this as comedy, and there were shouts and loud laughs at the climaxes of violence. And then, beneath these noises ... I could hear my neighbour saying, 'That's a good one ... Ooh-eee! She's got that coming! That'll teach her. That's right! Give it to her! She's learned her lesson ...' (Ebert, quoted in Boyle, 2005: 137)

Many 'rape revenge' films, such as *The Accused* (1988) and *Thelma and Louise* (1991), arguably adopt aspects of feminist ideas, in that they often portray the 'victim avenger' as both active and self-sufficient. However (spoiler alert) the rape victim in *The Accused* was ultimately 'saved' by male testimony. More recent films, such as *The Girl with the Dragon Tattoo* (2011), have been heralded as feminist, but in many ways it could be argued that the central character is yet another objectified female who fulfils the demands of the male gaze.

Discussion point

Sexy robots

Films such as *Ex Machina* (2014) and *Her* (2013) are arguably continuing a cinematic fascination with feminized robots programmed to be subservient, objects of visual pleasure and sexually obliging:

- List as many films as you can which have 'female' robots or machines.
- How many examples of 'masculine' robots are present in films?
- Are male and female robots presented differently? Consider which are characterized as subservient, authoritative, helpful, dangerous, sexy and so on.
- How could we use Mulvey's (1975) male gaze theory or Haraway's (1985) notion of the cyborg to analyze these?

LGBT+ on the big screen

Seidman (2010) notes that for most US citizens, there has been remarkable stability as regards the core sexual culture, heterosexual romance and marriage, and the ideal of monogamy and family-making since the end of World

War II, yet the scale and impact of popular culture have changed dramatically since 1945. In particular, there has been the development of television (especially cable TV, DVDs, Smart TVs and cinema complexes, the internet) and the emergence of youth cultures that both produce and consume popular culture. In many ways, he sees modern popular culture as performing the central cultural role previously performed by religion. According to him, it is virtually the most important structuring force for our sexual selves, giving us meanings, norms and ideals, and telling us who to have sex with, when, where and how.

In the US, the new visibility and assertiveness of gays and lesbians eventually pushed Hollywood – like the rest of the US – to respond. Many mainstream films in the 1970s and 1980s reacted to lesbian and gay activism in an unambiguously negative way. There was a 'stream of polluting, demeaning, and pathologizing images. The homosexual was represented as a serious threat to America's children, families, moral values, and indeed its national security. If the homosexual could no longer be silenced ... this figure could at least be portrayed as the polluted other to the pure heterosexual' (Seidman, 2010: 130).

For instance, the film *Sudden Impact* (1983) has an extremely negative portrayal of a lesbian character (Ray), which shows her as the very opposite of a respectable heterosexual woman. Ray is shown as the stereotypical, gender-inverted, mannish woman – who is also a sociopath and violent (the Dykeopath is another popular character in mainstream films – watch out for her!). In *Looking for Mr Goodbar* (1977), which depicts a world shaped by the sexual and gender liberationist ideas of the 1960s, the sexual relationship between two of the gay male characters is shown in highly stigmatizing ways. In films like these, the US is imagined as being divided into a heterosexual majority and a gay minority, a division with strong 'moral' overtones, with heterosexuality positioned as pure and same-sex desire clearly representing dangerous impurity.

However, beginning in the early 1990s, after much political campaigning, the status of the LGBT+ community shifted and Hollywood both reflected and promoted this change. In particular, 'it fashioned a new representation: the normal gay as the counter-part to the normal heterosexual. The normal gay and lesbian are presented as fully human or the psychological and moral equal of the heterosexual' (Seidman, 2010: 133). Yet there were clear limitations to this 'toleration'. Distinctions were made between the 'good gay' (settled, hard working) and the 'bad gay' (unconventional or promiscuous). A popular figure of 'acceptance' was the gay best friend (frequently played by Rupert Everett) in films such as *My Best Friend's Wedding* (1997). Such men, though gay, were 'safe', asexual and caring. Furthermore, these films also serve to reinforce a 'narrow ideal of heterosexuality' (Seidman, 2010: 137). The 'normal' gay man helps to create a social division between 'good' and 'bad' heterosexuals too. Such films shored up the institution of marriage, reinforcing the importance of legitimate monogamy. In this way, it is possible to see how social control shifts from focusing on the problems of same-sex desire to the normal/good sexual citizen.

More recently, we have seen films depicting trans bodies. Whilst there have been, arguably, independent films depicting trans identities for a while, it is only in the last few years that we have had trans represented in the mainstream: *Transamerica* (2006), with the trans woman played by a cisgendered woman, and Amazon's *Transparent* (2014–19), this time with the central character played by a cisgendered man. Are we witnessing a depiction of the 'good' or 'normal' trans woman? Are there equivalent mainstream representations of trans men? Arguably invisible, however, is the 'good' or 'bad' bisexual.

Discussion point

Good sexual citizens

With reference to contemporary films or television, what are the norms of 'good' or 'bad' sexual citizenship?

Which sexual identities are present? Who is missing and why do you think that is?

Many examples from television and film still place monogamous, loving partnerships on a pedestal, whether gay or straight. However, arguably, we are beginning to see a slow shift. In recent years, we have seen programmes such as *Trigonometry* (BBC Two), which depicts a couple tentatively exploring **polyamory**. Nevertheless, there are still plenty of films which reassert the importance and centrality of heterosexuality, and the necessity of this being restricted within the confines of a married couple. In fact, by the time people start to watch such films, they will already have been exposed to a raft of films and books which naturalize and normalize a particular expression of heterosexuality. For instance, Disney films such as *Snow White*, *Cinderella*, *Sleeping Beauty* and *The Little Mermaid* all have one theme in common: the story of heterosexual romantic love that ends in marriage. But it's not only film and television which mediates these sexualized norms – as we shall see, it proliferates in advertising too.

Sex sells? Advertising and sexuality

David Gauntlett (2008), perhaps rather controversially, stated that representations of men and women are not usually very conspicuously sexist.

Yet traditional stereotypical representations still exist. Whilst mums might not be going to Iceland any longer, they are still often locked in the kitchen or bathroom. Germaine Greer's book *The Whole Woman* (1999: 86) drew attention to the fact that advertising is produced by capitalists who want to cultivate insecurities for which they can then sell 'solutions': '... sophisticated marketing will have persuaded the most level-headed woman to throw money away on alchemical preparations containing anything from silk to cashmere, pearls, proteins, royal jelly... anything real or phony that might fend off her imminent collapse into hideous decrepitude'. This is a useful reminder that, despite decades of feminist criticism of such advertising, little has changed; in fact Greer concludes that things have become worse since she wrote *The Female Eunuch* (1970).

An area where sexualized images of women still proliferate is fashion photography and advertising – a clear example of the male gaze in action. As Zarzycka (1997) has argued, commercial fashion advertising results in women's bodies being reproduced as packaged, commodified, sex objects. Female bodies are represented in seductive poses and sometimes, as with a recent controversial *Dolce & Gabbana* advert (which was removed after a series of complaints), positioned in such a way as to arguably suggest gang rape. The *Wonderbra* 'Hello Boys' advert of 1984 is yet another example of an advert which shows the model, Eva Herzigova, as an object of the gaze.

However, have we seen a shift in recent times? It could be argued that the series of *Dior* adverts, staring Charlize Theron from 2011 to 2019, for example, resists the male gaze by having the model as protagonist, staring back at the viewer and challenging the voyeuristic gaze. Or is this an endorsement of the normalization of the pornographic, albeit with a supposed ironic twist (McRobbie, 2000)? Some, such as Lynne Segal (1997), have argued that male bodies have recently been sexualized in various media, presented for the viewing pleasure of a female, or gay, audience. The footballer David Beckham, for instance, famously assumed a pose more usually associated with the female muse, when he reclined sufficiently for the viewer to get an eyeful of his *Armani* pants in 2007. Can we, therefore, start talking of a female gaze?

Discussion point

Advertising diversity?

It's clear from some of the examples above, that advertising has frequently drawn on hegemonic understandings of heterosexual ideals in order to

(Continued)

sell products. However, perhaps we are witnessing a shift in recent years. Car sales advertising has traditionally been viewed as sexist, with women often pictured draped over car bonnets as a sales ploy. However, in 2019 *Renault* began an advertising campaign which centred around a lesbian couple, and *Starbucks* launched an advert in 2020 which follows the story of a trans man:

- Have a look at a range of lifestyle magazines aimed at straight and LGBT+ men and women. Look at the visual adverts within and identify the discourses of sexuality used. Which bodies are presented as 'sexy'? Are there BAME bodies? Are the bodies classed? Are there disabled bodies?
- Make a note of the adverts you watch on television over the course of an evening. Do any of these challenge hegemonic sexual norms?

Many feminists have long argued that a lack of diverse bodies in the media and constantly seeing representation of idealized, often photoshopped, bodies can have serious consequences. Susan Bordo (2004), for instance, in *Unbearable Weight*, points to the disproportionate number of girls and women who suffer from eating disorders such as anorexia nervosa and bulimia nervosa. The body, she argues becomes a contested terrain, a site where women and girls struggle to exert some control, a place where they attempt to reconcile their bodies in a highly sexualized culture. Arguably, we are also witnessing a rise in representations of idealized, and often unattainable, masculine bodies too (Wykes and Gunter, 2005). Certainly, some studies have suggested that eating disorders amongst young men are on the rise: one NHS Digital study (2018), looking at UK figures between 2015 and 2016, found that levels for men had risen at the same rate as they had for women. Levels of steroid use among young men had also quadrupled at the same time. If young adults, and older adults for that matter, are not feeling confident in their bodies, this can have a significant impact on their intimate lives (Ackard et al., 2000).

Media representations of sex acts

The BBC adaption of *Normal People* (2020) has been the subject of much praise for its treatment of consent in young heterosexual couples but has also found itself open to criticism for the screen time devoted to female nudity. In addition to constructing particular sexual identities and sexualized bodies, the media can also shape our responses to particular sexual practices. One interesting example, not least because it remains the most popular sex act, is masturbation. Richardson et al. (2013) argue that the contradictory responses we have about masturbation can be seen on screen too. Whilst masturbation is a practice that is, arguably, safe in terms of STIs and is free from the worry of unwanted pregnancy, as we saw in Chapter 1, it has been subject to social and moral control and is often, therefore, a source of embarrassment. Perhaps because of this contradictory nature, it frequently rears its head (sorry) in comedy. Richardson et al. give the examples of the US TV series *Roseanne* (1988–97) and the film *There's Something About Mary* (1998). Both examples feature young men masturbating – the stereotypical onanist. However, more recently, the media has given its audience female equivalents, in comedies such as the UK's *Fleabag* (2016–19) and US series *The Deuce* (2017–19). Whilst such scenes are also presented for comedic value, there is a sense the makers feel they are doing something risqué, which, of course, given the hegemonic constructions of female sexual passivity, they are.

Discussion point

(re)producing sex on screen

You could develop Richardson et al.'s (2013) observations about masturbation. How many examples can you think of in film or TV? What are we meant to think about the act or the masturbator? Is it presented as silly, shameful, dirty, sad, lonely? Who is doing it? Are they mostly men or women, gay, straight, trans? Are they white or black, young or old, (dis)abled?

Can you think of other sexual practices which are constructed in a particular way on screen and why they are presented in a certain way? What discourse frames the act?

Social media, new technologies and sexuality

So far, this chapter has perhaps focused rather more on the negative aspects of the media in relation to representations, or stereotypes, of sexuality. It is important to recognize, however, that most forms of media offer all of us moments of viewing, or listening, pleasure. New media and related technologies, such as the internet, emails, blogs, and podcasts, or social media platforms such as *Facebook*, *Twitter* and *Instagram*, are often seen as 'emancipatory', as they promote 'a user-driven, 'pull' culture in which people will no longer accept what is pushed at them by media conglomerates' (Curran, 2005: 138). For instance, it has enabled a global gay community which offers support for those whose sexual identities are stigmatized or punished (Gross, 2003). It has arguably blurred the lines between producers and consumers, and allowed users much more flexibility over what they consume. In particular, it has been argued (for instance by John Fiske, 1989 and Paul Willis, 1990) that these aspects of popular culture are potentially radical and subversive, as they give power to the masses and consumers and so undermine owners and elites in general.

In relation to sexuality more specifically, this has meant an almost limitless access to a variety of sexualized content, from pornography to sexual health information. We can communicate with people we wouldn't otherwise be able to meet, we can indulge in 'virtual' fantasy sex, we can construct an image of our sexualized self, alter it with a range of technologies, and place ourselves in cyberspace. In these unprecedented sexual times, we need to consider the impact these new forms of media are having on the ways our sexualities are shaped.

Arguably, new social media are particularly important in the sexual lives of young people, as their lives become increasingly enmeshed with the online world (Livingstone et al., 2015). Frequently, the academic focus has been around issues of risk and the impact that social media can have on young people's mental health (Cookingham and Ryan, 2014). Certainly, there is evidence to suggest that young people can find the role of social media in their (sexual) lives overwhelming because it is ever-present (Livingstone and Sefton-Green, 2016). Some research has focused on how social media platforms such as Facebook reinforce romantic and heteronormative ideals by placing an exaggerated emphasis on relationship status (De Ridder and Van Bauwel, 2013). There is also research to suggest that young people, particularly girls, are also succumbing to pressures to look a particular way and put their bodies under constant surveillance. The pressure to post photos and have them liked, it is argued, is a daily occurrence for many young people. A study carried out by Common Sense Media, with over a thousand 13–17 year olds in the US, found that seventy percent were on social media multiple times a day.

FACT FILE

New technologies, abuse and the law

Recent research has shown how new social media are being used for sexualized abuse. Many young people have been victims of 'revenge porn', which became a crime in 2015 in the UK, where private or sexual photos of someone are deliberately shared and made public via social media, such as Facebook, or by email, without their consent. In 2019 'upskirting', the practice of taking a photo under someone's clothes, became a criminal offence in the UK, under the Voyeurism Act. Many young people use their phones to take and send explicit photos of themselves via a digital device. Often this is done as a way to explore sexual identities and intimacies. Even so, any explicit image taken by a child of themself, if they are under the age of 18, is an offence, and if they share it, it is a further offence. However, sometimes young people are put under pressure to send or receive images they aren't comfortable with, and researchers are increas-ingly aware of the pressures many young people experience in such circumstances.

Nevertheless, there are also some interesting studies which point to the ways in which young people resist and negotiate sexual norms, showing how they have produced online stories which challenge hegemonic sexual dis-courses (Kehily, 2011). For instance, O'Neill (2014) looked at how young people had used public online spaces such as YouTube to share narratives about transgender lives. You can read more about social media and young people in Chapter 6 and Chapter 10.

As an everyday sexual practice enabled by the prevalence of mobile phones, sexting has also tended to be approached by researchers and the media as a problem. Young people, especially girls, are often cast as naïve and vulnerable. However, notwithstanding the many valid concerns related to this phenome-non, there are several recent studies which add to the debate by challenging conventional assumptions. Recent research has engaged with young people and suggest that sexting is an accepted and 'normal' practice (Roberts and Ravn, 2020). The young men they spoke to were very conscious of what con-stitutes good sexting practice, citing consent and mutuality as vital. Waling and Pym (2019) argue that girls feel less vulnerable than many studies would sug-gest and that instead, those men who send unwanted 'dick-pics' are viewed as creepy and sad. Setty (2020) has shown how some young men distance them-selves from sexting because of associations with shame. They also resisted and reworked dominant notions of hegemonic masculinity when they did share images of themselves.

Discussion point

Social guidelines

Barker et al. (2018) argue that these experiences of young people are examples of mediated intimacy. Programmes such as *How to Look Good*

(Continued)

Naked, Naked Attraction and *Embarrassing Bodies*, send clear messages to us about what is 'sexy', how we should look, and what we should do.

Social scientific research into problems or issues, sometimes results in suggestions for new policy, or it might lead to a toolkit, for an organization to use. Given that there seems to be some indication that social media is placing undue pressure on young people, in relation to their body image, put together a toolkit for young people themselves, on how to use and negotiate social media. Or write a proposal for related legislative change which would have a positive impact on young people's experience on social media platforms. You could have a look at Barker et al.'s (2018: 1343) 'five top tips for sex advice' first to get some inspiration.

Summary

Arguably, this chapter has shown that sex still sells, and particular kinds of sex. The media introduces us to ideas about sexuality, it shapes our expectations and understandings. Some identities and behaviours are visible, some are rendered invisible, some are celebrated, and others are presented as disreputable or downright dangerous. The media is the prompt for fierce debate too; fictional and non-fictional accounts of sexualities can spark public disputes and can often influence policy-making. In the representation and possible construction of sexuality, Connell (1987) suggests that the media has a key role in the maintenance of consent for current power relationships partly, for instance, through portrayals of emphasized and sexualized femininity, or through depictions of hegemonic heterosexuality. There are suggestions that the constant barrage of images with sexualized, slim bodies selling products or lifestyles is having a direct impact on men and women's relationship to their own bodies and sexuality. In fact, are we seeing an internalized gaze, which operates as a new, disciplinary power for anyone whose body doesn't fit the norm? Some have argued that the media is such a powerful influencer, that we effectively mimic, unquestionably, the images and behaviours we see. Others argue that as consumers we have more agency than that, and actually, in many ways, we are active collaborators in the production of sexual discourses.

There is so much more we could have looked at here – there are fascinating studies into anime and its impact on understandings of sexuality, we could have spent a chapter analyzing the music industry and sexuality (there are some relatively recently debates about *Blurred Lines*, for instance), or online gaming and sexualized representations. I hope that you take some of the themes and questions presented in this chapter and apply them to areas of the media which interest you.

> ## Key questions
>
> - What are the most influential aspects of media in your society in relation to sexuality? What sexual discourse is being promoted?
>
> - In what ways do new social media shape sexual norms? Can you identify moments of resistance?

FURTHER READING

Laura Mulvey's (1975) 'Visual pleasure and narrative cinema', *Screen*, 16 (3): 6–18, remains an extremely important essay, which allows us to think critically about the sexualization of both men and women in contemporary society.

For more on how violence and sexualities are constructed in print and on screen, Karen Boyle's *Media and Violence: Gendering the Debates* (Sage, 2005) is a good place to start.

If you are interested in exploring the impact of social media on young people's sexualities then I would recommend Sander De Ridder's (2017) 'Social media and young people's sexualities: values, norms, and battlegrounds', https://doi.or g/10.1177%2F2056305117738992

5

RELIGION AND SEXUALITY

_____ **Learning outcomes** _____

By the end of this chapter you should be able to:

- Identify key themes underpinning religious understandings of sexuality
- Provide an overview of the social regulation of sexuality through religion
- Critically analyze the impact of religious approaches to sexuality in contemporary societies

Introduction: 'Not at the table dear...'

Talking about sexuality and religion neatly combines two dinner party taboos; both can arouse strong sentiment, and both are considered to be private. As Turner (1991: 112) has noted, there is no one single religious approach to sexuality as 'religious orientations to human sexuality have occupied a variety of positions along a continuum between total denial and orgy'. Each tradition has its own norms, teachings and values, and is often itself subject to intense debate and diverging opinions on sexuality. Foster (1984) gives the example of the Shakers and Oneida Perfectionists. Both were Christian groups, based in the north east of the US, popular in the early nineteenth century. For the Shakers all sex was sinful and **celibacy** the desired state, whilst Oneida Perfectionists saw sex as a holy act. Both took the same version of the Bible as their justification. Zuckerman (2003) highlights the many diverse values in religions over time, from contemporary Mormon monogamy to Islamic poly-gamy, Buddhist sexual denial to Hindu Tantric sex as religious ritual. He notes, however, that despite such colourful diversity, there have also been some con-sistent themes across many religions. Most he argues, condemn male same-sex relations, though female same-sex appears to be less stigmatized and often ignored. The majority do not approve of sex for the sake of pleasure only and would view it as only acceptable within marriage.

This chapter, therefore, focuses on the role of religion in 'private' lives and the ways in which sexuality has been conceptualized. We consider how reli-gion contributes to shaping cultural attitudes to sex and the social organization of sexuality. Some religious traditions accept a diversity of human sexuality (Califia, 1997) whilst others are more rigid (Nussbaum, 1999). A focus on religion is particularly important given the rise of fundamentalist movements globally (Christian, Islamic, Hindu and Judaic) and the potential impact this will have on sexual lives.

A rise in fundamentalist faiths?

The growth of women's and gay rights organizations, their critiques of tradi-tional views of sexuality, and the greater permissiveness of the 1960s and 1970s, led to a backlash from fundamentalist religious groups. Such groups campaigned hard to undo legislation which, for instance, had granted abortion rights and (to varying extents) decriminalized same-sex relations.

Just one very recent example: the Satmar sect of fundamental Judaism recently issued a statement banning girls and married women from going to university, on the grounds that this was against the Torah (Fenton and Rickman, 2016). This group is based in the US and is the biggest Orthodox fundamentalist sect in the UK. Religions have had, and continue to have, a big influence on sex and sexualities. In 2016, 40 countries had anti-women laws – most of these inspired by religion.

Whilst some theorists of sexuality have called for collective 'un-sexualization', Mottier has pointed out that 'there is little in the current state of the politics of sexuality to lead us to conclude that an "unsexual" future is anywhere near, given the renewed propping up of traditional understandings of sex by the fundamen-talist backlash, as well as by scientific discourses' (2008: 126).

Since the 1980s, there has been a revival of fundamentalist religious (as well as biological) models of sexuality. The Catholic Church, for instance, still offi-cially sees gay men as 'objectively disordered' and defines same-sex relations as a 'moral evil'. The rise of Christian, Muslim, and other religious fundamen-talisms throughout large parts of the world has given new life to traditional moral condemnations of sexual 'deviancy'. In the US in particular, the Christian Right has voiced the strongest opposition to gay rights. As a social movement, its support in the US comes in part from the Catholic Church, but primarily from Evangelical Protestant groups whose aim is to restore 'traditional values' against what they see as the 'moral decay' brought about not just by sexual permissiveness, but also by feminist and gay rights campaigns which they see as undermining the patriarchal heterosexual family. Such groups include the following:

- The Promise Keepers: who aim to promote 'strong marriages and families' through, among other things, 'biblical values'. Their goal is to restore the traditional role of men within the heterosexual family.
- The Traditional Values Coalition: who see same-sex relations as immoral and a deliberate attempt to undermine society and 'recruit' young people. Consequently, they strongly oppose gay rights.
- The Westboro Baptist Church (Kansas): notorious for welcoming signs of divine wrath in the US, as a punishment for 'tolerating' same-sex relations, such as AIDS and 9/11. It claims that the US, along with Sweden, Canada, Ireland and Mexico, is a 'Godless sodomite culture'.

However, other fundamentalist religious groups are less extreme, e.g. many western societies have Christian support groups for gay men and women: such groups see same-sex relations as a 'misguided life-style choice', and thus offer 'help' to those who wish to lead a 'proper' heterosexual lifestyle. The largest of these, Exodus International, promises 'freedom from sexuality through the power of Jesus Christ' and offers 'reparative therapy' to 'men and women who struggle with unwanted homosexual attractions' (Mottier, 2008: 115).

Faced with the revival of such conservative religious fundamentalist crusades against the respect for sexual pluralism implicit in the various equal rights campaigns, authors such as Jeffrey Weeks and various queer theorists have attempted to elaborate what Mottier has described as 'alternative, "progressive" value models for sexuality' (2008: 115). However, there have also been liberal theologians, from various religious groups, who have publicly supported feminist and gay rights claims.

Discussion point

The influence of religion

Did you go to a faith-based school, or attend a club or youth group with religious affiliations? Perhaps you had to attend a place of worship, either regularly, or occasionally for religious festivals or ceremonies? If so, what did it tell and/or teach you about sex? If you had no such influence, what do you imagine the impact of such an institution on your ability to learn about sexualities might be? You could read Bartkowski et al's (2019) discussion on this.

Conceptualizations of sexuality: was the past permissive?

Not all religions have treated different sexualities negatively. Many ancient cultures have described and depicted gods with both male and female attributes, thus raising the possibility that people were not seen as rigidly male or female. This is borne out by the fact, as pointed out by Parkinson (2013: 12), that many cultures have references to the existence of intermediate sexes, 'third' sexes and 'hermaphrodites', which combined both sexes in one.

The Indian *Kamasutra* of the fourth century CE, for instance, refers to men who desired other men as having a 'third nature'. In Hindu religious mythologies, gender is often fluid, e.g. the male god Shiva is often depicted as wearing both masculine- and feminine-shaped earrings, while Hindu sacred texts exalt same-sex friendships as well as heterosexual desires. Some Hindu myths also have gods who change gender, while same-sex divine couples give birth to children. Thus, at least in principle, such diversity was accepted as a possibility in human sexuality. According to Vanita and Kidwai (2001: xviii), 'at most times and places in pre-nineteenth century India love between women and between men, even when disapproved of, was not actively persecuted. As far as we know, no one has ever been executed for homosexuality in India'. Sadly, as we shall see later in this book, such tolerant attitudes are being eroded.

In Ancient Sumerian civilization in Mesopotamia, the religious ceremonies surrounding the goddess Ishtar involved men whose masculinity she had turned to femininity. These men were known as *kurgarrus* (a 'third' sex) – while surviving poetry suggests that such men were seen as 'irregular', they were nonetheless an accepted part of the state religion and the divinely-ordained world order. In addition, Califia (1997) has explained how several Native American cultures recognized the existence of what they called 'two-spirit' people, e.g. those who were directed by 'the spirits' to live as a member of the opposite sex. Although such individuals were often teased, these societies nonetheless accepted the sexual behaviours chosen by such individuals. Various anthropological studies have also shown that most cultures have regarded as ordinary sexual behaviours that modern-day societies see as 'homosexual'.

Religion and repression

However, although this evidence hints that some religious traditions have accepted a diversity of sexualities, this is the exception rather than the norm. Most religions, especially the major religions, have condemned and even punished those who transgress what are considered to be the 'normal' sexuality codes. In fact, throughout history, and in the present-day world, women and LGBT+ people have often suffered inequalities, and even persecution, from various religions and/or the states influenced by such religions. In many ways this is not so surprising as most main global religions originated in conservative societies in the distant past. In addition, sociological studies (by those such as Durkheim, Marx and Weber) have shown how religions provide social cohesion by legitimating certain social structures and relations via creating a system of values that attempt to direct and control the actions and conduct of individual members of their respective societies. A very cursory examination of the main religions will quickly confirm that they have strong ideas about the 'proper' roles and behaviours of men and women, and all aspects relating to sexuality.

This is especially true of the various forms of fundamentalism, past and present, which attempt to force all individuals to live according to various supernaturally-revealed 'truths'. While most people today tend to think of fundamentalism as a modern phenomenon, it is important to remember that, for several centuries, most European countries were run according to fundamentalist religious principles, whether Catholic or Protestant. Furthermore, once those Christian societies began to establish colonies in the Americas, Asia and Africa, their fundamentalist views were imposed in their imperial territories on cultures which did not share the European dichotomy as regards sexualities and sexual behaviours.

Western Christianity and the Bible

As was the case in Ancient Greece, the concept 'homosexual' did not exist amongst the nomadic tribesmen of the Middle East, some of whom eventually produced the various 'books' of the Old Testament. As Wilton (2000) and others have pointed out, only two parts of the Old Testament, most famously the mythical story about Sodom and Gomorrah, but also one verse in Leviticus, dealt with what later became known as 'homosexuality'. One explanation for this is that, after these 'books' were compiled, they went through several translations, some of which led to later mistranslations and misinterpretations.

As we saw in Chapter 1, before the nineteenth century western Christianity drew on mythical accounts in the Bible of 'original sin' to depict women as dangerous, lustful temptresses, with lust being identified as one of the seven deadly sins. During the Middle Ages and the Renaissance (from about 900 to 1700), organized religion began to promote marriage and reproductive sex as an acceptable way to channel and control 'lust'. Emphasizing chastity, monogamy and sexual fidelity within marriage, Garton (2004) shows how early Christianity also often combined a profound distaste for sex with a particular horror of women's bodies and sexuality, casting them as corrupters of men. During the Industrial Revolution from the late eighteenth century, the Christian church contributed to ideas about the passive female and the housewife-mother role, and second wave feminists of the 1970s drew attention to how such religious beliefs buttressed a patriarchal ideology and the inequalities and oppressions which stemmed from it. In fact, most religions around the world defined women as subordinate to men.

In addition, although women often played a significant role within early Christianity, this increasingly troubled male Christian leaders, who struggled with reconciling female authority with their belief that the 'natural' role of women was servitude. By the end of the fourth century CE, authorities were of the view that women could not act as teachers or priests. However, some historians have pointed to the existence of several contemporary pagan cults which had similar attitudes to sex in general, and women's sexuality in particular, and have thus argued that 'the pervasive Christian condemnations of sexuality and the body were founded less on the teachings of Christ than on efforts to compete with these rival religious sects' (Garton, 2004: 50). Similarly, there are several examples amongst pagan philosophers of both classical and late antiquity, such as Seneca, who had similar attitudes to sexuality. A number of early Christian theologians drew on the works of these philosophers, and such examples were still being used as late as the thirteenth century. Despite these aspects, some historians, such as Elaine Pagels (1995), nonetheless stress the radical differences between Christians and pagans over sexuality, with Christianity seeing chastity as a way of freeing the self.

However, John Boswell, a medievalist historian, has argued that Christianity 'had a less dramatic impact on modes of coupling than its leaders wished and its apologists (and critics) have pretended' (1994: 108–9). Instead, he argues that both Roman law and Rabbinic teaching were greater influences on attitudes to eroticism. He also argues that there is evidence of early Christian acceptance of 'gay' subcultures in Europe, as had been the case in antiquity, and that the Christian Church 'accepted same-sex relationships and even had ceremonies paralleling and largely replicating marriage services solemnizing unions of men' (1994: 53). His exploration of ancient texts and sources has resulted in his argument for considerable continuities in western sexual mores, and for his rejection of the notion that early Christianity marked a clear discontinuity from these issues. Similar arguments are put forward by Bernadette Brooten who has focused on female homoeroticism. In *Love Between Women: Early Christian Responses to Female Homoeroticism* (1996), she makes the point that Boswell exhibits 'gender blindness', which causes him to focus almost exclusively on male same-sex relationships. Her main argument regarding continuity between pagan and early Christian attitudes is that both cultures exhibited 'persistent antipathy to love between women' (1996: 54). In particular, she argues that there are fewer turning points in the history of female homoeroticism:

> … because of the persistent structures of male domination. Love between women challenged the phallocentric cultures of pagan and Christian antiquity, and the response to this challenge has shaped the historical experience of lesbians ever since. In the hands of influential Church Fathers, such as St Paul, longstanding antagonism and fear of female homoeroticism found a very secure and continuing place within Christian doctrine. (1996: 54)

Many are in agreement that Christians were at war with the body and sexuality, and it was accompanied by the view that women were a corrupting influence.

Discussion point

A religious legacy?

How far do you think that traditional religious ideas about sexuality still affect sexuality and the rights of sexual minorities in the early twenty-first century? Does this explain the continued reluctance in many societies – even where the religion no longer holds political power – to permit same-sex civil partnerships and marriage?

Discussion point

Women and religion

How can religious institutions combat gender/sexual inequality whilst simultaneously contributing to it?

Seemingly secular? Cultural and social organization of sexuality

For many centuries, various religions, across the world, were central to the definition of morality and the organization of sexual behaviours. However, the process of secularization, beginning in Europe, in many ways, with Renaissance humanism, led to the gradual detachment of sexual values from religious ones. From the mid-nineteenth century, judgements about sexuality passed from the churches to various secular agencies – in particular, the medical profession. In both Britain and the US, feminists complained that doctors and sexologists were becoming a new 'priesthood', and were attempting, like religion, to control female sexuality. Yet the various religions have not given up their attempts to regulate and control sexual behaviours, e.g. the Catholic Church continues to influence such sexual aspects as birth control, abortion, same-sex relations and same-sex marriage. Similar attempts exist in most parts of the world, especially where various fundamentalist faiths have put issues concerning sexuality, gender and the body at the centre of their agendas.

Since the 1970s, a number of absolutist religious-political movements have arisen, usually referred to as 'fundamentalism'. According to Weeks (2011: 60), the term originally referred to the writings and activities in the early twentieth century of US and British conservative Christians (mainly evangelical Protestants) who campaigned against the threat to 'biblical truth' represented by Darwinian evolutionism. It was this movement which lay behind the infamous 'Monkey Case' brought against John Scopes, a biology teacher in Dayton, Tennessee, over his belief in evolutionism. Though found guilty, he was reprieved on appeal. As a result of the derision which this case attracted, the influence of these early fundamentalists waned.

Garton, among others, points out how, even in the early twenty-first century, many Christian church authorities still see anal and oral sex as 'against nature' because they are not acts for the purposes of procreation. This is in many respects just a continuation of the way that the Christian religion, and other religions in other periods, has tried to control sexuality. As Montserrat (1996: 163–6) has shown, this repressive attitude to sex and sexuality on the part of religion was not always the case – especially in the Ancient World, e.g. 'Canoptic life' suggested religion and sexual licence were not entirely incompatible.

Until the late eighteenth/early nineteenth centuries, Protestant theology was thus linked to an idealized view of sexual relations within marriage, and the popular idea of 'conjugal debt' (where both husbands and wives had a right to demand intercourse) indicated an acceptance of the 'naturalness' of marital relations. However, a re-emergence of Evangelical thought in England and the Second Great Awakening in the US, re-emphasized notions of virtue, restraint and morality. As a result, religious injunctions to practise abstinence marked an important transformation in Protestantism and came to influence religious views in Victorian Britain and the US. Religious moralist views were gradually swamped by the proliferation of medical texts on sex and the body in the nineteenth century. As a consequence, moralists gradually adopted medical/scientific ideas to continue their arguments for sexual restraint.

Diversity and rigidity

As Weeks (2011) and others have pointed out, for much of human history, sexuality has traditionally been seen by early theorists in terms of dominant ideas about 'right' and 'wrong', with the prime purpose of sex being reproduction, and therefore its 'natural' location is between men and women. The legitimacy of such views was upheld by religion and, increasingly, by the state. Other forms of sexuality, such as extra-marital sex, same-sex relations, prostitution, and non-reproductive sex were, conversely, generally seen as immoral aberrations from or even perversions of 'true' sexuality.

During the nineteenth century it became increasingly difficult to uphold such beliefs and this caused particular problems for religions. Both anthropological studies, and the new science of sexology, showed just how diverse and varied patterns of sexual behaviours were. In the twentieth century, social studies by the Chicago School and then, later, by Kinsey and his colleagues, confirmed the existence of diverse sexualities beneath the conventionally-approved patterns of sexual behaviour (see Chapters 1 and 2).

However, as Weeks points out, 'An emphasis on the social shaping of sexual cultures does not mean they are ephemeral, or easily changed. A striking feature about sexual cultures is how deeply embedded they are, taking on the air of naturalness and inevitability, even when they are near neighbours or coexist with one another' (2011: 181). For example, within Europe, the religious divisions reflect clearly different sexual cultures, despite the spread of secularism in that continent. Eder et al. (1999: 6–10) have detected four distinct religious-moral patterns:

- North West Europe, largely Protestant since the sixteenth century, has tended to emphasize the nuclear family, while variously disapproving of, or condemning, extra-marital sex and same-sex relations. Prostitution, while also condemned, has often been tacitly accepted in practice.
- In Southern Europe, the Catholic countries, whilst often having stricter moral codes which condemned various sexual 'sins', also had a covert acceptance of same-sex relations, as long as it did not breach gender norms.
- In Eastern Europe, the Orthodox countries, which, in earlier times, were often famed for sexual licentiousness, became from the early modern period much more morally conservative, and often imposed strong divisions between men and women.
- In South Western Europe, where Islam was dominant for some centuries, and now is influential in many north European cities, there were strict moral codes. However, as regards men, there was a significant difference between theory and practice – as long as sexual behaviours remained private and gender norms were not publicly violated.

From the early 1980s, the Christian Right mounted campaigns against same-sex relations as well as against paedophile activism which had emerged in the 1970s, erroneously linking the two. For instance, in the US, the conservative Anita Bryant headed a 'crusade', which she named *Save Our Children*, against what she said was 'the threat of homosexual recruitment of our children'. As Mottier (2008: 107) points out, this 'portrayed all gays – and gay men in particular – as potential child molesters and triggered the start of organized opposition to gay rights organizations in the US from the late 1970s'.

During the 1980s, when AIDS became public knowledge, many religious fundamentalists and the religious Right claimed that it was 'divine' retribution for the sexual permissiveness of the 1960s and 1970s. In particular, in the early years when AIDS seemed to just be a problem within the gay community, fundamentalists saw it as proof that same-sex relations were against God's or Allah's teachings, and should therefore cease and/or not be tolerated. This was particularly marked in Thatcher's Britain and Reagan's USA, where religious fundamentalists criticized and actively opposed abortion, feminist views on women's sexuality and the claims of gay rights activists. Such religious groups called for the state to intervene in order to bring about 'moral regeneration'.

Such religious views also tried to shape discussions about what prevention policies were best suited to dealing with AIDS. Although medical experts agreed that, apart from total sexual abstinence, the most effective measure was the use of condoms, the Catholic Church and various fundamentalist religious groups rejected condom use as preventing procreation and/or promoting sexual promiscuity. Thus, in the US and elsewhere, 'Just Say No!' campaigns were developed to promote sexual abstinence, while unmarried young people with a 'sexual past' were encouraged to become 'born-again virgins' by making a pledge to refrain from further sexual activity until marriage. Conservative US sexologists, such as Helen Singer Kaplan, Theresa Crenshaw and Masters and Johnson, who rejected the idea of 'safe sex', were often prepared to ally with such religious groups in order to contain AIDS by reducing sexual activity (Money, 1991).

The rise of fundamentalisms

As Weeks and others have pointed out, after the Enlightenment, many rationalists assumed that, in the face of reason and science, the influence of religion would decline. None of the main theorists of social science in the nineteenth century – Marx, Durkheim and Weber – were 'believers', while Freud saw religion as 'a response to infantile needs'. Yet despite the march of modernity, and the spread of secularization, the late twentieth and early twenty-first centuries have seen 'faith' make a significant comeback. Apart from often fierce cultural clashes and political divides linked to religion, in many parts of the world there has been a marked rise in fundamentalism. As Weeks states (2011: 157), 'God is back ... And sexuality is at the heart of this apparent religious revival on a world scale'.

All religious systems have always been preoccupied, in one way or another, with people's bodies and their various sexual desires. All religions, whether polytheistic or monotheistic, have certain attitudes to sexuality, though there is no consistency in their various dogmas and ethics on this issue. Some religions, such as Judaism, are highly prescriptive and proscriptive about family, gender and sexual ethics. Although some have spoken about the 'radical legitimacy of the practice of sexuality in the Islamic world', there are clear, and sharp, exceptions. For instance, same-sex relations are 'violently condemned' by Islam, while extra-marital sex for women can, even in the twenty-first century, lead to such women being stoned to death in several fundamentalist Muslim countries (Bouhdiba, 1985: 159, 200). As regards Christianity, its mainstream traditions have long had a deep and troubled relationship with the body, especially women's bodies. In the Middle Ages, Christianity drew up a list of 'sexual sins' which were seen as worse than rape (because rape could at least lead to conception): these included masturbation and sodomy. Although from the sixteenth century Weeks argues a 'new eroticism' began (mainly at first within Protestant groups) to enter conjugal relationships, this was often accompanied by an intensification of strictures against non-marital and same-sex relations (MacCulloch, 2009).

Even though, in Europe, enforcement of laws against sexual 'misbehaviour' began to move from the Church to the State from the early modern period, such acts continued to convey the idea of 'sin' as well as crime: 'Sodomy, too awful to be named amongst Christians, according to an English jurist in the seventeenth century, remained both [a sin and crime] into the nineteenth century, and only in the twentieth century did religion and the law gradually separate' (Weeks, 2011: 157). Across Europe, the most secularized part of the world, issues such as birth control, abortion and divorce remained entangled with religious beliefs until the late twentieth century.

Between being and doing

Despite various differences, orthodox/fundamentalist faith systems do have some things in common, i.e. the subordination of women and the punishment of same-sex relations. This is despite the fact that Christianity, Islam and Judaism have often proclaimed the **equality** of women within their faiths. In many instances, practice is often different from theory. As Weeks points out:

Muslim men in the twenty-first century are allowed four wives under sharia law, a wife one husband. Men are allowed to marry outside the faith, women can only marry into the faith. In Islam and Orthodox Judaism, segregation of worship is still normal. Women are respected, but overwhelmingly in their domestic roles as mother and wife. In the Christian churches women's admission to the priesthood has been a hazardous journey. (2011: 158)

However, the greatest controversies surround not women's formal roles within faiths, but that of their sexual autonomy. In orthodox or fundamentalist countries such as Saudi Arabia and Iran, or in areas in Afghanistan, Iraq and Syria controlled by such fundamentalist groups as the Taleban and ISIS, the re-imposition of the veil and *burka* on women marks what is often a violent rejection by men of modernity and the effects it has had on women. In Western Europe, paradoxically, the adoption of the veil and burka by Muslim women is often portrayed as a mark of their autonomy against the sexualizing influences of modern culture.

In addition to struggling with women's sexuality, many fundamentalist faiths have found it difficult to cope with the emergence of affirmative gay and lesbian identities. In the past, same-sex relations often coexisted alongside various religions, though usually uneasily. Islamic countries in North Africa often tolerated same-sex relations between men, as long as they did not 'impinge on a man's gender identity' (Weeks, 2011: 158). In England, in the late nineteenth and early twentieth centuries, it was widely known that there were many gay men within the Anglican priesthood. Yet this issue proved to be especially fraught; both the Church of England, and the Episcopalian Church in the US, came close to schism over gay priests and bishops (Bates, 2004). It became such an issue largely because LGBT+ members of those churches were no longer willing to accept 'discretion' as the price of acceptance. Since the 1970s, various movements arose both within and without Christian churches in the US, Western Europe and elsewhere to affirm the faith of LGBT+ Christians. Similar movements have emerged amongst gay Muslims and Jews.

Discussion point

LGBT+ marginalization

- Is it fair to say that religion sometimes fosters **heterosexism** and **homophobia**?
- You may find Wedow et al.'s (2017) discussion of their research useful.

Life in the margins? Continuities and change for LGBT+ communities

Academic scholarship is increasingly showing the ways in which LGBT+ people are able to explore their sexuality within a religious context. Research reveals the ways in which they cope and sometimes thrive under what appears to be religious oppression (Yip, 2009). Krista McQueeney's (2009) research ('We are all God's children, y'all: race, gender and sexuality in lesbian and gay affirming congregations') compared a black, working-class, lesbian congregation within an evangelical church with a white, mainly middle-class and heterosexual congregation in a liberal protestant church. Despite worshipping within an apparently conservative Christianity, where God's will is believed to be expressed in the heterosexual family, with men and women seen as complementary and sex an act purely for procreation, both congregations also had a firm belief in the inherent dignity of people, women's suffrage and the abolition of slavery. LGBT+ people were able to negotiate their identity within this context in various ways. Some 'reproduced politics of respectability' (Warner, 1999): they used Christian discourse to normalize their own identity. Less positively, others minimized the importance of sexuality and constructed it as separate from Christianity. Some reproduced the politics of normalization by making a distinction between good and bad lesbians; monogamous couples were good and 'others' were bad. Some of the working-class black gay men she observed performed a form of 'Christian manhood'; as heads or leaders, they were able to construct a masculinity which was viewed to challenge stereotypes of gay men. For some women, their identity as 'good mothers' became an important way of being good Christians *despite* being lesbian. In other words, what was happening was sometimes a complex mix of minimizing, moralizing and normalizing strategies, which often left the idea of same-sex sin unchallenged and benefitted those closer to the mainstream at the expense of those on the margins (Cohen, 1997).

The intersection of sexuality and gender: LGBT+ women and Judaism

As with other religions, sexual acts between women are not envisioned and hence not specifically mentioned in the Torah. Within it, sanctions focus on male same-sex desire (Fox, 1983). Women remain largely unnamed within this book, though where they are named it is as sexual objects (as opposed to subjects). Female sexuality, in particular lesbianism, is only mentioned briefly in later interpretations of the law by Rabbinic scholars. These condemn women 'playing around with others' as 'the practices of the Egyptians'; in this sense, lesbianism is 'othered' as a deviant practice belonging to another culture or religion. Ideas of female sexuality are constructed by men; they are passive and sex is penile penetration (Biale, 1984: 196).

Various cultural texts, however, have attempted to force questions around religion and female sexuality, though often they have found themselves the focus of controversy. In 1923, for instance, the play *God of Vengeance* was shut down on morality charges just weeks after opening on Broadway because of its depiction of LGBT+ women. Although formal teaching of Judaism has not changed in its stance on lesbianism in the last four hundred years, the twentieth century saw shifts reflecting wider social changes; after reform within conservative denominations women and LGBT+ people have been able to become rabbis and cantors, however Orthodox Judaism has been slower to change (see Sarah, 1995). The recent film *Disobedience* (Lelio, 2018), takes up the mantle and highlights key issues pertaining to religion and sexuality. Based on Naomi Alderman's fictional representation of her own experiences, the film explores the ways in which female same-sex desire is viewed in an orthodox Jewish community. She cited a 2001 documentary, *Trembling Before G-d*, as being an important influence for her novel. The documentary looked at the ways in which many were torn between their religion and their LGBT+ identity, feeling unable to reconcile the two.

Slowly, attitudes are, perhaps, shifting. The British chief rabbi Ephraim Mirvis has recently published a guidebook, entitled 'The Wellbeing of LGBT+ Pupils', requesting that Jewish schools in the UK take a zero-tolerance approach to homophobic and transphobic bullying, and to teach all children to regard others and themselves with respect and kindness.

However, the rise of more fundamentalist forms of religion across all the major faiths has seen active campaigns against same-sex relations, which are designed to mobilize the 'faithful' and re-establish traditional boundaries around the respective 'true faiths'. The Catholic Church has faced real problems because, as well as continuing to hate the 'sin' of same-sex relations, it has been the subject of many accusations of child abuse by priests. In some parts of the Islamic world such hostility has taken a more violent form, with many gay men either being executed or murdered for their sexual identity.

In many ways, these fundamentalist groups, despite their strong rejection of modernism, have used twenty-first century communication technologies to propagate their beliefs. Many of those drawn to them are people, mainly young men, who see fundamentalism as a haven from the rapid changes and insecurities of modernity and globalization, and a way of affirming traditional conservative values, especially as regards family and gender roles, and sexual conformity.

Arguably, in the 1970s, a newer and more general type of fundamentalism began to develop around the world. This new version has gone beyond conservative Christianity, and now also includes mass movements associated with Islam, Hinduism and Judaism.

Despite obvious differences between these religions, they have certain features in common (Bhatt, 1997):

- Textual literalism as regards their respective 'holy' texts.
- A forceful rejection of what they see as the collapse of 'morality' and growing secularism.
- A strong and absolutist belief that only their faith possesses the 'Truth'.
- A passionate preoccupation with gender, sexuality and the body.

With the rapid spread of **globalization** and its often disruptive impact on traditional ways of life, and the collapse of secular 'grand narratives' of change and improvement (especially Marxism after 1988–89), many of those affected turned to fundamentalist religions as these seemed to offer alternative sources of meaning and identity. In particular, those in the non-western world were attracted by the older beliefs' opposition to the values of western liberalism, secularism and relativism (Bhatt, 1997: 61).

In the context of spreading modernism and globalization, many of these fundamentalist groups focus in particular on women who do not conform to traditional ideas of femininity, and men and women who challenge conventional binaries of sex, gender and sexuality. They are framed as being responsible for the destruction of traditional social order and family life.

According to MacCulloch (2009: 990), the changes to traditional orders associated with modernity resulted in anger, especially amongst displaced young men. In his view, this anger embodied 'the hurt of heterosexual men at cultural shifts which have generally threatened to marginalize them and deprive them of dignity, hegemony or even much usefulness' (MacCulloch, 2009: 61). Giddens (1994: 80) has identified such threats to the integrity of traditional life patterns as very often being seen as profound attacks on the integrity of the self. Such reactionary movements, whilst, in a real sense, are attempts to return to traditional values and a past long-gone, are also rooted in the present, being reactions against the fast pace of the changes and uncertainties associated with modernity and globalization.

Islamic feminism: a tool for change

A significant feature of religion, as we have seen, is the endorsement of misogyny through doctrine and religious scriptures which shape and embed misogyny into society (Cervantes-Altamirano, 2013; Shackle, 2013). For example, Politt (2013) examines sexual equality in the alleged afterlife of the three main Abrahamic faiths of Judaism, Christianity and Islam. Doctrine was written by men for men who themselves have based their interpretations on personal biases (Cervantes-Altamirano, 2013; Mir-Hosseini, 2004).

The need to control the nature of women's sexuality, and its perceived danger, is evident across the three major Abrahamic faiths. This is apparent in the Christian attitudes towards sex and celibacy which have arguably been detrimental to both men and women (Politt, 2013). Another example is within Islam, where menstrual taboos prevent men from having sex with their wives while they are bleeding (Shackle, 2013). Furthermore, as we have seen, there is consistency in the preoccupation with policing female virginity or fidelity and women's modesty (Politt, 2013). For example, within British Muslim communities, perceived cultural practices such as so-called 'honour'-based violence have been effectively utilized to ensure the control of women (Brandon and Hafez, 2008; Sanghera, 2007). More emphasis, too, is placed upon regulating the sexuality of Muslim women compared to Muslim men where, for example, women are required to dress 'modestly' (Badran, 2011). In Islam, such modesty comes in the form of the veil; this is used in its broadest sense to include modest clothing and the *hijab* (headscarf). The *niqaab* (face veil) may be 'promoted' to the extent where it is sometimes perceived as a form of oppression (Joppke, 2009; Khiabany and Williamson, 2008). It is worth noting that in the UK Muslims are heterogeneous, having distinct cultural and social traditions from their respective communities, and therefore each will interpret religious scriptures differently (Khiabany and Williamson, 2008). Feminism has played an important role for such women and has provided a way of negotiating their religious and sexual selves (Badran, 2011; Shackle, 2013).

The rise of political Islam in the Middle East has arguably fostered binaries of west versus east, and secular versus religious (Mir-Hosseini, 2004). Political Islam has conflated feminism with the west and therefore constructed it as anti-Islam (Mir-Hosseini, 2004). In reality, Badran (2011) argues that in the early stages of feminism in Egypt, Muslim women utilized the teachings of their religion to bring awareness to their individual rights and responsibilities. Parallels can be drawn with Christian women who used religious texts to highlight their God-given rights (Politt, 2013). Political Islam, therefore, claims it is impossible for a Muslim woman to identify as a feminist; Islam and feminism are mutually exclusive concepts (Segran, 2013; Siddiqui, 2006). Nevertheless, in the face of such consternation, many women are determined to challenge the oppression they face.

Islamic feminism has its roots in the aspirational Sisters in Islam (SIS), based in Malaysia during the 1980s. They were organized around giving marginalized Muslim women a voice and, therefore, autonomy. Focusing on the issue of domestic abuse, they used the Quran, along with *hadiths*, to give women advice. Previously accepted oppressive practices of domestic abuse had been justified by flawed readings of the doctrine. The challenges by SIS empowered the lives of many. A contemporary global movement entitled Musawah, Arabic for 'equality', has been setting the standards for advocating the rights of

Muslim women in an Islamic context (see Segran, 2013). Drawing on contemporary human rights and equality discourse, along with Islamic jurisprudence, Islamic feminists have increased the rights and responsibilities afforded to Muslim women; Badran (2011) has called this Muslim holistic feminism. Organizations such as Musawah, have meant that women do not always have to choose between their faith or their rights.

Women have been able to utilize Islamic knowledge to assert their sexual rights, e.g. some have been given the confidence to refuse to participate in unprotected sex with husbands who have AIDS or other sexually transmitted infections. Previously, this would have been perceived as an obligation of marriage. SIS, who work in collaboration with Musawah, provide literature and deploy activists to inform women of their rights and agency in an Islamic context, which empowers them and enables them to utilize Islamic jurisprudence to argue against ill treatment, such as that of husbands who neglect them or have affairs outside of the marriage. The response the victims of patriarchal structures operating in Muslim communities give with regard to the deployment of Islamic jurisprudence is a positive one, as their husbands and families are more likely to make positive changes that are respectful of their individual rights and responsibilities (Segran, 2013).

Summary

In this chapter we have begun to explore the role of religion in shaping attitudes to sexuality. Clearly, there is no single religious approach to sexuality, and even within an overarching faith such as Christianity, there are diverging views. In order to understand any given religion's attitude to sexuality, there are many complex political, social and cultural influences which need to be considered. Women's sexuality still seems to be a thorny issue, which is perhaps not surprising when 'theological appreciation of the feminine does not necessarily lead to a positive evaluation of real women' (Hawley, 1986: 235). Ongoing debates within the Roman Catholic church about birth control and abortion show the potential for heterosexuality to disrupt religious discourse. Sexuality, and especially LGBT+ sexuality, is still often framed as a sin, a problem to be denied or controlled (Mellor and Shilling, 2010). We have seen that religion remains a strong influence on how many of us feel about sexuality (Parrinder, 1996). Even those who are atheist, may well absorb the religious attitudes of their culture. Yet this is not necessarily problematical – we have also seen that many religions have developed more tolerant attitudes to sexualities, allowing their followers to negotiate their sexuality by feeling they belong to their faith (Valentine and Waite, 2012). It is vital, therefore, if we are to have a fuller understanding of sexuality, to pay attention to the religious beliefs and practices which continue to exert an influence over our under-standings of sexuality (Denison, 1998).

Key questions

- In relation to any given religion, what aspects of sexuality are its key concern?
- In the case of competing equality strands, should one be given more weight than the other?

FURTHER READING

An interesting exploration of the ways in which Muslim men negotiate their gay identities, is to be found in Tom Boellstorff's (2005) 'Between religion and desire: being Muslim and Gay in Indonesia', *American Anthropologist*, 107 (4): 575–85.

If you wish to read more about sexuality as written within the New Testament, you could start with William Loader's *Sexuality and the Jesus Tradition* (Eerdmans, 2005).

Jonathan Magonet's *Jewish Explorations of Sexuality* also provides some very interesting essays on the tensions between tradition and modernity (Berghahn, 1995).

John Boswell's understanding of sexualities has come under fire for taking a somewhat 'essentialist' approach (notably by David Halperin) but you might want to look at *Chrisitanity, Social Tolerance and Homosexuality: Gay People in Western Europe from the Beginning of the Christian Era to the Fourteenth Century* (Chicago University Press, 1980), to see if you think the criticisms have validity.

6

INTIMACIES

─────── Learning outcomes ───────

By the end of this chapter you should be able to:

- Understand the ways in which intimate relationships vary across cultures and over time
- Examine some contemporary theories which tend to study wider intimacies as opposed to the 'traditional' family unit
- Identifiy some of the social changes which shift the ways in which people construct and maintain intimate relationships in the twenty-first century

Introduction

What traditionally has been known as the sociology of the family (with a focus on the structure of the idealized, white, nuclear family) is increasingly being conceptualized as the sociology of intimacies and relationships, in order to capture some of the ways in which we have organized our intimate lives differently. The twenty-first century has seen a raft of policy changes concerning marriage and adoption in the **global north**. People are getting married later, divorce rates are higher than they were fifty years ago, many people have increased access to reproductive techniques (though of course such privileges are classed and 'raced'). There is also, arguably, increased social acceptance of childbirth outside of marriage and LGBT+ families.

This chapter introduces and explicates the main ways in which we organize our sexual identities, through institutions such as marriage and parenting, in such a context. The family, as an institution, has frequently been cited by feminists as one which has traditionally legitimated the commission of violence against women and children. This chapter, therefore, will also examine the 'dark side' of intimate lives in a variety of contexts. Following this will be a discussion of the rise of new technologies and their role in the transformation of intimate sexual lives. Included within this, will be a discussion of social networks and 'virtual communities', and the potential for new technology to transform erotic practices. Boundaries between the public and private in relation to sexual practice are becoming increasingly blurred, and sexual communication can now take place across global spaces. This chapter will consider some of the implications of this 'cybersexual smorgasbord' (Plummer, 2003) – the pleasures and dangers of the digital age. For example, have new technologies created opportunities for new forms of exploitation? Does sexuality always have to be about the interaction of flesh and blood (Weeks, 2007)?

Discussion point

The charmed circle

Rubin (1984: 101) argued that all cultures have a sexual hierarchy, a set of sexual identities and practices which conform to hegemonic norms and thus are postioned within a 'charmed circle', such as monogamy and (heterosexual) marriage. Other forms of intimacy are placed within the outer limits of the circle, or excluded altogether, e.g. same-sex relations and kink practices.

- Have a look at Rubin's diagram and have a go at updating it. Consider what may have changed and what has remained the same.
- How might intersectional thinking help us to better understand this circle?

Family and friends

The family, for many, may seem like a 'haven in a heartless world', a source of comfort and security. Such a commonsense and, perhaps, romantic view of the family is an easy image to succumb to when it is an institution that most of us feel we know. This conventional perception, stereotype even, of the family is questioned and explored from different perspectives by sociologists. As Berger and Berger (1976: 93–4) argue, 'the family is an essential component of almost everyone's taken-for-granted world. It is all the more necessary to gain some distance from this taken-for-granted perspective if one is to understand what the institution is all about ... Familiarity breeds not so much contempt as blindness'.

Many families are based on kinship – a social bond of blood ties, marriage or adoption – but who is included under the umbrella term 'family' changes over time and across different cultures. Rather than being a 'natural' unit, therefore, the family could be said to be another example of social construction. Many social theorists have suggested that the family is interesting to study because of the way it is shaped by society, and the way in turn it helps to shape society. The family is also interesting and important in other ways as an object of sociological enquiry, as it is:

- a legally sanctioned institution and central to many governments' policies and party-political rhetoric;
- also at the centre of one of the fundamental paradoxes in our lives: the fact that we are individuals but we are also social beings;
- often seen as playing a central role in reproducing and producing links between the individual and society.

In the context of this book, many of us first learn about sexuality and sexualities within such units. Sociological understandings of the family and relationships have shifted over time, as is reflected in the title of this chapter. This shift in emphasis allows for a more flexible focus on the emotional content of relationships (Smart, 2008). As such, it then becomes possible to include a variety of relationships between friends, sexual partners, family and kin, instead of perceiving the traditional family as the only possible model for personal relationships.

Discussion point

Intimacies

What advantages do you perceive in exploring intimacy, in its fullest sense, as opposed to 'the family'? Why might this be an important conceptual shift for understanding sexualities?

The family is a social unit traditionally understood as those affiliated by legal or blood ties, or by co-residence. Intimacies or intimate relationships refer to those relationships whereby people may not necessarily be linked by blood or legal ties, but nevertheless see themselves as constituting a meaningful unit. Jamieson (2002) suggests there are four key types of intimacies: couple relationships; parent–child relationships; sexual relationships; and those between friends and kin.

Theories of the family

There are three broad theories of family life that have been developed alongside trends in mainstream sociology and these are summarized as follows.

Marxist interpretations of family life

Marxist theories regard the family as an exploitative institution, which serves to reproduce social inequalities and uphold capitalism (Zaretsky, 1976). Engels (1972 [1884]), in *The Origin of the Family: Private Property and the State*, analyzed the emergence of the nuclear family and male dominance in western societies, suggesting that the growth of private property and patriarchy evolved together. Within the nuclear family, it is argued, women are relegated to the private sphere, enabling men to work in the public sphere and accumulate wealth, the suggestion being that if women were able to participate in the public sphere their lot would be improved. Delmar (1976: 287) has argued that Engels' major contribution was to suggest that 'women's oppression was a problem of history, rather than biology'. Identifying that women were oppressed because of social convention as opposed to biological fate entails that changes in society could improve the situation of women.

Whilst Marx might not have treated the women in his life particularly well, his theories, along with those of Engels, are useful for a consideration of sexuality more generally, and provide a useful insight into the oppression of women in particular. As Reynolds (2018) notes, Marxist formulations of sexuality can be traced back to the late nineteenth century, with Magnus Hirschfeld supporting 'homosexual' and transgender rights (see Weeks, 1985), or Eduard Bernstein defending same-sex sexuality during the trials of Oscar Wilde. Through the early moments of the Bolshevik revolution, there was a hint of a more enlightened approach to sexuality. Alexandra Kollontai's arguments in the 1920s, for instance, echoed feminist concerns about women's exploitation in society within marriage and prostitution. She placed an emphasis on private property and class inequality as causal factors in reinforcing gendered inequality and sexual oppression. Many contemporary feminists have been sceptical, though, of the suggestion that if women had more involvement with the economy their status would be improved. There is evidence that women who go out to work are also left with the majority of the housework, the so-called 'double burden' of domestic and paid labour (Campbell, 2013). Women also often take on 'service' work which can be seen as an extension of their housework, e.g. nursing, and such work has a relatively low status, and low pay, in our society.

Functionalist theory

Functionalist approaches have viewed the family as an important 'organ' in the 'body' of society (see for example, Parsons and Bales, 1955). For functionalist sociologist George Murdock (1949), the 'traditional' nuclear family with its rigid gender roles of the father as breadwinner and mother as carer and house-wife, provides the best opportunity for the socially controlled expression of the (heterosexual) sex drive. More importantly, they argue that the family serves an important role in society in terms of maintaining social stability and order by socializing children and stabilizing adults. Part of this socializing involves conveying understandings of what is appropriate sexual expression. For functionalists, this is an important part of being a parent. Karen Martin (2009) has shown that many families fulfil this expectation very effectively. Through looking at what parents say to their children about sexuality and reproduction, she found that even with children as young as three years old, parents routinely assumed their children were heterosexual, that they would get (heterosexually) married, and that cross-gender interactions between chil-dren were markers of heterosexuality. Alongside this kind of socialization is an additional emphasis on normative sexuality – compulsory monogamy – where families reinforce norms about the importance of exclusive romantic and sexual relationships, with marriage being valued over other kinds of relation-ship (Willey, 2016). Such expectations of the family are reflected in many of the governmental initiatives outlined below. Although the work of Parsons and Murdock is important in that it acknowledges the importance of the family unit in society, there have been various criticisms of functionalist perspectives on the family. A key problem is that functionalist theory places the hetero-sexual (and arguably white and middle-class) nuclear family as the 'norm', and renders other forms of kinship as dysfunctional or deviant – which is problem-atic when in fact very few families conform to the nuclear family ideal. Functionalist theory also does not pay enough attention to the gendered eco-nomic and power inequalities within many intimate relationships, and the harms that these can lead to, an omission that feminists have criticized.

Feminist approaches to 'the family'

A third approach emerged with the early second wave feminist theories of the 1970s, providing some of the most comprehensive challenges to understand-ings of the family. These are dealt with elsewhere in this book, so this section will be brief, however, early arguments were that family structures are in no way natural or inevitable, and that the family is a major site of the subordina-tion of women (Mitchell, 1971; Oakley, 1972). Feminists revealed that the gendered divisions of the family were socially constructed and served to per-petuate patriarchy. Sylvia Walby (1989) describes patriarchy as 'a system of social structures and practices in which men dominate, oppress, and exploit women' (Walby, 1989: 214). A key way in which the family shored up patri-archy was through sexual oppression. Black feminists also highlighted the ways in which functionalist theories privileged white, middle-class family structures, rendering immigrant households or those with alternative structures as 'other' (Collins, 2008). Feminists also drew attention to the false separation of the public sphere from the private in relation to sexuality. Firstly, they argued that women were excluded from participating in the public sphere because of their reproductive duties in the private realm of the family. They also called into question the understanding of the family as private, due to the fact that the household and their roles within it are heavily scrutinized and policed by state policies – hence the famous feminist slogan 'the personal is political'.

Discussion point

Reproduction of the family

Have a look at contemporary policies on families and intimate relationships. These might be to do with marriage, adoption, divorce. Which of the three broad approaches are reflected most obviously in these policies?

Compare this to how families and intimate relationships are portrayed on television, e.g. in soap operas, or dramas. What is their role in relation to sexuality?

Shifting patterns and ideologies of intimacy

Many recent studies into family life have pointed to the various ways in which behaviours changed by the end of the twentieth century in the west. As mentioned earlier, this includes consistent patterns of delayed marriage, increased divorce, re-marriage, having children later in life, and, more recently, changes in cohabitation such as Living Apart Together (LAP). This period saw greater emphasis being placed on personal choice and happiness. A new form of society emerged, therefore, a period of 'high modernity' (Giddens, 1992) or 'reflexive modernity' (Beck, 1994). A positive consequence of high modernity, for Giddens, is a loosening and blurring of the structural frameworks that underpin heterosexual relationships and the separation of sex and reproduction. Increasingly, he argues, men and women are compelled to reflexively create their identity through day-to-day decisions. This enables individuals to choose partnerships on a basis of mutual understanding, leading to 'pure relationships'. By a 'pure relationship' he refers to:

A social relationship [which] is entered into for its own sake, for what can be derived by each person from a sustained association with another;

and which is continued only in so far as it is thought by both parties to deliver enough satisfaction for each individual to stay within it. (Giddens, 1992: 58)

Partnerships entered into for their own sake, it is suggested, give rise to greater democracy and equality in relationships. Giddens focuses on same-sex relationships as leading the way in creating more democratic relationships. There have however been many criticisms of his work, e.g. he has been accused of neglecting to address continuing inequalities such as those based on social class, ethnicity and gender (Crow, 2002; Smart and Neale, 1999). Despite such criticisms, many sociologists have found Giddens' work of use, particularly in relation to same-sex partnerships (Weeks et al., 2001). Stacey (1996), for instance, argues that same-sex relationships represent an ideal postmodern kinship because their conscious efforts to form relationships are freed from the traditional patterns of family. Lacking any traditional role models or guidelines, such couples have had to be creative when forming intimate relationships. A criticism of such a rose-tinted view of same-sex relationships might be that they don't exist in a vacuum and in fact all of us, heterosexual or LGBT+, are taught very early on, that a particular type of heterosexuality is the only 'proper' way to be. Sexology taught society that same-sex desire was an inversion, and whilst this is now dismissed as a theory, it has had a lasting impact on how LGBT+ communities arrange themselves (Foucault, 1979). Many same-sex couples have formed around heterosexual dynamics, the **butch/femme** couple, for instance, weren't necessarily knowingly subverting gender norms. Nevertheless, Giddens' work in many ways prefigured some of the work on the friendship/family continuum (Pahl and Prevalin, 2005).

Much has been written about friendship within sociology, frequently drawing on the work of Aristotle who defined three types of friendship – friends of virtue, friends of pleasure and friends of utility (Pahl, 2000). A recent aspect of work on intimacies is a consideration of friendships as constituting 'families of choice'. 'Elective families' (Beck-Gernsheim, 1998) are often seen as being pioneered by gay men and lesbians, though they are by no means confined to them (Giddens, 1992). Several studies have shown that friends become a chosen family when they engage in similar practices, providing support in times of crisis, coming together for the major rituals of life surrounding birth, death and other occasions that mark progress through the life course (Charles et al., 2008; Pahl and Spencer, 2004). Giddens (1992) argues that the pursuit of personal happiness and stability through such relationships is of increasing importance in late modernity with the decline of a cohesive moral and social world. An increasing number of researchers have suggested that in fact friendships are so important in personal lives that we are witnessing a shift from the centrality of the couple to a more fluid network of intimates (Roseneil and

Budgeon, 2004; Spencer and Pahl, 2006). In fact, in recent years the phrase 'friends with benefits' has come into common parlance (Jonason et al., 2011). It refers to friendship with sex, a relationship which blends the emotional intimacy of friendship with the physical closeness of a romantic partnership. This is perhaps an indication of the ways in which the boundaries between friendship and intimate partnerships have become more relaxed. This (new?) relationship has prompted the film *Friends with Benefits* (2011) for instance, but it is interesting that in many fictional representations, the relationship usually ends up as a conventional romantic one, an indication of the strength of compulsory heterosexuality perhaps (Rich, 1980). Nonetheless, Garcia et al. (2014) found that women, in particular, had much to gain from these looser ties of intimacy in terms of psychological wellbeing. Some argue, however, that in fact we are over-emphasizing social change. Crow (2002), for example, states that family relationships have always shown plurality and diversity, that there have throughout history been single parents, same-sex couples and co-habitees, and what has changed are our labels for them. Others point to the continued importance that individuals place on intimate relationships (Ribbens McCarthy et al., 2003).

Intimate relationships and the State

Perhaps in response to such apparently liberal approaches to intimate lives, in many ways governments' views of the family frequently follow that of functionalist approaches, in that they tend to see the family as the foundation for an ordered and moral society (Gillies, 2008). In the *State of the Nation Report: Fractured Families*, for instance, Conservative MP Iain Duncan-Smith talked of how the 'report paints a worrying picture of family breakdown in the UK. We now have one of the highest divorce rates in the western world and the fabric of family life has been stripped away in the past thirty years' (2006: 5). Dark days indeed! Much has been written about the ways in which the state shapes and perhaps even controls our intimate relationships. Media attention tends to portray the UK, for instance, as a 'nanny state' in which the government scrutinizes every aspect of family life, from how many fruit and vegetable portions children are given, and keep-fit classes for over-weight parents, to the use of compulsory parenting classes for those parents with 'problem' children. Many sociologists have noted that such intrusions into family life are highly classed, and that those families who do not fit with the ideal middle-class model of family life are demonized. Walkerdine and Lucey's (1989) UK study, for example, showed how middle-class childrearing practices are articulated as normal and desirable.

The state has also played a significant part in determining what is (and what is not) regarded as a legitimate relationship. One clear example is the ways in which same-sex couples have been treated in government policies. Section 28 of the Local Government Act 1988, an Act that has been described as the most successful piece of homophobic legislation since the 1800s (Smith, 1994), was passed under Thatcher's government. It stated that a local authority 'shall not intentionally promote homosexuality or publish material with the intention of promoting homosexuality' or 'promote the teaching in any maintained school of the acceptability of homosexuality as a pretended family relationship'. The Act caused many to feel they had to hide their sexual identity in certain situations because of a perceived rise in anti-gay feeling. Certainly, the Act does seem to have had an influence on the ways in which society responded to same-sex relationships, as during the conservative Thatcher administration, homophobic attitudes in society increased markedly. The British Social Attitudes Survey recorded sixty-two percent of respondents disapproving of gay relationships in 1983. By 1985 this has risen to sixty-nine percent and rose again to seventy-four percent in 1987. That figure had reduced by 1992 to fifty-eight percent. Section 28 was not repealed, however, until 21 June 2000 in Scotland and 18 November 2003 in the rest of the UK. There have also been differing ages of consent for heterosexuals and gay men (lesbians have not historically been included in age of consent laws, not because their relationships have been socially accepted but more because when the first age of consent laws were passed there was a fear that talking about lesbianism would 'spread the contagion'; see Weeks, 1989). In 1967, in the UK, the age of consent for gay men was 21, compared to 16 for heterosexuals; in 1979 it was reduced to 18. It was not until January 2001, under the Sexual Offences (Amendment) Act, that the age of consent for gay men was reduced from 18 to 16 in line with that for heterosexuals for the first time. There was, however, much objection from the moral Right and religious groups at the time. Whilst 16 is the most common age of consent across the globe, there are still, of course, several places where it is still illegal to be gay. The state also decides who can and cannot be married, e.g. until relatively recently, same-sex couples could not register their relationships in many countries across the globe. However, since the start of the twenty-first century, more and more nations are extending this right. We should be mindful of the fact, however, that rights given can easily be taken away again. The Trump administration, for example, has recently sought to reverse health care protections for trans people, and to make it legal for people to be fired on the grounds of being gay or trans.

Violence and intimate relationships

The family may be commonly regarded and indeed recast by governments as a 'haven in a heartless world'; the reality however is that for many, the family, or our intimate relationship, constitutes a dangerous place. Since large numbers of women experience domestic violence perpetrated by men (almost 1 in 3 women in England and Wales, according to the ONS 2019), the assumption is that it is, therefore, performed by a substantial percentage of men and not the act of a pathological 'few' (Price, 2005). As Bourke argues, when domestic violence happens so frequently it can begin to look 'normal', and for this reason, many feminist sociologists have argued as a necessity to think beyond psychiatric (men who are violent in relationships are sick) approaches or theological (such men are evil) approaches (Bourke, 1999). This different perspective requires examining the social structures that allow and permit male violence against women. A critical explanatory concept for many feminist theories of men's violence is patriarchy. In other words, patriarchy can be explained as a consistent pattern of ideological and structural practices that serve to justify and perpetuate men's oppression of women. Walby identified six mechanisms of patriarchy: the mode of production; the realm of paid work; the state; realm of sexuality; cultural institutions; and crucially for this chapter, male violence against women, all of which serve to subjugate women, which, in turn, permits a range of violent acts.

The family, as an institution, has frequently been cited by feminists as one which has traditionally legitimated the commission of violence against women and children (Kelly, 1988). Historically, the dichotomy between the public and the private with regard to domestic violence, has often been reflected in the ambivalence of most agencies, including the police, towards getting involved in situations which occurred 'behind closed doors' away from public view (Yllo and Bograd, 1988). Violence in the home between intimates was frequently, and perhaps still is, perceived as different from violence against a stranger in a public place (Stanko, 1985). The parameters of the 'family' were traditionally set aside as paradigmatically 'private' (Oakley, 1981). This public/private binary has resulted in attitudes that rendered domestic violence as not 'real' police work, and therefore not associated with criminal investigation, because police work was about maintaining public order, whereas domestic violence was about marriage counselling and social work and not appropriate to their role (Yllo and Bograd, 1988). Many would argue that much domestic violence has been regarded as trivial, and to a certain extent even considered normal, inevitable and excusable, because it was also 'domestic' (Fineman, 1994; Stanko, 1985). Edwards (1986) concluded from interviews with police officers that domestic violence was seen by many as a 'normal' part of family life and hence not a matter for their concern except in severe cases. There was, and perhaps still is, a covert toleration of domestic violence. While it continued to be seen as a 'private matter', it was virtually impossible to redefine it as criminal. For example, until as recently as 1991 men could not be charged with raping their wives. The issue of privileging a 'private' domestic situation, where men are abusing women within a household, took much political campaigning on the part of feminists, in order to expose the hypocrisy and use of power against women's interests (Corrin, 1996). This is an ongoing battle; Home Secretary Theresa May cited 'shameful' police attitudes in 2016, which included referring to female vicitms as 'slags' and 'bitches', such language being a clear example of the intersection of violence and patriarchal norms of sexuality. The family has also been recognized as an institution which places the very young and the elderly at risk. For instance, it is estimated that at least half of the children living in abusive households will themselves become the victims of abuse. Although statistically men are overwhelmingly more likely to be perpetrators of, and women and children victims of, domestic violence, this does not mean that men cannot be victims and women are incapable of violence. Recently, for example, there have been studies on violence in same-sex relationships (Hester and Donovan, 2014 – this will be discussed in a little more detail in Chapter 12). We are also becoming increasingly aware of the men who are victims of abuse perpetrated by the women in their lives, with statistics suggesting as many as 1 in 6 men may experience dometic abuse (Bagshaw and Chung, 2000). The important work to understand the impact of violence and abuse in men's lives, began in earnest in the 1990s, with contributions by scholars such as Stanko and Hobdell (1993). Hester (2012) has continued this research by anlysing the contexts in which women use violence against their male partners and men report such abuse to the authorities.

Intimacies online: a new sexual revolution?

People may be conducting their sexual lives offline in different ways, but it seems they are also finding new, and innovative, ways to pursue love, romance and sex online too. The relationship between intimacy and technology is a fascinating and ever-changing one. Increasingly, people are using the internet to find love and sex and they are not short of places to find it. Pornography abounds, sex work has moved online, and there is a range of sexual communities available to suit most requirements. Technology is even advancing to the point where we could have sexual relationships not just with sex robots but with a virtual partner. Some have argued that we are witnessing a sexual revolution of sorts, with technology transforming the ways we negotiate and conduct our intimate lives. Many people have been using apps such as *Tinder* and *Bumble* to meet people for some time now, and online dating is so normal it's positively old hat, with more and more people meeting their long-term partners this way. Chat rooms and web cams have also enabled remote sexual practices. However, arguably a new generation of digisexuals – people who use new technologies for sexual purposes as a primary expression of their sexuality – is on the rise

(McArthur and Twist, 2017). Virtual sex with an avatar, using cyber/teledildonics controlled by a computer, is a practice growing in popularity. Indeed, at the time of writing, the social distancing rules as a result of the Covid-19 pandemic have likely fostered a range of innovative ways to 'do' sex.

Films such as *Ex Machina* (2014) (see Chapter 4) have perhaps served to normalize robotic sexuality (Gibson, 2020). Various companies, such as the *Real Doll* company and *Realbotix*, have developed 'realistic' sexbots: robots which can talk, move, have warm skin and 'self-lubricating vaginas' (which are dishwasher friendly!). Sex-doll brothels exist in many countries and have done for some time, but do these and robotic dolls ask new questions of how we understand intimacy and sexuality? We have already seen, for instance, moral panics about a so-called masculine 'celibacy syndrome' in Japan, fuelled by an alleged taste for manga, online games and anime (Hinton, 2015). Therefore, we need to examine what are the likely, and possibly legitimate, concerns raised by virtual sex or robot sex. Some have argued that prolonged use of technology for such purposes could cause obsession and depression, much like protracted use of the internet or gaming more generally seems to have negative impacts on mental health and wellbeing. Too much sex online, or with a robot, it's argued, could lead to an obsession with digisex – a digiattachment (McArthur and Twist, 2017). Others have warned that intimate relations with an inanimate, essentially non-consenting and subservient entity, could lead to harmful abuses of other humans (see Gersen, 2019). In other words, treating something, or someone, as an object, not worthy of concern, may become habitualized and normalized. Other rights-based questions might concern the robot. For instance, as artificial intelligence develops, will there be a point at which we might have to ask whether the robot has given consent to practices which, in another scenario, might be seen as abusive. Again, popular culture has got there ahead of the game with TV series such as *Humans* (C4) asking those very questions. Many feminists are rightly concerned about the development of real dolls which look like children. The producers claim they are providing a useful service to society, arguing that men who are attracted to children can use/abuse a doll rather than a living child. That particular argument doesn't really stand, however, as evidence suggests that where there are brothels or sex clubs, assaults on women increase (Bindel, 2004). It could be said that socially sanctioned child abuse, even if it is of a doll, is a dangerous precedent. The dolls are sexualized, objectified, and their production arguably normalizes an abusive and damaging practice. We could also question to what extent these are changes in intimate practices. Blow-up sex dolls, for instance, have been a comedy trope for many years. Are we witnessing the emergence of an old sexual story (the objectification of women) onto a new platform (the alleged 'democratic' cybersphere)?

It is apparent, therefore, that a particular transformation of intimacy is taking place. The big question mark is the extent to which it is a transformation to be welcomed.

Discussion point

Good enough to eat?

- Read about Armin Meiwes and Bernd Juergen Brandes.
- Does the use of technology and internet software shift the nature of sexual interactions?
- What ethical questions arise from cybersex?

Summary

There would seem to be no doubt that our intimate relationships have undergone a transformation in recent years and there is no reason to think that this will not continue as the twenty-first century progresses. Post-industrialization has led to the de-traditionalization and individualization of social life. Does this mean, then, the end of family life as we know it? Although society has seen a rise in the divorce statistics, we are still, it would seem, heavily invested in marriage and 'coupledom'. For example, although almost half of marriages will end in divorce, more than forty percent of marriages are remarriages. Remarriage often creates blended families, or re-configured families, consisting of a combination of biological and step-parents/siblings. There has also been a rise in the numbers of couples co-habiting. December 2005 saw the first official civil partnerships in the UK (the legal union of same-sex couples) and in the first year 18,059 ceremonies took place and many more same-sex couples married after that became legal in 2014. Numerous LGBT+ people raise children from previous heterosexual relationships, or they have adopted children. Increasingly, LGBT+ people are also choosing to have their own biological children, using a variety of reproductive technologies (Gabb, 2008).

The work of David Morgan (1996) and others has shifted the field conceptually, through the development of the idea of family practices – families are what they do rather than being defined exclusively by kinship and marriage. The field has shifted so much that academics such as Jamieson (2001) and Smart (2008) refer to 'intimacies' and 'personal life' rather than 'the family'. Such terminological changes mean that when we talk of family it is less rigidly identified with the idealized nuclear family of the 1950s. Indeed, new developments in technologies may well mean that the ways in which we conduct our intimate lives will be radically transformed in years to come. Just as dating apps have been normalized, will sex robots be an everyday part of our futures? Is it the case that our bodies, and not just our identities, are becoming more fluid, transgressing traditional boundaries? This is hard to predict but research reveals the fact that, for now, we seem to be heavily invested in intimate personal relationships.

Key questions

- Does the state still have as strong a role in shaping our intimate lives as it did even twenty years ago?
- To what extent do you think families are still responsible for reproducing sexual norms?
- What do you anticipate will be the key shifts in our intimate lives in the coming years?

FURTHER READING

The *Sociology of Personal Life* (Red Globe, 2019) by Vanessa May and Petra Nordqvist offers some very accessible explorations of personal life in contemporary society.

Jacqui Gabb's 'The relationship work of sexual intimacy in long-term heterosexual and LGBTQ partnerships' (*Current Sociology*, 2018) has some interesting comparisons between the attitudes of men and women and looks at how humour is often deployed in 'fallow' periods.

For a consideration of trans intimacies, I would recommend Rosenberg et al.'s (*Sexuality and Culture*, 2019) '"I couldn't imagine my life without it": Australian trans women's experiences of sexuality, intimacy, and gender-affirming hormone therapy', and Riggs and Bartholomaeus's (*Sex Education*, 2017) 'Transgender young people's narratives of intimacy and sexual health: implications for sexuality education'.

7

POLITICS AND POLICY

———————————— Learning outcomes ————————————

By the end of this chapter you should be able to:

- Identify some of the key themes and issues in debates around the politics and policies of sexuality
- Critically analyze existing policies related to sexualities
- Identify and engage with contemporary political campaigns around sexuality

Introduction

As we have already seen, sexuality connects in a range of important ways to issues of power in relation to gender, class and ethnicity. These connections and understandings of sexuality itself are shaped by social and political forces. Since the late 1980s sexuality has been high on western political agendas, covering such issues as teenage pregnancy rates, prevention of STIs, the regulation of prostitution and pornography, the sexual abuse of children, same-sex marriage and adoption, and hate crimes. In addition, issues of sex trafficking and tourism, AIDS or rape as a weapon of war, illustrate the ways in which the politics of sexuality is a global concern. Policies reflect, in many ways, the values of those involved in the policy-making process.

As seen in Chapters 1, 2 and 5, cultural understandings of sex have in the global north been shaped by three models of sexuality, which Mottier (2008) identifies as:

- the moral/religious model;
- the biological model;
- the social model.

According to Mottier, although these three models have, historically, emerged successively, they currently run alongside one another, with all three having influence over the production and reproduction of sexual politics and a significant impact on the potential for (or lack of) political transformation. Arguably, as we shall see later in this chapter, these models have had an impact on the frameworks of equality underpinning demands for LGBT+ 'equality', with the political rhetoric shifting towards equality in 'sameness' rather than 'difference' (Richardson and Monro, 2012). Many normative assumptions about sexuality also, arguably, shape social policy and welfare practices. Most often, it emerges in policy when it is viewed as problematic, as with single parents, STIs, prostitution, teenage mothers and abortion. Policies often can be grouped around concerns to protect perceived vulnerable individuals and populations, or to protect the public from behaviours or groups understood as dangerous or undesirable (Carabine, 2009). Not surprisingly then, sexuality can provoke heated political debate and shows the ways in which what is considered 'normal', in terms of sexuality, is a notion that is very much contested. Carabine also makes clear that policies do not have to overtly be about sexuality in order to regulate sexual behaviours and identities. Policy on housing, education, health or income support, for instance, can communicate particular ideas about what is deemed acceptable in terms of relationships or behaviours. Common to many of these policies is an assumption that heterosexuality is normal, and it is thus privileged and protected through the laws on marriage, tax, inheritance, or rights to residency. As such, (a particular expression of) heterosexuality can be said to be institutionalized (Ingraham, 1994).

However, whilst states might attempt to regulate and control sexuality, these processes can be, and often are, challenged and resisted. We will explore some of these social movements, inevitably focusing on minority group organizations. As we do so, we will consider whether there has been a transformation in action. Have the internet and other forms of technology enabled the increased connection, and therefore the activation, of social movements? As you read through the chapter, you might want to refer to the timeline at the beginning of the book to put some of the events in context. This chapter, therefore, will look at a range of ways in which sexuality can be understood as very much a public and political issue and not the private concern it is often cast as. We will begin to develop an understanding of the conditions and factors promoting changes in the legal and social status of differing sexualities. The chapter will raise critical questions about sexual citizenship, e.g. access to resources for family planning, and protection from risks in relation to health and violence, are all issues of sexual citizenship. We will also examine key historical 'moments' in the changing status of heterosexual and LGBT+ identities, beginning with women's liberation movements and the sexual 'revolution', before moving on to LGBT+ liberation movements.

Feminist movements and sexuality

As seen previously, the first women's movement in the late nineteenth century was mostly concerned with the struggle for civil and political equality for women. Yet women's sexuality had long been subject to moral and then, later, scientific scrutiny. So, despite the main focus being on equal legal and political rights, sexuality also emerged as a central concern. In particular, it increasingly became an area for developing a critique of existing gender relations. Early feminists drew on biological 'justifications' for the double moral standard which existed as regards sexuality and sexual behaviour – that men were 'naturally' more promiscuous, while women were 'naturally' passive and chaste – to develop a critique of male sexuality as being the origin of sexual oppression. Political activism in Europe and the US of the nineteenth century often focused on prostitution and the related spread of STIs. Some feminists argued that these issues were at the heart of why women were denied the vote; men wanted to protect their ability to sexually exploit women.

Their campaigns against prostitution called for an end to 'white slavery' (in which poverty forced young working-class girls (and to a lesser extent boys) into sexual exploitation by wealthy middle-class men (see Chapter 10 for a discussion of the journalist W.T. Stead). However, their efforts to 'rescue' such 'fallen' women – a narrative which persists today – resonated with the growing general moral view that prostitution was both a vice and a major public health risk, though mostly as regards the health of men. Prostitutes came to be seen as a source of pollution which put men's lives at risk. Many states, fearing that STIs would make male bodies too weak for military purposes, took steps to control prostitution. Significantly, no steps were taken to prevent men from infecting prostitutes, instead prostitutes were forced to undergo medical inspections: if they were found to be infected, they were imprisoned and forced to undergo medical treatment. In fact, during the First and Second World Wars, prostitutes were often depicted as 'helping the enemy' by 'contaminating' the nation's soldiers. During the First World War, the US government put thousands of suspected prostitutes into internment camps, while the German military command in several occupied territories punished women who, knowing they had an STI, nonetheless had sex with soldiers, with prison sentences of up to a year.

Interestingly, given some recent discussions about the legalization of prostitution and brothels, nineteenth-century feminists in Europe called on the state to ban prostitution altogether, not just to control it, because being a regulator meant the state was in effect acting as a 'pimp'. As early as 1875, an important organization – the British and Continental Federation for the Abolition of Government Regulation of Vice – was formed to campaign for abolition. In particular, it focused on the international traffic in women for the purposes of prostitution (as you will see in Chapter 8, this is still a global concern). In 1904 the first 'International Agreement for the Suppression of the White Slave Traffic' was enacted; as a result, there followed a slow but general legal prohibition of brothels in most western nations.

However, the views of such feminist campaigners were, to an extent, based on the 'scientific' views and categorizations of nineteenth-century sexologists, i.e. that there were biological differences between men and women which led to different sexualities and behaviours. Yet not all feminists shared such a binary view of femininity and female sexuality. In fact, several prominent nineteenth-century feminists were involved in contemporary radical sex movements which, among other things, campaigned for greater sexual freedoms for both men and women. Such reformers campaigned against obscenity and anti-homosexual laws, and for things such as access to birth control information, abortion and 'free love' between equal partners. In some ways, these movements echoed the earlier criticisms of the marriage 'contract' made by Mary Wollstonecraft in 1792, who saw this institution as both arising from and confirming men's economic and physical control of women.

Free-thinking anarchist and socialist feminists were active in many countries, e.g. Emma Goldman and Lillian Harman in the US, and Ito Noe in Japan. In Germany, the League of Progressive Women's Associations suggested boycotting marriage and demanded sexual pleasure for women as well as men. Alexandra Kollontai, a feminist and communist who played a leading role in the early Soviet state, argued that the family, like the state, was a capitalist institution: 'Instead of the conjugal slavery of the past, communist society offers women and men a free union which is strong in the comradeship which inspired it' (1920: 19). Because she saw female sexual exploitation as being linked to the economic dependency of women on men in the capitalist system, she believed prostitution would disappear once capitalism was overthrown. Such a revolution would, she argued, also allow both men and women to enjoy their sexualities in freedom.

Nonetheless, Kollontai's views were soon sidelined in the new Soviet state, whilst in the East, traditionalists were outraged by the arguments of these feminists, e.g. in 1923 Ito Noe was murdered by the Japanese military police. In addition, mainstream feminist movements, such as those campaigning for the right to vote, believed such sexual liberationist views would undermine the social respectability of their struggles. However, there was broad agreement on a woman's right to refuse 'unreasonable' male sexual demands and excessive numbers of pregnancies, and to ownership over their own bodies, promoting the concept of 'voluntary motherhood'. In particular, such feminists campaigned for greater access to sex education and contraceptive information and methods. The attitudes of many of their male contemporaries can be judged by the comments of William Acton, a leading Victorian physician, who, in 1875, argued that 'during the last few years, and since the rights of women have been so much insisted upon ... numerous husbands have complained to me of the hardships under which they suffer by being married to women who regard themselves as martyrs when called upon to fulfil the duties of wives. This spirit of insubordination has become intolerable' (Acton [1875], quoted in Jeffreys, 2001: 66).

Discussion point

Sexual policymaking

Find an example of contemporary policy relating to sexual rights around an issue such as sex education or access to contraception (many of these will be readily available via government internet pages). Consider the following questions:

- Are there particular values written into the policy? Whose views are being reflected here?
- Does this policy grant or restrict rights?

The sexual 'revolution'

Although only limited progress was made, many of the demands of first wave feminism, such as a right to legal abortion and access to contraception, were later taken up and developed by the women's movements which emerged in the 1960s and 1970s. Second wave feminists put the politicization of sexuality at the centre of their agenda. These movements developed in societies in which many aspects of traditional gender relations had been transformed, to a greater or lesser extent, by the massive post-war entry of women into the workforce. The greater economic independence of many women was also the result of increasing state provision of social welfare which provided various support mechanisms. These changes, in addition to certain transformations relating to the institutions of marriage, the family and gender, helped undermine some of the traditional aspects of gender relations between the sexes, though largely for middle-class women.

It was in this context that, in 1960, the modern contraceptive pill for women first became widely available in the west. Combined with new reproductive technologies (such as IVF), the pill essentially uncoupled intercourse from reproduction and, at least in part, contributed to what became known as the 'sexual revolution' of the 1960s and 1970s. Many feminists initially saw this 'sexual revolution', and its attendant sexual liberation, as being crucial for women's liberation generally. However, this revolution – which, amongst other aspects, often promoted the idea of 'swinging' – was in many ways quite different from what the earlier feminists had advocated. In the main, the cultural transformations were led by men, and as a result the unequal gender power relations were largely reproduced: as Sheila Jeffreys (1990) argued, it seemed to be more about fulfilling male fantasies about female availability than a genuine increase in sexual freedom for women, and arguably gave men more control over women's bodies. As the feminist writer Beatrix Campbell wrote:

> What it did not do was defend women against the differential effects of permissiveness on men and women ... It was about the affirmation of young men's sexuality and promiscuity ... the very affirmation of sexuality was a celebration of masculine sexuality. (Campbell, 1980: 1–2)

The personal is political

In addition, the sexual 'revolution', and its associated abolition of many obscenity and morality laws, far from undermining, let alone overthrowing, capitalism, actually led to a massive expansion of the national and international sex industries, and the **commodification** of sex to unprecedented levels. In particular, 'free love' actually led to a great increase in prostitution (along with pornography), rather than the expected decline. As a result, feminists returned to the issues of prostitution and pornography. Second wave feminism increasingly focused on sexuality, and many argued that sexual oppression of women was a central – or even the most central – area of male power over women. In particular, many advanced the slogan 'the personal is political', questioning any clear public/private division, arguing that women's lives were rooted in gender inequality. The 'private' thus became politicized, and from the 1970s sexuality became a main feature of feminist theory and activism, especially around such issues as contraception, abortion, rape, sexual abuse, pornography, prostitution, and sexual harassment. In addition, many areas traditionally seen as belonging to the 'private' sphere of the family and the home, such as the right to say 'no', the right to sexual pleasure, were also politicized and taken into the 'public' arena.

Another example of how the politics of sex emerged is that provided by Shere Hite (1976). Focusing much of her work on the female orgasm, she argued that women's lack of sexual satisfaction was part of their oppression, an oppression most women were unconscious of. In fact, she saw the apparent lack of female enthusiasm for sex, shown by various studies, as a very political act of 'passive resistance', similar in some ways to Gandhi's passive resistance to British rule in India.

Others concentrated on the topic of political lesbianism. In the early 1970s, US feminist Ti-Grace Atkinson argued that feminism was a theory and that lesbianism was the practice, Jill Johnson (1973: 180) stating that 'feminists who still sleep with the man are delivering their most vital energies to the oppressor'. She influenced others, such as Sheila Jeffreys, a member of the Leeds Revolutionary Feminist Group, who argued that women should avoid relationships with men for as long as the power relations between men and women remained unequal, though she did not argue that, in place of male partners, women should instead have sex with other women. Jeffreys and the Leeds group went on to argue that lesbianism was a matter of political choice rather than a biologically determined sexual identity, and promoted a political version of the social model of sexuality.

FACT FILE

Gouines Rouges

Co-founded by French novelist Monique Wittig in Paris in 1971, the *Gouines Rouges* [Red Dykes], the first political lesbian group in France, campaigned for women's and gay rights but felt somewhat sidelined by both movements (the women's movement was seen to be dominated by a focus on heterosexual issues, the gay rights movement came to be dominated by men). It was a similar story in Italy, as the formation of *Identita Lesbica* [Lesbian Identity] was a result of a largely anti-lesbian feminist movement and a gay rights group *FUORI!* [OUT!], which was dominated by a focus on gay men's issues.

There was also the influential Women Against Pornography (WAP) group, founded in 1976, by such feminists as Andrea Dworkin, Shere Hite and Adrienne Rich. During the 1980s, there were many debates amongst feminists about pornography and prostitution. Rejecting some of the arguments of the sexual revolution, which had seen the legalization of these institutions as part of moves to greater sexual liberation, many feminists saw both pornography and prostitution as playing key roles in the oppression of women generally.

Feminists such as Susan Brownmiller (1975) and Andrea Dworkin saw prostitution and pornography as examples of male violence against women (see Chapter 13), arguing that violence was the underlying foundation of all male sexuality. Kate Millett also saw rape as a weapon of patriarchy. This perspective thus saw pornography as essentially another manifestation of male violence against women, as regards both production and consumption.

However, some feminists, such as Gayle Rubin and Lynne Segal, have criticized this anti-porn approach, for instance, for not distinguishing between pornography involving men and women, and that produced for lesbians by lesbians, and for adopting political and legal strategies which threatened aspects of free speech, or which led them to form political alliances with the religious Right who, at the same time, were actively opposed to women's and LGBT+ rights. For example, the Feminist Anti-Censorship Taskforce was established in the US in the early 1980s to oppose attempts by feminists such as Dworkin to legislate against pornographic materials. At the same time, women working in the porn industry and/or involved in prostitution, who rejected feminist views which saw their activities as degrading for women, formed interest groups and unions to fight for legalization and better conditions in the sex industry.

Contemporary feminist activism

There are many contemporary campaigns which continue the work of first and second wave feminists. For instance, the ongoing political campaign for women's right to abortion across the globe has recently achieved hard-won success in Northern Ireland, where abortion was decriminalized in 2019. Another key issue is that of female genital mutilation (FGM), which has had support from prominent figures such as the African American feminist novelist Alice Walker. FGM, which affects over 200 million girls and women, leaving many dead, ill or in life-long pain, refers to the alteration of female genital organs for non-surgical reasons and often involves cutting the clitoris and labia. As a result of various international campaigns, FGM was declared a violation of human rights by both the UN and Amnesty International. Since the mid-1990s, it was made illegal in many western and several non-western countries. Yet Alice Walker's novel *Possessing the Secret of Joy* (1992), and the documentary film *Warrior Marks* (1994), which she co-produced, both of which oppose FGM, have been attacked for what some feminists (such as Germaine Greer) saw as their cultural imperialism and neo-colonialism, and the imposition of an ethnocentric US vision of African cultural practices. In addition, western feminists in general have been accused of focusing on the cultural practices of the **global south** whilst ignoring the rapid growth in the west of cosmetic surgical 'interventions' on women's genitals, such as vaginoplasty. Somali-born campaigner Hibo Wardere (2016), however, argues that FGM is a practice which violates human rights.

Discussion point

Ending FGM

Read the interagency statement on FGM *Eliminating Female Genital Mutilation* (WHO, 2008) and an academic article on the topic such as Fellmeth's (2008) 'State regulation of sexuality in international human rights law and theory'.

- Are there credible arguments for FGM as cultural practice?
- In what ways can FGM be seen as a violation of human rights? Which existing policies and treaties does this relate to?
- What are the difficulties involved when one nation (or nations) makes a statement about another?

Another recent and high-profile mainstream campaign, drawing attention to the politics of the body, was the #MeToo movement in which prominent women in the media shared stories about the abuse and harassment they had experienced at the hands of powerful men. Via social media, #MeToo and its French equivalent #BalanceTonPorc (CallOutYourPig) have encouraged women to come forward about abuse they have experienced. Celebrities such as Gwyneth Paltrow and Lady Gaga did so and shared their experiences in the hope that this would give voice to other women. Perhaps most famously, in 2017 the film producer Harvey Weinstein faced several allegations about misconduct towards women he had worked with, including accusations of rape. He was sentenced to twenty-three years in prison in 2020. Not everyone, however, has been in favour of this approach. Germaine Greer accused the women of 'whingeing', and in an open letter to *Le Monde*, French actress Catherine Deneuve argued that men should be 'free to hit on' women, even persistently. She accused the movements of being puritanical, and said the [male] sexual urge is 'wild and aggressive' and that things had turned into a 'witch hunt … rape is a crime, but trying to seduce someone, even persistently or clumsily, is not – nor is men being gentlemanly a macho attack'. However, #MeToo has shown women that collectivity is possible and can bring about social change. Millions of women have found the courage to talk about their painful experiences and many men have been called to account.

LGBT+ movements

As we have started to see, the 1960s and 1970s was a period of politicization of sex in the global north. It led to some important challenges for thinking about sexual identities and practices. Despite such critiques, however, mainstream public considerations of sexuality were arguably firmly wedded to the assumption that sexuality = heterosexuality. Even popular sex manuals of the time largely ignored non-heterosexuality. For instance, Mottier (2008: 100) highlights that the popular 1969 sex manual, *Everything You Ever Wanted to Know About Sex But Were Afraid to Ask*, had this to say about lesbianism: ' ... like their male counterparts, lesbians are handicapped by having only half the pieces in the anatomical jigsaw puzzle. Just as one penis plus one penis equals nothing, one vagina plus another vagina still equals zero'.

The sexual 'revolution' of the 1960s, including the feminist movement's politicization of sexuality, was, as Sheila Jeffreys pointed out, essentially a heterosexual revolution. Nonetheless, the reduction of legal and moral controls over aspects of sexuality created social conditions in which, to use Michel Foucault's term, non-heterosexualities could flourish more publicly (Foucault, 1979). Many have argued that the founding moment of the modern LGBT+ movement was the police raid on the New York gay bar Stonewall in 1969. This bar was routinely invaded by the police but on that particular night, the clientele defended themselves and a riot ensued. Following this, the National Gay Liberation organization was set up in the US, while in Britain, the short-lived Gay Liberation Front was set up in 1970. Similar organizations emerged in many other countries. Some, such as Lambda in the US, focused on reforming discriminatory policies via legal actions or lobbying.

Political impact of HIV/AIDS

However, as explored elsewhere (see Chapters 8 and 9), it was the development of the AIDS crisis that had a special impact on political mobilization, especially on that of gay men. Within a short time, **HIV/AIDS** had resurrected earlier traditional attitudes which associated sex with danger and risk, and in particular cast LGBT+ people as the dangerous 'other'. Whilst the politics of the sexual revolution in the 1960s had coincided, in many countries, with the political Left often being in power and prepared to promote sexual reforms, the AIDS crisis unfolded in a very different political climate, especially in the US and Britain, where the Right were in power. The 'moral agenda' of the Right was essentially shaped in opposition to feminist critiques of patriarchy and traditional understandings of femininity and female sexuality, and by the claims of gay rights activists. Religious groups worked with the 'moral Right' in attempts to persuade governments to control sexuality. Although LGBT+ people had successfully established new public identities during the sexual revolution, the emergence of the HIV/AIDS crisis in the early 1980s revealed, as noted by Jeffrey Weeks, that traditional associations of homosexuality with disease and 'abnormality' had not been fully destroyed during the sexual revolution.

The fact that AIDS initially devastated large and already vocal gay communities in San Francisco and New York helped to unite communities across the globe and prompt political protest. Groups such as the US's ACT UP (AIDS Coalition to Unleash Power, established in 1987) pursued more unconventional and confrontational tactics, using direct action and civil disobedience, such as chaining themselves to the VIP balcony at the stock exchange, to make their voice heard. Similarly, the British queer movement OutRage!, set up in 1990 and including prominent member Peter Tatchell, was formed in response both to a series of homophobic murders and an increase in police targeting gay and bisexual men. More recently, we have seen the rise of LGBT+ Pride events and marches across the globe. As a result of such groups, many nations in the west have passed a range of LGBT+ rights policies in relation to employment, marriage, adoption, age of consent, and the military. These political and social developments have thus helped undermine the idea of 'sexual normalcy' as constructed by nineteenth-century sexologists who had used the concept of the 'pervert'. As a result there have been recent positive steps, such as Northern Ireland allowing same-sex marriage in 2020. Are we, though, seeing a new **homonormative** 'normal' within the LGBT+ population, with new divisions being drawn between the 'good' and 'bad' gay (Warner, 1999)? We have seen also that technology has transformed sexual practices (Chapter 6), but we need to consider the impact this might have had on political spaces. The internet has enabled members of sexual minority cultures to reach each other across the globe, and no doubt it plays a central part in mobilizing contemporary political movements too, as it does for *Extinction Rebellion*, but could we argue that it has come at a cost, the cost being physical, social and political spaces? In other words, are gay communities dying, leading to a 'diaspora of gays from traditional urban enclaves' (Rosser et al., 2008: 588)?

We must remember as well that attitudes can very quickly take a backward turn, as we have seen in parts of the European Union. In 2019, 80 Polish municipalities declared themselves LGBT+-free zones, forcing LGBT+ campaigners to fight for rights they thought they had won long ago. At present, anti-LGBT+ hate speech is not punishable by law and, along with several other countries such as Romania and Slovakia, same-sex civil partnerships are not allowed.

The silent 'T'? Trans activism

As we have seen elsewhere in this book (Chapters 3 and 9), there has been a tendency to treat the 'T' of LGBT+ as an add-on, if it is acknowledged at all, despite their shared histories (Stryker, 2008). In recent years, trans activists have drawn more attention to the ways in which the trans community face similar discrimination to the 'LGB', as a result of restrictive views of gender and sexuality. Trans people were part of 'key moments' in lesbian and gay liberation, such as the Stonewall riots and the setting up of GLF (Hines, 2009). Nevertheless, the relationship between the trans community and both feminist groups and LGB groups has been a troubled one. Arguably, the ways in which trans identities have problematized the relationship between gender and sexuality, revealing the limitations of sexual and gendered identities, have contributed to this exclusion (Monro, 2005). Transgender studies and politics emerged, according to Stryker (2006) in the 1990s, with the publication of Stone's (1991) *Posttranssexual Manifesto* and Feinberg's (1992) *Transgender Liberation*. Stryker (1998) argues that these led to politicized communities and saw the formation of groups such as Transgender Nation in the US, whilst in the UK the lobbying group Press for Change emerged after a high-profile case around issues of marriage and privacy rights.

The growth of a visible trans activist movement has been behind some of the recent legislative changes we have witnessed in the west. There is the proposed US Employment and Non-Discrimination Act (ENDA), which would prevent discrimination on the basis of gender and sexual orientation, and in the UK the Gender Recognition Act (GRA) (2004), which came into effect in 2005. ENDA is, to date, the subject of heated debate, with many despairing of Trump's attitude. The GRA was, in some ways, an important piece of legislation, giving transgender people the right to change their birth certificates and to marry in the gender of their choice. However, many have argued that it is seriously out of step. For instance, trans people have to endure an extremely lengthy and costly (both in terms of finances and mental health) process to 'prove' their gender identity, until which point they are viewed as having 'gender dysphoria'. Thus, recently there has been a somewhat divisive consultation, which lasted for 16 weeks in 2018, around the act, with fierce debate between some radical feminists and trans activists over widening the definitions of gender. The reforms have been postponed but the debate continues. There has also been attention brought to various, related, mental health policies across the globe. Campaigners had to fight to have 'homosexuality' eventually removed as a mental health disorder in 1990, but the issue has been ongoing for the trans community. In the UK, for instance, the Mental Health Act has 'transgender' on the Psychiatric Disorder Register, which many view as discriminatory. It took until 2019 for the WHO to declare that transgender is not a mental health condition. Instead it will be classified under sexual health, though the changes will not come into effect until 2022. Arguably, such changes should mean that it becomes possible for trans people to update their documentation without having to be diagnosed with a mental health illness. Such steps are an important part in depathologizing trans identities, not just politically but culturally too. These changes are part and parcel of a more general move to an acknowledgement of sexual citizenship.

Discussion point

Activism in action – the GRA

The consultation over the UK's GRA, has resulted in fierce, perhaps even toxic, debate. Firstly, have a look at the wording of the Act as it currently stands. You could then look at the *Guardian*'s (19 October 2018) article 'Shifting Sands', which contains the views of various lawyers and legal scholars. Finally, have a look at the views put forward both by trans activists and by feminist groups, such as the Gender Identity Research & Education Society (GIRES) and womansplaceuk.org's guidance on the proposal.

- What are the key issues relating to the proposal?
- What should be the outcome of this consultation?
- What will be the possible impact of not making the proposed changes?
- What will be the possible impact of going ahead with the changes?

Disability, rights and sexuality

Another area of scholarship that has received scant attention is that pertaining to disabled people's sexuality. Early research largely accepted hegemonic narratives of disabled bodies as 'deficit' and 'asexual', but these have gradually been challenged as a result of a politicization of disability in relation to sexuality (Paterson and Hughes, 2000). Recently, attention has been drawn to the ways in which disabled people have been routinely subject to a range of restrictions and medical procedures as a result of government policies. In Britain, in the nineteenth century, a Royal Commission argued that intermarriage between deaf, 'dumb' or blind people should be discouraged. A later Royal Commission (1908) report on the 'Care and Control of the Feeble-Minded', argued the case for compulsory sterilization, something which Winston Churchill was in favour of. Under the Nazi regime at least 200,000 disabled people were killed, but over twice that many people were sterilized. Calls for eugenics in Britain remained loud well into the 1940s, and several proposals for legislation were brought to parliament. Although none were successful, there is evidence that many people were coerced into sterilization. Such policies may well be, more or less, a thing of the past, but in very recent years sterilization of disabled people has been common.

Shuttleworth (2007) has argued that because of the dominance of the medical module of disability (over a social module), more focus has been placed on correcting perceived deficiencies rather than looking at the capacity for sexual pleasure or reproduction. The key turning point came with the publication of Shakespeare et al.'s (1996) *The Sexual Politics of Disability* (see Chapter 3). This led to sexuality taking a firm place on the agenda of the Disability Rights Movement. As a result there have been some interesting debates of late around social exclusion, sexuality and disability, such as whether disabled people should be exempt from laws prohibiting sex work (see Appel, 2010; Di Nucci, 2017).

Sexual citizenship

Much of what we have looked at thus far concerns sexual rights. In other words, it is about the demands that various groups have made to be allowed full citizenship. What is meant by the term 'sexual citizenship' is, according to Richardson (2018), still being defined. For some, the term specifically refers to the sexual 'rights' either granted or denied to various social groups; others however discuss sexual citizenship in much broader terms. Regardless of how the term is defined and conceptualized, there is increasing interest in sexuality and its connection to citizenship, and the need to develop a 'specific notion of sexual or intimate citizenship'. Richardson argues that 'In this regard, we need to consider the question not just of access to citizenship, but also the basis upon which such access is granted or denied' (2018: 11). In particular, it is necessary to examine the question of what rights and obligations are the concerns of sexual or intimate citizenship. This is a very important question with regard to the impact on those groups for whom rights are being claimed – the debates over the rights and wrongs of same-sex marriage, for instance, from within the LGBT+ community, give a flavour of just how hot those political potatoes can be.

Summary

Politics and government policies clearly have a role to play in shaping understandings of sexuality. We have seen significant changes over the past forty or fifty years, as a result of political campaigning and legislative change. New rights are being won all the time: many more women across the globe have access to contraception and abortion; traditional understandings of heterosexuality as monogamous and only rightfully experienced within marriage have been challenged; HIV/AIDS is now a manageable, chronic condition (for those who can afford, or are offered, the medication) and attitudes towards populations with the condition have, for the most part, changed for the better; same-sex couples are more culturally visible and marriage rights have been extended in many nations; pornography, partly as a result of the internet, has been normalized.

However, there are clearly limits to the changes, and reminders that conservative views are never very far away. Sex workers remain stigmatized, single mothers are still frowned upon, many people still do not have the right to get married or adopt, many have no access to contraception or abortion. And hard-won rights can very easily be taken away. Policy related to sexuality remains highly contested, and whilst it can change, as a result of protest or lobbying, it still reflects the prevailing values of those in power.

Key questions

- What aspect of sexuality is currently being used as a political weapon in your society? Can you predict areas which are likely to be a focus in the future?

- Is the granting or winning of sexual rights sufficient to achieving sexual justice? Might rights-based successes or narratives have unintended results?

- To what extent should one nation be able to enforce their policies (and thus their values) on another?

FURTHER READING

For students wanting to read about political social movements in relation to sexualities, there are a number of suggestions. For a thorough and detailed introduction to the feminist movement, have a look at Sally Scholz's *Feminism: A Beginner's Guide* (Oneworld, 2018). Mark Blaisus offers a useful exploration of trans rights in *Sexual Identities, Queer Politics: Lesbian, Gay, Bisexual and Transgender Politics* (Princeton UP, 2001). For more on the politics of disability and sexuality, Tom Shakespeare et al.'s *The Sexual Politics of Disability* (Continuum, 1996) is still a good read.

There are also a number of texts which give more of a focus to policies relating to sexuality. Have a look at Richardson and Monro's *Sexuality, Equality & Diversity* (Red Globe, 2012). Or Mike Cole's *Education, Equality and Human Rights: Issues of Gender, 'Race', Sexuality, Disability and Social Class* (Routledge, 2011).

8

GLOBAL SEXUALITIES

--------- **Learning outcomes** ---------

By the end of this chapter you should be able to:

- Develop an understanding of the varied understandings and expressions of sexuality in cross-cultural contexts
- Understand and analyze the politics and limits of 'western' terminology regarding globalized sexualities
- Consider the ways in which ideas of sexuality around the world have been constructed and/or constrained in particular ways, as a result of specific cultural contexts

---

What we now call intimacy, and its importance in personal relations, has been largely created by globalizing influences ... A world where no-one is 'outside' is one where pre-existing traditions cannot avoid contact not only with others but also with many alternative ways of life ... The point is not only that the other 'answers back', but that mutual interrogation is possible. (Giddens, 1994: 95, 97)

Introduction

'Globalization' has been something of a buzz word in the social sciences for some time now, however, as a concept, it is still extremely relevant in relation to studying sexualities. The term 'globalization' is generally taken to refer to the process of global integration of economic, social, cultural and communication activities which has increased at a rapid rate since the 1980s. As a result, this dynamic force is generally seen as having transformed 'social relations at all levels on a worldwide scale' (Weeks, 2011: 71). While there is continuing debate about the precise meaning of this term, and about the extent to which the concept of globalization is a new one, there can be no doubt that the levels of global connectedness, through the movement of people and ideas, are unprecedented.

On one level, the term is seen as a neutral one, which merely describes transformations in global interactions. Held, for example, sees it as a series of interlinked processes which, together, are transforming human interactions at all levels (2000: 54–5). However, since the 1990s, globalization has also been seen as a transnational political and cultural project, specifically linked to **neo-liberalism**, the modern free-market version of capitalism. As a consequence, this phenomenon has, in turn, led to the emergence of transnational anti-capitalist and anti-globalization movements.

Sexuality is just one of the many social and cultural areas affected by globalization: the confrontation and contestation of different beliefs, behaviours and assumptions, results in a process of reshaping the context and meanings of intimacy and the erotic (Weeks, 2011: 72). Inevitably, this has impacted significantly on the ways in which sexuality is imagined, experienced and regulated in different parts of the world. Studies of global sexualities have emerged both from a variety of sources such as anthropology, geography and feminist considerations of sexual and reproductive rights of women across the globe and the focus on strategies to deal with HIV/AIDS. As touched on in other chapters in this textbook, globalization has affected several areas of sexuality, such as health (HIV/AIDS), religion, human rights **discourses**, popular culture and identities, and sexual abuses associated with war (Bourke, 1999).

Discussion point

The politics of terminology

As you progress through this chapter and go on to read other texts, think about the vocabulary which is used and its implications. Comparison is frequently drawn between the global south and the global north, but more than two-thirds of the world's population live in the south, therefore, is this a useful distinction? However, other terms used, such as the Third World, are not without problems. Austerity measures across Europe have shown us that it is possible to live in Third World conditions, whilst living in a First World society. Another option is to distinguish between developed or developing countries, usually in terms of industrialization (though all too often it has moral overtones too), but this suggests that some countries

---

have a long way to go until they 'progress' whilst suggesting that others are already there. This is problematic, not least because of the global devastation wrought by so-called progress (wars, economic deprivation, climate catastrophe and so on). Many feminists refer to 'one-third world' and 'two-thirds world' to draw attention to the imbalance. However, for the purposes of this textbook, in line with many theorists of sexuality, I will mostly make reference to the global north and south and the west, the political thrust of the terminology denoting the inequity between.

- Which terms make most sense to you?

The politics of naming reflects the highly contentious nature of globalization, something which this chapter will go on to consider in more detail. Hemmings et al. (2006) reveal the impact of the globalizing processes, while affecting all parts of the world, as uneven because individuals and groups, states and regions, are enmeshed in huge disparities of power and gross inequalities. This accounts for persistent inequalities between different cultures, and in sexual injustices, 'especially against women, children and lesbian, gay or transgender identified peoples' (Weeks, 2011: 72). In many ways, globalization accentuates pre-existing inequalities in both the global north and south, where economic pressures force those at the bottom of their societies into an unequal marketplace, including the sexual marketplace.

As earlier chapters have shown, there is no universally accepted understanding of sexuality, but most conceptualizations would link it to ideas of the body and culture. Often, the various ways in which processes of globalization shape sexuality are left unconsidered. Sadly, this chapter cannot introduce you, in any depth, to all of the myriad ways in which globalization impacts on sexuality. Instead, it aims to introduce you to some key concepts in this area. We begin by briefly considering the impact of globalization on understandings of sexuality more generally, and we assess the extent to which these processes are new. The chapter then moves on to look at some key issues in relation to the globalization of sexuality, such as whether we can talk about global sexual rights, the impact of war, health, sex tourism, and human trafficking.

Global sex: an uneven flow?

The flow of beliefs and practices as regards sexuality is arguably, as with other aspects of globalization, such as economic and cultural relations, an unbalanced one, with western culture having a stronger reach. In fact, unequal globalization in the field of sexuality is not new. As Connell has shown, European conquests on the 'new lands' in the sixteenth century contributed to the shaping of European gendered subjectivities (Connell, 2003: 49), while European colonization from the late nineteenth century resulted in a great wave of globalization which, among other aspects, saw sexual colonization and exploitation – including human trafficking. Altman (2001) has argued that the much bigger globalization wave, which began in the 1980s, has resulted in what he has called 'global sex'. In addition, Berger (2004) asserts that, as regards the unequal impact of globalization on sexuality, it is necessary, when thinking about HIV/AIDS, to be aware of the competing hierarchies of class, gender and ethnicity. As Binnie (2004) has pointed out, aspects of class and wealth and the unequal impact of globalization on sexuality are also shown in relation to the issue of sex tourism.

FACT FILE

Sex and the Empire

Hunter S. Jones (2018) has argued that the Victorian era, a period when Britain became the richest in the world through industrialization and exploiting its vast Empire, was a time when sex became a commodity. This contrasts with the stereotypical view of the Victorian era being one of prudery and sexual repression. It was a time which saw a significant and rapid division between the rich and poor; the very rich had a lifestyle of leisure and pleasure, the destitute often had to turn to selling themselves. The conditions were set, therefore, for prostitution to flourish. Specialized brothels and guidebooks to brothels in London set the precedent for such activity further afield, with Victorian mores travelling to the US, for instance, where, during the Gold Rush, women were shipped in from all over the world for the benefit of the miners, and guidebooks in the style of British ones were produced for visiting businessmen. British rule in India and Africa, whilst not inventing prostitution, brought vast social change, including the requirement for local men to move to single-sex barracks to access work. Women then often created camps near to these barracks and offered food, companionship or sex. Ignoring their own impact on sexual dynamics, this allowed the moralizing Victorian rulers to argue that their presence was needed to 'tame' the local populace. These were just some of the legacies of Victorian attitudes to sexuality in the south (Cruz-Malave and Manalansan, 2002).

Many have suggested that globalization, and its related growth in consumerism, has led to an homogenization of standards of (heterosexual) beauty and masculinity, and cultural practices. For instance, in parts of East Asia there has been a movement away from the tradition of arranged marriages in favour of marriages of 'choice' (Jones, 2010; Raymo et al., 2015). However, it has been argued by others that globalization does not necessarily mean homogenization; in particular, they maintain that it is necessary to challenge or unpack local/global, powerless/powerful binaries. There are, for instance, many fascinating examples of 'transculturation', whereby the meeting of different cultures does not simply result in the adoption of the dominant culture, but also changes aspects of the dominant culture itself (Arrizon, 2006; Bergmann, 2007). For instance, the global availability of LGBT+ identities has made new modes of identity formation possible.

Discussion point

As Herdt and Howe (2007) point out, by switching on the television in just about any country across the globe, it is possible to see evidence of what has been called 'US-styled' sexuality, via syndicated TV programmes, films and advertising. This poses the question of whether, as a result of global neoliberal capitalism and the spread of information technologies, sexuality across the world – including the global south – has become 'Americanized'. However, it is also possible to argue that US sexuality is being impacted by alternative conceptions of sexuality flowing from other countries and cultures.

- Think of what you have watched recently. Can you think of examples of 'Americanized' sexuality?
- Alternatively, have you witnessed examples of sexuality in the west influenced by understandings from across the globe?

It is important to consider the production of knowledge too. As Foucault (1979) has suggested, current knowledge about sexuality emerged from western/northern, 'scientific' understandings of sexuality, which relied on the rigid binary of hetero/homosexuality. However, as we will see throughout this textbook, there are plenty of expressions of sexuality which challenge such a narrow way of thinking about sexuality, and this goes for experiences of sexuality in the global south also (Tucker, 2009).

Early studies of global sexuality arguably researched and described it within an exoticizing framework (Epprecht, 2008). Orientalism, or constructing cultures outside the west as exotic 'Others', can be seen as an instrument of domination (Said, 1978). Whilst this tendency to 'other' the global south has, arguably, largely disappeared from other fields of study, some have asserted that there is still a tendency to subject the global south to an exoticizing 'gaze', either by suggesting certain expressions of sexuality are 'authentic', or by seeking to protect 'traditional' sexualities from the processes of 'global queering' (Altman, 1996).

Bhambra and Santos (2017) have argued that there is a distinct asymmetry between studies into sexuality produced by the west and elsewhere. A quick look through various texts on sexuality reveals the paucity of writing on global sexualities, especially from scholars who reside outside the west. As scholars of sexuality, we are often only obliged to learn about our own worlds, and if we are encouraged to glance across the globe, it is often only ever briefly. Ken Plummer notes the problems with attempting to 'go global' in relation to sexualities given the ubiquity of western theoretical approaches (2013: 761). For instance, there appears to be a tendency in some literature to see western articulations of sexuality as 'modern'. Arguably, this is especially so in relation to non-heterosexual sexuality. LGBT+ life is recognized if it fits with understandings from the **metropole**. Those expressions of sexuality which don't map onto western understandings are often constructed as 'traditional' (Wilson, 2006). Connell agrees, stating that in 'the era of neoliberal globalization, the metropole continues to be the main site of theoretical processing' (2015: 51).

We need to ask whether there is a theoretical and research hegemony of western scholarship. How is sexuality interwoven into everyday experiences, and how do individuals and groups make sense of their sexual identities in a variety of socio-political cultural contexts? Is the west always taken as the benchmark against which the sexual mores of 'others' are measured or understood? Is there an assumption of progress, in which some (the west/north) are perceived as further ahead on the trajectory than others (the south/east)? How is 'difference' read – are scholars attributing it as always due to culture or tradition or do they recognize the impact of politics, economics?

As you continue with this chapter and we move on to consider globalization in relation to a variety of issues, you might want to question what is happening on a global scale. We need to think about the relationships and interconnectedness of cultures. Western colonialism has undoubtedly impacted on many cultures; with it came assumptions about gender, Christianity and its notions of sin, and new laws. But the relationship is never one-way as, the technologies and practices of the colonies of Empires impacted on them too (Bhambra, 2007). Are we witnessing a globalized proliferation of western sexual discourses, with dominant or hegemonic meanings of straight and LGBT+ identities translated at a local, national and international level – in other words, a new form of colonialism? Or can it be said that what is happening is an intersection of western ideologies with local identities and practices, with a flow of understandings and experiences between the two (Blackwood, 2005)?

Sexual citizenship: rights and wrongs across the globe

As Hemmings et al. have shown, globalization has given sexuality a 'central significance within global regimes of power' (2006: 1); this is shown by the many inequalities between cultures, and especially in the continuing sexual 'wrongs' and injustices. It is especially true of those committed against women and children, and against LGBT+ people. However, global awareness of how different sets of values are often in conflict with each other has increasingly led to the view that the sexual wrongs arising from these conflicts *are* 'wrong' – whether according to standards of western liberalism (and even of post-colonial paternalism), or 'wrong' by emerging global values of human solidarity (Weeks, 2007: 213). Globalization has enabled an awareness of wrongs and sufferings across the world which previously were largely unknown. The globalized media – not just TV and newspapers but increasingly also the internet and social media – often interview those who have suffered injustices and abuses. Most recently, of course, we are increasingly aware that many of the refugees fleeing to Europe are fleeing from persecution of their sexuality. As Copestake has shown, for instance, growing persecution by the Shia in Iraq 'has led to a rapid increase in the numbers of Iraqi homosexuals now seeking asylum in the UK because it has become impossible for them to live safely in their own country' (2006: 31). As the section on war and sexuality below shows, such increases in sexual injustices are often associated with conflict.

Globalization has also affected sexuality by giving rise to new forms of conflict in less-industrialized societies over, for example, the reproductive rights of women, or the rights of women to escape restrictive or violent family and communal relationships. The processes of engagement between cultures, and movements across national boundaries, have in turn given rise to new discourses of human rights on a global scale, which are already having a significant impact on sexual politics in several countries. These discourses have shaped ideas of what constitutes sexuality and global sexual justice, and have contributed to the remaking of sexual lives.

As early as the nineteenth century, an international awareness of sexual injustice began to develop, in part, into the long struggle to abolish the slave trade. For instance, in 1875, the International Abolitionist Federation was set up by Josephine Butler, the British feminist, to campaign against state support and regulation of prostitution. As early as 1885, an international conference to stop sexual trafficking took place in Paris, and the aim of ending the so-called 'white slave trade' quickly became an important plank in feminist campaigns against sexual exploitation. Other attempts to impose new international standards and 'sexual rights' included the Hague Convention of 1907, which prohibited rape as an act of war (Altman, 2001: 114, 123). During the 1920s and 1930s, Magnus Hirschfeld's World League for Sexual Reform was an international attempt, involving people from both western and 'Third World' countries, to tackle such issues as the sexual exploitation of children, rights for LGBT+ people, liberalization of attitudes to birth control and divorce, and steps to control sexual disease. Interestingly, these issues are very similar to those that are now the main concerns in present-day debates about globalization and sexuality.

However, these early positive attempts to establish global standards about sexual rights were set back by the rise of fascism and then the outbreak of the Second World War. Strangely, issues of sexuality were 'noticeably absent from the new declarations of Universal Human Rights that signalled the birth of the post-war world, despite the ostensible protection of rights to family life and privacy' (Petchesky, 2000; Weeks, 2007: 204–5). It was not until the 1970s that attempts were made again to revive concerns about global sexual rights. Since then, a newer and more extensive and intensified wave of globalization has affected the world in many ways.

In particular, globalization has seen the emergence of global standards of what constitutes justice, a growing acceptance of difference and human variety as regards sexuality, and an understanding of the power differentials which underpin differences. From such developments, new human sexual values and rights are emerging. These rights concern both negative and positive freedoms. Negative freedoms include such aspects as freedom from violence, legal oppression, the criminalization of sexual behaviour and harassment, all of which are necessary preconditions for living an autonomous life. The positive freedoms include the right to privacy, the recognition and acceptance of different ways of life, and free choice in relationships (provided these freedoms do not cause harm to the rights of others (Weeks, 2007: 222; Wintermute, 2005). Such claims have been central to debates about intimacy and sexuality since the 1960s, but globalization has enabled them to become part of the discourse of human rights.

Arguably, many of the sexual injustices in the global north and south which have been inflicted to uphold religious beliefs have been, and are, imposed on women. This is graphically illustrated by the comments made by the Mufti of Australia, Sheikh Taj Aldin al-Hilali, on the gang rape by 14 Muslim men of an 18-year-old woman in Sydney, Australia: 'If you take uncovered meat and place it outside … and the cats come to eat it … whose fault is it, the cats' or the uncovered meat's? The uncovered meat is the problem. If she was in her room, in her home, in her hijab, no problem would have occurred' (quoted in

Sieghart, 2006: 7). The other group frequently subjected to harm are those who are non-heterosexual. Bishop Desmond Tutu has made the case that such attitudes and behaviours constitute crimes against humanity in exactly the same way that apartheid did. He further sees opposition to the persecution of people because of their sexual orientation as a 'matter of ordinary justice' (Baird, 2004; Tutu, 2004: 5). However, as Weeks points out, 'ordinary justice is what is so often lacking when questions of sexuality and intimacy come to the fore, and the fears, anxieties, threats and risks are compounded when the local feeds into the global, and the global in turn feeds back into the local' (Weeks, 2007: 201).

Although there have been real gains in some of the wealthier parts of the world as regards same-sex relations, these must be set against many negative developments, particularly as regards sexual injustices. For some time, in fact, the world has seen a wave of sexual harms. For instance, there has been an increase in homophobic violence, often the result of an increase globally in the operation of conservative sexual moralities (Hemmings et al., 2006: 1). In many parts of Africa and the Caribbean, post-colonial regimes have condemned same-sex relations as western cultural behaviours which, under imperialism, had been imposed on their societies (Phillips, 2000, 2003; Alexander, 2003). LGBT+ people are violently persecuted in Uganda, Zambia, Zimbabwe and Jamaica. In some Latin American countries, in particular, Argentina, Brazil and Venezuela, trans people are frequently murdered in the streets (Baird, 2004: 8). In Mexico, there is considerable deep-rooted violence against LGBT+ communities, especially when they are associated with 'transgressive' gender behaviour (Ortiz-Hernandez and Granados-Cosme, 2006).

However, it is important to recognize that such problems are not just found in the global south. As Weeks has noted, in post-Soviet Russia, LGBT+ claims for rights receive 'vitriolic opposition from Russian Orthodox, Muslim and Jewish leaders' (2007: 200). In June 2013 a new piece of legislation was passed, as an amendment to existing child protection laws, which criminalized the distribution of materials which support non-traditional sexualities. Religious leaders have variously called for LGBT+ people to be flogged or have equated them with those suffering from leprosy. Extreme nationalist groups have issued death threats against LGBT+ people and attacked them (McLauglin, 2006: 40). Similar developments have been particularly pronounced in some of the new EU accession countries, such as Poland, where a Catholic fundamentalist regime was accused by Human Rights Watch of presiding over 'official homophobia' (Page, 2006: 43). After the fall of other eastern and central European communist states in 1989, similar forms of homophobia emerged quite quickly.

According to Plummer, all sexual lives face the divisions of social location. Class, caste, gender, age, ethnicity, national identity and religion, for instance, intersect to impact on the ways in which people experience their sexuality, as seen in Table 8.1: 'They face the "pathologies of power" whereby many come to be marginalized, colonized and subordinated. In the simplest terms, wealthy white men have usually ruled the world; poor indigenous women have usually been pushed to the margins of the wretched. Their sexual worlds have differed accordingly' (Plummer, 2015: 64). These deep global divisions between rich and poor clearly have major consequences for sexual lives and sexualities.

Table 8.1 Types of inequalities of sexuality

Type of sexuality	Characteristics
Pauperized sexualities	Associated with the extreme poverty faced by 2.2 billion people across the world. For such people, 'are the best things in life really free?'
Unhygenic sexualities	2.5 billion people lack basic sanitation – 'how to have sex with the great unwashed?'
Emaciated sexualities	2 billion people lack sufficient nutrition – 'how to have sex when you are hungry, emaciated, looking for food?'
Sickness sexualities	50,000 people die each day from poverty-related causes – 'how to have sex when you are very ill?'
Homeless sexualities	150 million people globally are homeless – 'where do you have sex when you have no home?'
Exiled sexualities	70 million people are refugees – 'where do you have sex in a refugee camp?'
Public sexualities	'You have no private space, no way of being alone – who do you have to have sex in front of?'

(*Source*: adapted from Plummer, 2015: 64–5)

Cosmopolitanism

As a result of globalization and modernity, what Plummer calls 'cosmopolitanism' and 'cosmopolitan sexualities' have only relatively recently become actual possibilities for the many – and increasingly so, as communication paths across the globe multiply. For him, globalization offers the chance to connect people's distinctive sexual and gendered individualities with human solidarity and belonging. In particular, it becomes possible to bridge people's plural sexual differences with collective values, and their sexual uniqueness with 'multiple group coherence' (Plummer, 2015: 74).

Attempts to create global human rights regimes have involved on-going debates about a series of issues. As we shall see in this chapter, these include debates on sexual violence, abuse and the right to a 'safe' body, including issues such as rape, rape in war, FGM, and so-called 'honour' crimes. In addition, there are wide-ranging debates, within and between world health groups, on sexual practices and care linked to health, but especially HIV/AIDS. There are also on-going debates on global trafficking and sex work: sex worker groups have become concerned with rights and conditions, while anti-trafficking crusaders argue that trafficking is another form of violation of rights and is, in effect, a global slave trade.

Of particular relevance is the Sexual Rights Initiative (SRI). Set up in 2006, it is a coalition of organizations from all regions of the world that has been advocating the advancement of human rights as regards gender and sexuality. It aims to advance sexual rights as a particular set of rights and as a cross-cutting issue within international law, especially in relation to the UN's Human Rights Council. The SRI regularly monitors the situation in all UN countries concerning a wide variety of sexual rights issues and links its findings to the UN's Universal Periodic Review (UPR). Similar issues and investigations are also pursued by ARC International which was set up in 2003. ARC International focuses on advancing LGBT+ rights and it tries to facilitate access to UN mechanisms. Like the SRI, they have an office in Geneva and advance relevant issues within the UN human rights system. In particular, they played a key role in the development of the Yogyakarta Principles on the application of International Human Rights Law in relation to sexual orientation and gender identity.

A particular problem for cosmopolitanism is how, given that sexual cultures are multifarious and have specific historical formations, to distinguish between claims for rights that have universal relevance and those which are highly culturally-specific. This applies to all claims for specific rights, as well as to assertions of universal human sexual rights, especially as in some cultures and societies such rights are possibly distasteful to large numbers of citizens. Given that human 'rights' do not exist naturally but have to be invented and constructed in specific complex historical situations, the possibility of creating minimum common global values requires sustained dialogue.

Although, at both national and international levels, human rights remain contested, they are the necessary standards by which it is possible to challenge ways of life that deny freedom to sexual minorities, and also to challenge a relativism that refuses to make any distinctions at all. As Nussbaum has argued, a global/universal concept of human justice need not be insensitive to the various traditions that shape human lives, nor should it become the mere

135

projection of particularist western values onto more traditional societies (1999: 8). Because the global development of human sexual rights has been a process that 'engages the Other', it has involved a dialogue across differences. As a result, the concept of a global, cosmopolitan sexuality which is emerging allows both the space and opportunity for difference to flourish within a developing discourse of our common humanity (Weeks, 2007: 222–23).

War and sexuality

Globalization increasingly means what happens in distant countries can affect us, even if we are far from such countries. War is perhaps the most obvious and dramatic example. In the years following the US-led invasion of Iraq in 2003, both positive and negative developments occurred: in particular, the re-emergence of fundamentalist Shia Islam, which had previously been held in check by Saddam Hussein. This became part of a wave of transnational fundamentalist Islamic revivalism which, among other things, increasingly targeted those such adherents considered 'immoral'. Gay men have been particularly targeted. As a result, a spate of murders – problematically framed as 'honour' killings, according to the new Iraqi penal code, which protects from murder charges those who kill those seen as acting against Islam – of gay men by murder squads has led to many fleeing from Iraq.

As Herdt and Howe point out, 'The role of war, militaries and peacekeepers are things not often associated with sexuality. However, it is very clear, especially in recent years, that these are deeply interrelated' (Herdt and Howe, 2007: 12). From the twentieth century onwards, hyper-masculinity, sexual humiliation and rape have been used increasingly often as tools of war. And as the 2003 Iraq invasion showed, sexual conquest and sexual humiliation continue to be utilized as tools of war in the twenty-first century also. War tends to distort gender roles and exaggerates male prowess and conquest, while prostitution and rape become tools of war. We are increasingly aware of the numbers of boys and men who are raped during war, both civilians and soldiers (Murdoch et al., 2014). By the twenty-first century, as we have seen, there developed growing recognition of sexuality as a human right, and there is now increasing international recognition that war has helped create prostitution or commercial sex throughout world history. However, although it is increasingly recognized as a tool of war, it has only recently been accepted as a crime against humanity, with the International Criminal Court finding a Congolese rebel commander guilty of such in 2019.

Wherever wars break out, or even when armies are simply deployed, sexual commerce and inevitable rape, sexual abuse, and prostitution quickly follow, while STI epidemics often break out after conflicts end. Though women are the main targets, men also have been used as a way to humiliate enemies. These developments have a long history: during the Roman Empire, prostitutes (some of them sexually enslaved or colonized as 'spoils of war') were a constant feature accompanying the Roman legions, wherever they went. Studies have shown that similar activities were associated with the British Empire in India, South Africa and Borneo. Gilbert Herdt states that, in New Guinea, the Sambia mythology of the Great Man/War Leader resulted in a situation of extreme gender training in which a man did not become a 'real' man until he had stolen the wife of an enemy. More recently, during the Second World War, there was the 'Rape of Nanjing', committed by Japanese troops in December 1937 during their invasion of China. This was a very brutal sexual assault, mainly on women and children: 'there were many cases of rape … Many women were killed after the act and their bodies mutilated. Approximately 20,000 cases of rape occurred within the city during the first month of the occupation' (extract from the judgement of the International Military Tribunal for the Far East, held in Tokyo after the war, quoted in Boister and Cryer, 2008: 536).

In Europe, the Nazis sexually humiliated women as part of a systemic violation of all human dignity and rights: this resulted in dreadful abuses being inflicted on heterosexual women and on LGBT+ people in the concentration and death camps. According to Herdt, 'cruel sexual commerce was therein created, one of the most shameful chapters of the Holocaust' (Herdt, 2007: 196). More recently, during the wars in the former Yugoslavia, it was reported that thousands of women, and young girls and boys, were raped by enemies.

The impact of war on sexuality is often seen in the exaggerated gender images depicted in films and the media, with accompanying themes of sexual intimidation, conquest and rape. For instance, US armed forces were central to the epidemic of syphilis during the two world wars. To control the spread of the disease, prostitutes were quarantined and interned, and thus denied their human rights. After 1945, sexual liaisons between US troops and Japanese and Korean women quickly led to the growth of sexual commerce. This was particularly marked in the Philippines and Vietnam and other parts of Southeast Asia. In some ways this built on an earlier French influence which, before they were forced to withdraw from the region, had created a huge sex industry in Thailand. The practice of US troops taking 'R and R' was sanctioned by the military authorities, and was implicitly financed by the US government through the salaries paid and the transport provided to take the men to places of 'relaxation'. As many have argued, such behaviours foreshadowed what was to come in the form of sex tourism. This is just one aspect of the dreadful impact of war on gender roles and sexual intimacy: there are also consequences such as unwanted pregnancies, HIV/AIDS, and the wholesale sexual conquest of people. It is worth noting that, so far, the US refuses to recognize rape as a war crime (it has refused to ratify the International Criminal Court's

Rome Statute which ruled that rape is a crime of war), or even to explicitly forbid rape as a weapon of warfare.

But as Paul Higate has shown, sexual violations, particularly, but not exclusively against women and girls, are not just restricted to wars and conflict societies. A series of sexual assaults, and the growth of prostitution, have even been noted in UN mission areas in post-conflict societies. Studies have also revealed some humanitarian workers in refugee camps in various African countries who have 'exchanged' food and other survival essentials for sex. More recently Oxfam, alongside accusations of **sexism** and 'colonial' behaviour, was accused of not reporting accusations of child abuse by its aid workers in Haiti. According to Higate, 'these and numerous other reports appear to point to the flourishing of an aggressive sexuality that fails to discern between minors and adults and that may even result in the rape and death of vulnerable female and male civilians (such as occurred in Somalia) in conflict and post-conflict societies' (Higate, 2007: 198). He sees the existence of prostitution and the sexual violation of children in mission areas as showing the negative impact that hypermasculinity associated with war and the military can have on attitudes towards women.

Whether it is war zones or post-conflict societies, it is clear that any aspects of sexuality in such situations cannot be seen 'as simply a set of negotiated desires between consenting adults' (Herdt and Howe, 2007: 169). Until attitudes change, sexual violence and brutality, forced prostitution, sexual slavery and sexual exploitation as consequences of sexual conquest will continue to blight the lives of tens of thousands of people.

Sexual health and HIV/AIDS

As a result of globalization, a world has emerged in which the nature and experience of risk has altered. The most obvious and tragic example is the HIV/AIDS epidemic, which began in the 1980s and rapidly became the first new global health crisis or pandemic in the age of 'heightened globalization'. This brought to the surface many anxieties and ambiguities about sex and sexual orientation, and led to a wide 'variety of moral, cultural and social responses' (Weeks, 2007: 212). By the end of 1985, there were just over 20,000 reported cases; by the end of 2005, the number of reported cases was 40 million, with over 25 million deaths worldwide during those twenty years.

Such a crisis quickly raised the need for international responses and mobilization, e.g. the World Health Organization developed programmes during the 1980s before UNAIDS was established. However, many of these responses have been shaped by 'certain ways of understanding the epidemic which are gendered, ethnicized and embody certain assumptions about sexuality. AIDS has also sexualized identities, or at least has led to a gradual shift towards concept-ualizing sexuality as a central aspect of identity inparts of the world where HIV programmes have played a prominent role' (Weeks, 2007: 212).

As well as highlighting the need for both international and specific local responses, and the fragility of political borders, the AIDS epidemic also revealed the uneven development of societies in the global north and south. Global inequalities of power have inevitably shaped responses to AIDS in various ways. For instance, according to Weeks in 2003 over three-fifths of those on life-saving anti-viral therapies were from rich countries where, by and large, the epidemic was under control (Weeks, 2007). The picture, however, was often quite different in many poorer countries. In such countries and regions, extreme poverty, sexual moralities (those which subordinated women and/or punished gay men) and religious beliefs and practices (such as the Catholic Church's refusal to condone the use of condoms) have variously weakened or prevented the practice of safe sex and the easy distribution of the newer, more-effective, anti-viral drugs. In sub-Saharan Africa, in particular, the stigma surrounding HIV/AIDS has had a serious impact on women and children (Campbell et al., 2006: 132–8).

The impact of different cultures on weakening international responses was shown during a UN conference on AIDS in 2006. Whilst agreement was reached to double the money to combat AIDS, several conservative Islamic countries blocked any attempt to specifically mention the most vulnerable and stigmatized groups at risk such as intravenous drug users and gay men. In addi-tion, female delegates were unable to achieve a full discussion of the particular plight of women as regards AIDS. Another vulnerable group which was also denied specific mention and consideration was that of sex workers.

A focus on global sexualities and health highlights the need to think about the relationship between sexualities, spaces and places. We need to consider not only how sexualities are experienced in different places across the globe but also how certain places become sexualized, at the local, national, interna-tional and transnational levels. Hanna Hacker (2007), for instance, has argued that development funding for HIV projects has the effect of globalizing west-ern ideas about sexuality. Those understood as somehow 'less developed' are encouraged or co-opted to align themselves with identities and practices approved of, or understood by, western standards. For instance, many have pointed to so-called 'gay-conditionality' policies. As such, financial aid to countries in the global south is dependent on the quality of LGBT+ rights. There are several key aspects related to this. The first is historical amnesia, i.e. many of these formerly colonized countries had anti-LGBT+ laws established through European colonial law (Han and O'Mahoney, 2018). The second relates to the fact that in these 'dialogues' between those states needing aid and those deciding whether or not to give it, the voices of those people stuck in the middle, the sexually 'diverse', are left unheard (Seckinelgin, 2018). Articulations of LGBT+ identity, from both potential aid-receivers and givers, construct an identity category which does not necessarily relate to people's lived experience of their sexuality.

Discussion point

Global norms?

Is there, or can there be, a *global* norm relating to sexual rights and sexual health? Is it possible to formulate a set of globally recognizable and acceptable attitudes and values, given the diversity of cultures and traditions?

In order to answer these questions, read some of the debates about female genital mutilation (FGM). Is it a violation of human rights? Or is it a 'manifestation of a cultural ethos surrounding women's sexuality' (Herdt and Howe, 2007: 169)?

Sexual exploitation: tourism and trafficking

Sex tourism

> In the third world, even the 'third rate' American or European tourist is king or queen. (O'Connell Davidson and Sanchez Taylor, 2005: 87)

One area of sexuality significantly affected by globalization is that concerning sex tourism. In order to increase tourism in general, many countries have adopted policies that also specifically encourage western sex tourism. According to O'Connell Davidson and Sanchez Taylor this has created 'sexual Disneylands', where western (usually male) sexual tourists, both heterosexual and gay, are able to indulge their fantasies relatively cheaply (2005: 84). For instance, the early stages of the Thai 'economic miracle' were significantly funded by Thailand's role as a 'rest and recuperation' centre for US troops during the Vietnam War. Even now, sex tourism is, in practice, a major element in Thailand's economy (Renton, 2005). Nonetheless, sex tourism often frequently unbalances struggling economies: formal tourist economies frequently develop more informal sexualized economies, which emphasize the huge disparities of power, wealth and opportunity across the globe.

It is very difficult to estimate the extent to which sex tourism happens, due to its often informal, hidden and illegal nature. Many governments, in both the global north and south, are unwilling to acknowledge its existence. It is also very difficult to define; many sex tourists do not travel with the express intention of purchasing sex – it is often spontaneous. What we do know is that it is an industry which has grown massively since the 1990s. In many respects, tourism is understood more generally as a search for difference and as Wonders and Michalowski (2001) have posited, women are the embodiment of difference in a patriarchal world.

The sexual exploitation of children and young people by sex tourists has become a particular international concern. The concept 'Commercial Sexual Exploitation of Children' (CSEC) brings together 'the varying forms of child exploitation, including child prostitution, child pornography and trafficking in children' (Weeks, 2007: 211). This new definition came into existence, after over twenty years of work, at two World Congresses in 1996 and 2001. It is based on the belief that childhood is fundamentally different from adulthood, thus children should be protected from becoming victims of sexual commerce and exploitation.

The regulation of sexuality, at national levels, has long been practised via legal systems – either by specific laws, or by various state services, such as welfare provision, housing and planning regulations, educational policies, and immigration controls. However, the growth of sex tourism as a feature of globalization has led to international attempts to regulate these aspects of sexuality. For instance, the various NGO campaigns to protect children have led to national laws which permit individuals to be prosecuted for offences committed abroad. In the UK, for instance, there is now legislation which allows the prosecution of those British citizens engaging in 'sex' with children abroad. The first successful prosecution under this law was in 2004, when a man was jailed for two years for attempting to arrange sex with a child in Sri Lanka.

Lesbian and gay sex tourism to developing countries has been seen by many as more 'progressive', as it often challenges colonial patterns, and allows for new forms of identification. Yet, as Weeks has pointed out, 'there has been an insistent note of sexual colonialism throughout modern gay history' (2007: 210; 1990). Binnie (2004) has identified a continuing trend in which the right to travel and to resist homophobic pressures is often opposed to concerns about the local cultures of those countries which have become desirable locations for sex tourists. For instance, some local pro-gay organizations, e.g. in Hawaii, have questioned the 'hidden' or 'unnoticed' violence of both tourism and sex tourism, which depends on the exploitation of many workers (especially women, young people and children) via low wages, and which, in the long run, frequently displaces poor peoples from their own lands and communities (AFSC, 2002: 211). Even the internationally renowned Sydney Mardi Gras has been criticized for its marginalization of working-class and BAME LGBT+ people (Markwell, 2002: 81–100). However, developed countries have also made sex tourism a feature: both London and Manchester have emphasized their positive gay attractions, whilst European cities, such as Amsterdam, have long been attracting sex tourists.

Less written about are the women who travel for sexual encouters. Often, such tourists are constructed as being in search of romance, however, recent research has troubled such a normative account (Bauer, 2013). Some point to the parallels between the global economic inequalities and sexualized racism at play in 'conventional' sex tourism and women paying for sex abroad (Ourahmoune, 2013). In such dynamics, male sex workers are subject to exploitation and constructed as hypersexualized 'studs' by the women who pay them for sex (Sanchez Taylor, 2006).

The reality, however, is that it is mainly men who purchase sex (whether from women or men), and the vast majority of the world's sex workers are women and girls. While there is a long history of male dominance as regards sexual 'rights' for women, the phenomenon of western men travelling from wealthy countries to buy sex in economically deprived societies is largely a consequence of the relations between rich and poor countries, and especially of the existence of a globalized marketplace. It is those global relations that enable men from wealthy western countries to take advantage of widely available and relatively inexpensive opportunities to travel, and also to take advantage of the fact that the cost of living, and the cost of sex, are far cheaper than in the west. As Rahman and Jackson (2010) argue, both the demand for prostitution and the supply of sex workers are the result of complex and intersecting local and global inequalities. All these issues and factors, in the end, reflect how the global commodity market is impacting on gender and sexual relations. It is often women who are the most disadvantaged by the intersections between global and local exploitation (Alexander and Mohanty, 1997; Mohanty, 1997).

Sex tourism, in many ways, is a continuation or re-articualtaion of the colonial relationship between the west and the exoctic 'other', a relationship of domination and subordination. The body of the colonial subject is produced through notions of sexual excess and civilized 'lack'. The border is, so often, a Deriddean (1991) 'absent present'; particular bodies are allowed to move freely across borders, whilst others are either disallowed, or as we shall see, forcibly moved. The sex tourist also has access to permeate the physical border of the sex worker.

Sex trafficking

Trafficking is a common feature of sex tourism, with sex workers often being shipped to where the money is. Thus, the sex tourist is not the only one travelling. Bird and Donaldson (2009) have argued that this often happens in advance of high-profile international football events such as the 2010 FIFA Soccer World Cup. It is estimated that approximately 21 million men, women and children are trafficked for forced labour around the world. This includes those trafficked for sex: estimates of the numbers involved vary from 500,000 to 1.8 million. However, as Plummer points out, the measurement and regulation of the sex trafficking trade 'is notoriously difficult' (Plummer, 2015: 59–60).

There have been various attempts to account for this growing global commodification of sex and sexualities. Richard Poulin (2003) is one of several who argue that routine sexual marketing is a direct outcome of growing exploitation under capitalism. Although it is impossible to estimate the market value of all its various forms, it is undoubtedly a major global industry which amounts to multi-billions of dollars.

This global capitalist exploitation, in particular, involves the sale and use of women's bodies and thus becomes connected to the development of neopatriarchy. The radical feminist Sheila Jeffreys (2008) sees this global exploitation as being linked to a vast 'Industrial Vagina', where an often violent and extensive world of regulating women's lives becomes more and more entrenched. While the increasing involvement of (mainly) women from poorer parts of the world in sex work can be seen as enabling them to save money and support their families, many see this global explosion of sex work as part of an abusive and often brutal exploitation of people via various forms of human sex trafficking.

The trafficking of men, women and children for sexual labour, whether forced or voluntary, involves many networks, border crossings and financial transactions. Sexual trafficking also raises the question of what constitutes 'voluntary' involvement in prostitution. With so many women and girls struggling for basic survival in so many countries, 'survival sex' or 'subsistence prostitution' exposes such issues as the commodification of sex, and the economic, social and governmental structures that have led to these situations. Young women and men (often kidnapped in Southeast Asian countries such as Burma and Nepal) brought into this sex trade are not only exposed to dreadful suffering at the hands of traffickers and their clients, but also suffer from the horrors of the AIDS epidemic which can spread swiftly amongst sex workers. Despite programmes designed to teach about safer sex and to provide condoms, the painful legacy of sexual tourism remains; in part, this is the result not just of global economic inequalities, but also of the impact of war on these countries (see earlier section).

Women in particular, therefore, can be thought of as a resource or commodity for globalization. Women go into sex work, either being trafficked or through **coercion** or force, or they may remain in their home countries to service global sex tourism (Kempadoo and Doezema, 1998). The process of globalization, deregulation, privatization and swingeing cuts to investments in the public sector affect women adversely (Pyle and Ward, 2003).

Moghadam (2000) argues that globalization has contradictory effects for women – on the one hand offering greater opportunities in the workforce, for instance, but on the other the risks of sexual exploitation and trafficking.

Summary

Technology, communication, finances and politics have become globalized, but so too, it would seem, has sexuality. The point at which cultures meet is an interesting and at times difficult area to consider. As we have seen, what we mean by 'sexuality' is contingent on all manner of things – history, politics, economics – and hopefully through some of the examples in this chapter, it is clear that understandings of sexuality will also vary depending on which part of the globe we are from. We need to recognize the different tempos and rhythms of oppression, and the different regimes of sexuality that shape individual ways of being. As sexuality scholars, it is our duty to consider whose sexual story is included in debates about sexualities in the global north and south, and whose narratives remain unheard (Plummer, 1995). We must also think through the ways in which men and women's 'lives are imbricated in the forces of globalization' (Shohat, quoted in Howe, 2009: 420).

Weeks (2007) has pointed out how the world of sexuality is being transformed by the new global connections and flows associated with globalization. These flows include people moving from traditional rural communities into towns and cities, from country to country, and from the global south to the affluent west. As we have seen, globalization movements also include those associated with war: sexual abuses and rape, and sexually transmitted diseases, including HIV. In addition, the issue of STIs has led to global mobilizations and programmes for improved sexual health, which have brought their own issues. There are also movements of people escaping from persecution because of their sexualities (Bamforth, 2005), waves of pornography, in what has become a massively lucrative global industry (Altman, 2001), and flows of sexual tourism which are giving rise to new or intensified forms of sexual exploitation. We have not even touched on other recent debates such as those around terrorism and sexuality (Corrêa et al., 2008; Puar, 2007) or discussions regarding new media technologies, flows of drugs with erotic uses or cybersex.

However, on the positive side, we have begun to consider the ways in which global developments can create new opportunities for overcoming the limits and restrictions imposed on sexualities via demands for human sexual rights and social justice. Globalization has enabled flows of social movements, such as the global feminist and LGBT+ movements, which have had significant impacts on aspects of identity and ways of being (Adam et al., 1999; Threlfal, 1996). Globalization has also allowed for the intermingling of identities, and forms of cosmopolitanism and hybridity. There have also been global organizations which were set up specifically to deal with concerns about the impacts of human trafficking and sex work. The kind of world that will result from these different consequences of globalization remains to be seen.

Key questions

- Is it possible to conceptualize sexuality on a global scale and what are some of the moral (and practical) implications of doing so?

- How can we avoid a western-centric focus on sexuality?

- What do you think will be the key issues in relation to globalization and sexuality in the coming years?

FURTHER READING

For students who want to read about globalization more generally, George Ritzer's *Globalization: The Essentials* (Wiley-Blackwell, 2011) might be a useful starting point, or for a more critical interrogation of globalization, you might want to look at the work of Pierre Bourdieu, such as *Firing Back Against the Tyranny of the Market 2* (Verso, 2003), or David Harvey's *The New Imperialism* (Oxford UP, 2003).

Jon Binnie's *The Globalization of Sexuality* (Sage, 2004) offers an interrogation of the relationship between globalization and sexuality, capitalism and nation-states. Focusing on same-sex desire, he argues against the idea that 'global gay' consumer culture has erased local sex cultures and identities.

For an interesting ethnography looking at the impact of globalization on Vietnam's sex industry, look at Kimberley Hoang's *Dealing in Desire* (University of California Press, 2015).

And see Anouka van Eerdewijk's (2005) study, 'Being a Man', into safe sex and masculinity in Dakar, which explores global processes in a local setting, considering the tensions between the two and the ways in which individuals negotiate these processes (in Davids and van Driel, *The Gender Question in Globalization*, Aldershot: Ashgate).

PART III

ISSUES

9

IDENTITIES

Learning outcomes

By the end of this chapter you should be able to:

- Begin to think critically about the ways in which sexual identities are constructed
- Consider why identity, particularly sexual identity, has become important in contemporary society
- Begin to assess the limitations of understandings of sexual identity in a global context

---

Introduction

Identities matter. They give us a sense of who we are and how we relate to others. They mark the ways in which we are the same as others who share our identities, and they highlight the ways in which we differ from those who don't share our identity. As members of society, we have multiple identities, e.g. student, employee, parent. The formation of an identity involves a knitting together of the social, cultural and psychological; our identity is what links us to our social world. The purpose of this chapter is to explore the issue of how sexual identities are socially produced. In doing so, we will be challenging the persistent and pervasive view that sexual identity is the one realm of our identity which is a result of our genetic inheritance. We will consider the ways in which sexual identity might be experienced as fragile, in that it is often reliant on rigid notions of sameness and difference, and the oppositional binaries such as masculine/feminine or heterosexual/homosexual, binaries which, as we shall see, may not fit comfortably with people's experience of their sexual identity. Identities are, of course, political, hence in the exploration of sexuality and its diversities there will be a consideration of the intersections with sexuality and gender, ethnicity and class. We begin this chapter by looking at why identity is such an important aspect of contemporary society, moving on to focus on sexual identity more generally. We will then look at a few specific sexual identities and consider their relationship to each other. This is not a comprehensive review of all sexualities – it would take a text of encyclopaedic length to do that – instead we focus on some identities which have perhaps had less of a presence in the book thus far.

Identity and society

> Everyone has to ask himself the question 'who am I', 'how should I live', 'who do I want to become'… Self-construction of the self is, so to speak, a necessity. Self-confirmation of the self is an impossibility. (Bauman, 1988: 62)

The question of identity has been a preoccupation of social scientists for some time, arguably, as identity is central to our understandings of who we are (as individuals). In the 1930s, sociologists such as George Herbert Mead (1934) argued that identity was modified through everyday interactions. In a similar way to Enlightenment thinkers of the seventeenth and eighteenth centuries, he felt there was an inner core of self, but unlike them, he didn't think this was unchanging. In this sense, his work was foundational for contemporary understandings of identity as inherently connected to the social.

However, by the late twentieth century, many scholars were interested not only in the increased importance placed on identity in our social lives (and a related rise in academic identity discourse), but also at the same time its rapid fragmentation. Thinkers such as Stuart Hall (1996) were arguing that there was no coherent, fixed inner core. Instead, identity was a continuous process. As a result of the rapid and widespread changes taking place in societies across the globe, driven by transformations in technology, politics and the economy, the traditional fixed meanings of national and cultural identity are disrupted by the global marketing of style, consumerism. Such changes meant that aspects which might previously have been a given, such as social class, can no longer be assumed to be static: we might be born working class, but through education, work or lifestyle, end up middle class. Changes in social and economic structures also mean that many people no longer stay in the area they were born in, or even the country they were born in. Thus, national identity is also more complicated for more people than ever before. In this sense, we are living in times which might be experienced as more uncertain or risky (Beck, 1992; Giddens, 1991); such unpredictability often brings with it anxiety. Therefore, the conditions are ripe for identity to become more important than ever before. If identity, however, is not given or certain, it must be created, hence its formation comes to be seen as the great 'project' of late/postmodernity. This 'compulsive and obligatory self-determination' of 'liquid' modernity (Bauman, 1988: 5) is a never-ending quest. Identities 'can be adopted and discarded like a change of costume' (Lasch, 1979: 29). However, in a world driven by competition and the pursuit of profit, the conditions of global, neoliberal capitalism mean that not everyone can choose as freely as others. Political and economic systems become so large that many people feel it is impossible to challenge or resist them. It is a society which emphasizes the importance of individuality whilst taking away many people's ability, or will, to act. Thus, Lasch and others argue, we turn to the project of the self and instead focus on diet, exercise, beauty regimes. In this sense, identity becomes embodied (Featherstone, 2010).

Areas of enquiry which concern social theorists are also transformed under these conditions. Academics have long been interested in issues to do with social justice and equality, and with a new focus on identity, this area of interrogation might shift to matters of recognition. An interest in the political process may well turn to look at concerns about the human rights around identity politics. It has also led academics to posit that it is a time of increasing boundary formation. To identify who one is, we are simultaneously saying who we are definitely not; is this a time of 'identification wars' (Bauman, 1988: 11)?

Sexuality as an identity

Just as community collapses, identity is invented. (Young, 1999: 164)

Many of us take for granted that not only is sexuality an identity but that it is also at the core of our identities. As such, it has become a central marker of self in the twenty-first century. However, as we saw in Chapter 2, having a sexual identity is a relatively new concept and it is certainly not one shared across the globe: for some of us, sexuality is simply something we do. Seidman (2010) has suggested that rapid industrialization and changing social arrangements in the early twentieth century, where traditional gender divisions were blurring (men found themselves in white-collar work using so-called 'feminine skills', and women were gaining 'masculine' freedoms and rights such as the right to vote or have an education) invoked a degree of identity panic. In order to counter this seeming collapse in the social order, it became increasingly important to affirm clear gender roles and reconstruct an apparently dichotomous understanding of gender. The vehicle for this, according to Seidman and others, was to assert a heterosexual identity, reliant on a rigid and ordered understanding of gender difference and sexual attraction to one's supposed 'opposite'. In effect, this ideological belief in gender polarity become a central organizing principle in many western societies. As a fragile construct, heterosexuality absolutely relies on an assertion of difference. Sexual identity needs to be understood as relational. Just as understandings of masculinity rely on its polar opposite, femininity, for heterosexuality to make any conceptual sense, it needs to be understood alongside its assumed opposite.

This points to the fact that sexual identities are never neutral 'facts of life', they can only be understood within the specific social contexts in which they occur. They become enmeshed in 'normative expectations – that is, for example, wrong or dirty for young children, exploratory and exciting for adolescents, reproductive in heterosexual coupledom, and somewhat distasteful in older age' (Shildrick, 2009: 131). One example is the way in which gender and sexuality are reproduced through our relationship with food. On a recent visit to a popular holiday resort, I noticed a menu advertising breaksfast for 'dads' which consisted of a heartattack-inducing amount of dead pig, unlike the breakfast for 'mums'; here, heterosexual masculinity is shored up through consumption of meat (Sumpter, 2015). Another arena which has played a role in constructing dominant notions of sexuality is sport, where ideals of the sporting body are constructed around a notion of masculine heterosexual proficiency. This leads to a 'homophobic zeitgeist' enacted on and off the playing field, effectively rendering sport a heterosexual and male preserve (Anderson, 2011: 565). Recently, with more and more celebrity sports people 'coming out', we have perhaps seen a shift in sporting culture and performances of gender and sexuality. Sexual identities are therefore political, subject both to formal or legislative constraints (see Chapter 7) and other, less formal sociocultural expectations. Foucault (1979) showed how such processes constructed sexuality through 'disciplinary practices', with those who reject normative standards being seen as a threat to the very fabric of society. As we saw in Chapter 7, there have been several political resistance movements which have challenged dominant, normative constructions of gender and sexuality, and in addition to achieving political recognition they have (re)claimed a sexual identity. The appearance of Queer Nation, in particular, is cited by many as heralding a significant turning point in sexual politics and notions of sexual identities (Richardson, 2000).

Discussion point

Changing sexual identities

In 1994, Judith Lorber argued there were ten sexual identities: heterosexual male/female; lesbian; gay man; bisexual male/female; **transvestite** female/male and transsexual female/male. By 2019, a quick Google search showed that the number had risen to 50+ to include such categories as 'sapiosexual', 'vegansexual' and 'skoliosexual'.

- Write a list of as many sexual identities as you can think of, then compare them with lists you can find online.
- What does this apparent proliferation of sexual identities tell us about attitudes towards sexuality?
- Why do you think there has been this shift?
- Organize these into a hierarchy which reflects their relative status in society.
- Is it possible to engage in any of the related sexual practices without being given a label or identity?

Language, culture and sexual identity

We keep coming back to the importance of vocabulary, but it is hard to escape; language frames how we think. Before we start to look at a few examples of sexual identity, it is important to consider the implications of our 'tools of analysis'. Foucault (1979) drew attention to the importance of language in relation to sexual identities. He argued that the sexologists effectively brought us into being with the labels used to categorize sexual behaviours. Language is also important in relation to its usage; the words we choose or reject can be an act of identity. The re-appropriation of 'queer', for instance, was an act of identity, and the use of Polari, which was common among gay communities of the 1960s in the UK, was an important part of the construction of a particular gay identity (Baker, 2002). Language is also reflective of cultural attitudes towards sexuality – the very concept of having a sexual identity may not always be pertinent. As we have seen in Chapter 8, in the context of globalization, sexuality becomes very complicated. The western 'lesbian' in many ways maps onto the Japanese 'onabe', yet there are differences, in that *onabes* are not attracted to lesbians (*rezu*) or other *onabes*. Many of the sexual identities we will be looking at in this chapter will not be universally recognized. In India, the *hijra* who present themselves as 'feminine' and are attracted to 'masculine' men, do not exactly equate with an understanding of the gay or trans identities of the global north (Boellstorff, 2006).

Asexuality

We are going to begin with a subject position that many texts on sexuality barely mention. Asexuality in relation to sexual identities, where it is present, is usually discussed as part of the stereotype of ageing sexualities. It has also been used to define ideal feminine sexual passivity, 'romantic' friendships between lesbians or disabled sexuality (Shakespeare, 2006). Frequently, asexuality is conflated with celibacy. Or it is often assumed that someone who is asexual has no interest in sex at all, or does not find people attractive – an identity which is stereotyped as being characterized by a lack or absence. However, in recent years there has been more mobilization around the identity, and as a consequence, we can argue that it is much more nuanced and complicated as a sexual subject position. Asexuals have a diverse range of identities and might not be sexually attracted to men or women, or they may be attracted but not want a physical relationship. This does not necessarily mean they do not experience romantic or aesthetic attraction, sexual arousal, or that they do not want intimacy in their relationships. As such, asexual people can have heterosexual or same-sex preferences. Asexuality is, like so many other areas of minority sexuality, under-theorized, and has largely been interrogated under a medicalized gaze, but social reactions to asexuality are interesting and tell us much about the sexualized society we live in (Scott and Dawson, 2015). Carrigan (2012) argues that asexuality requires us to fundamentally question aspects of human identity previously considered the norm, the sexual assumption of contemporary society.

Heterosexuality

If the established norm is heterosexuality, however, often there is no perceived need to explain heterosexuality, especially a heterosexuality that conforms to traditional moral principles of marriage and monogamy. As a result, while there have been many studies into the 'causes' of same-sex desire, there have been very few studies of heterosexuality. As Saraga (1998) points out, attempts to study heterosexuality have often been met with incredulity. In one study which asked women to reflect on their experiences of being heterosexual, many said they felt uncomfortable with the label 'heterosexual'. One woman realized it was an aspect of her identity that she'd never considered before and others reflected on their discomfort at being labelled by others. It is important, though, to think critically about dominant groups, to remove the blanket of invisibility that comes with privilege.

As an 'invisible' majority, heterosexual sexuality is, in many respects, 'unmarked', however there have been some interesting studies that highlight the ways in which heterosexuality is performed (Butler, 1990). One such example is Kira Hall's (1995) study of a group of telephone sex workers, who referred to themselves as 'fantasy makers'. One woman described a process, whereby she constructed an idea of female heterosexuality through language: 'I can describe myself now so that it lasts for about five minutes, by using lots of adjectives … it's not just wasting time, because they need to build up a mental picture in their minds about what you look like, and also it allows me to use words that are very feminine' (Hall, 1995: 199–200). In this way, Arlie Hochschild's (1979) notion of affective, or emotional, labour can be used to think through issues related to sex work. Such workers have to construct an idea of the self which their clients interpret as 'authentic', a reflection of men's power to construct the 'truth' and part of a much older tradtion which renders the body of women the 'constitutive outide' (Derrida, 1991: 63). Other women go on to explain the kind of talk they engage in as reproducing eroticized notions of being young and also somewhat 'ditzy'. There are also plenty of other heterosexual subcultures (dogging, swinging, BDSM), which allow us to start thinking more critically about the majority norm which frames all our lives.

We are also told that (male) heterosexuality might be said to be going through something of a crisis, that its foundations have had a bit of a shake-up. For instance, in recent years we have seen the formation of heterosexual (usually male) rights groups. One such example would be the spate of Heterosexual Pride events. These started on US campuses as a backlash against a presumed LGBT+ acceptance, and in 2019, a call to hold a straight Pride event in Boson caused international controversy. The (brief) rise of Incels – a portmanteau of 'involuntary celibates' – is also striking. These are groups of men, who often commune via the internet, or the manosphere as it's often known, and lay the blame of their lack of sex life at the feet of feminism. Are these men placing themselves on Connells' (1995) hierarchy of hegemonic masculinity and finding that they are lacking in this regard? This particular type of heterosexual masculinity makes for an interesting comparison with the professional pickup artists or (PUAS), who use a combination of coercion and manipulation to get women to have sex with them. Again, these groups use the internet to share techniques, and we are seeing, perhaps, another form of mediated identity and intimacy (O'Neill, 2018).

Masculinities and sexuality

Recently, sexual identities associated with masculinity have been the subject of various academic debates, which have tended to problematize the predominant understandings of this particular sexual identity, and how these understandings have influenced the politics and practices of sexuality.

Female masculinities

If masculinity is seen as a social variable, it can then be applied beyond men, thus 'female masculinity' is a possibility. There is a long history of associating masculinity with lesbianism, as a result of the work of the Victorian sexologists (see Chapters 1 and 2). Butch culture became an important part of lesbian communities and identities. Kennedy and Davis (1993) examined the classed nature of butch/femme identities in working-class lesbian communities in Buffalo, New York, in the 1950s. For many working-class lesbians, they argue, based on examinations of oral history documents, a butch identity was important because it allowed women access to hitherto 'male' areas of work, which was essential since they could not necessarily rely on a husband's wage. The common linkage of butch with working-class lesbian communities may also be related to the fact that, as Hennessy (2000) argues, it is simply cheaper to adopt a butch look than it is a femme one. Nevertheless, such figures have, historically, been subject to abuse. Perhaps because, as Reeser has stated, 'when masculinity is disassociated from the male body … masculinity might suddenly become very visible because it is seen to reside somewhere it is not normally or naturally housed' (2010: 3). The work of Judith Halberstam (1998) on female masculinity was instrumental in bringing to prominence as a research priority the experiences of butch lesbians, through an analysis of fictional narratives and cinema. More importantly, perhaps, she 'troubled' conventional understandings of masculinity. Visible 'masculinity' in heterosexual women is also usually constructed as problematic, and often comes with the label 'laddish'. A common assumption is that women who have casual sex, for instance, are somehow subverting conventional femininity and appropriate modes of behaviour. This is a common trope in popular culture – the 2015 film *Trainwreck*, for instance, has a central female character who enjoys lots of sex with different men, but we are shown, albeit humorously, that this is not appropriate behaviour.

Generally, then, masculine identities are constructed as relational and part of binary logics. Thus, an individual's sense of identifying themselves as 'masculine' often involves self-definition, either in concert with, or in opposition to, others. Here, 'masculinity' is defined against 'femininity' – in other words, that which it is not.

Gay masculinities

While it is clear that multiple masculinities exist, it is also clear that hegemonic forms of masculinity also exist (Connell, 1987). In general these masculinities are heterosexual, and come with greater social power than, for instance, gay masculinities. As a result, some gay men have responded by creating hypermasculine identities and styles – such as 'the clone', which is an identity often associated with post-Stonewall gay subcultures, and frequently characterized by short hair, checked shirts, tightly-fitting T-shirts, denim jeans and neat moustaches (for a time, Freddie Mercury of Queen dressed as a clone); or 'the leatherman', another type of hypermasculinity, with dress/style references to

156

bikers and cowboys, which, with its roots in biker culture of the 1950s, acted as an alternative to dominant connections between being gay and 'effeminacy'; or 'the bear' (bear-identified men tend to be a bit 'bigger', more mature and have beards), an identity which emerged in the 1980s, where, some have argued, the larger body shape was eroticized as a marker of good health in the era of AIDS (Wright, 1997). The internet has played an important part in the ongoing presence of these subcultures, with Egan (2003) arguing that for many men without recourse to specific bars, it acts as a place to make social and romantic contacts. The gay community generally places the youthful, slender and smooth 'twink' as the ideal, and several studies have noted how this places disproportionate pressure on gay men to achieve a slim body, which can lead to eating disorders (Berry, 2001). Several of these identities offer a counter to this ideal, and perhaps reduce the marginalization many gay men may feel in the gay community, as well as mainstream society. However, we could ask to what extent such identities subvert hegemonic heterosexual masculinity or reify it.

The relationships between gay and straight masculinities are clearly complex, and it is argued by some that the homophobia involved in rejecting gay identities serves the purpose of disciplining all men to stay within social norms. This discipline is seen as being necessary because of the blurry boundaries between male same-sex desire and what has been called 'homosociality'. In addition, there are tensions of dominance and ambiguity relating to masculinity within male heterosexual identities, as seen in Robinson et al.'s (2011) study with gay and heterosexual male hairdressers (see Chapter 3). We can also see the potential influence of queer masculinities on heterosexual masculinities with the relatively recent trend of body hair removal, though this may also be an influence from sporting culture (Miller, 2019). Thus 'masculinity' – and the various types of masculinities – can be seen as potentially unstable identities and performances, subject to cultural anxieties, expectations and prohibitions which individuals may either accommodate or resist.

Discussion point

Top dog?

As part of the gender order theory, where hegemonic masculinity is seen as the practice which legitimizes men's dominance in society, Connell (1987) argued that gay masculinities were the most oppressed of all within a hierarchy of masculinities because of their conflation with femininity.

(Continued)

- Is this still the case?
- Where would transgender and transsexual people be placed in this hierarchy?
- Construct your own hierarchy of masculinities.

BDSM

BDSM refers to the various sexual practices and identities of:

- bondage/discipline;
- domination/submission;
- sadism/masochism.

Several of these sexual practices and identities, as with many minority sexual identities, have been the object of various psychiatric theories, criminal laws, and moral disapproval. According to Andrea Beckmann (2009: 1), 'sadomasochism' as a sexual identity is a social construction based on 'a mystification of social reality'. 'Sadism' is closely associated with the writings of the Marquis de Sade (1740–1815), and is taken to mean an erotic love of cruelty or domination, whilst the term 'masochism' was first used by the German sexologist, Richard von Krafft-Ebing (1840–1902), and refers to the erotic love of pain and submission (derived from the semi-autobiographical tales of Leopold von Sacher-Masoch (1836–95) of subservient men admiring dominant women). Therefore, this is an identity which, among several others, under the medicalized gaze became labelled as a 'sexual perversion'. The work of Mary Douglas (1966) might be useful for considering social responses to such practices, looking at the ways in which certain bodily acts or behaviours are constructed as polluting and therefore dangerous. Acts which cross 'revered' boundaries such as skin or orifces, like blood-play or anal penetration, challenge the socially constructed binary of clean/dirt.

Awareness of these various sexual identities reached a wider audience recently, via the 2011 film *Fifty Shades of Grey*, which was based on the erotic novel of the same name, by British author E.L. James. The film was notable for its explicit scenes showing elements of bondage/discipline, dominance/submission and sadism/masochism. This attracted some criticism from various quarters, including from some of those within the BDSM communities. These claimed that the film both confused BDSM with abuse, and depicted it as a pathology that needed to be overcome. In addition, they pointed out that it showed incorrect and possibly dangerous BDSM practices.

In fact, it is important to distinguish between, on the one hand, sexual practices which involve consensual roleplay which can be violent, and on the other, non-consensual physical and/or mental cruelty. Related to this, is the fact that some feminists have criticized the film – and BDSM in general – because of the links to the heterosexual domination of males over females, and also for its objectification of women (Kelly, 1988). In particular, as such practices seem to assert the inevitability of inequalities within relationships, whereas feminism seeks to end such inequalities, there is the fear that BDSM 'enacts and mimics the kinds of violence from which feminism seeks to free women' (Eadie, 2004: 216).

However, because mutual consent and prior negotiation, with the use of 'safewords', are the basis of BDSM practice, participants state that this shows their activities do not, in fact, involve abuse of power. On the contrary, they argue that this is often unlike the most common, 'normative' socially accepted sexual practices, in particular, heterosexual sex. Such 'vanilla' sex, it is pointed out, often ignores 'the power inequalities embedded in assumptions about what sexual partners will do' (Eadie, 2004: 215).

Essentially, BDSM identities belong to sexual communities which are organized around the derivation of erotic pleasure from role play, and the giving and/or receiving of varying degrees of consensual physical and/or mental pain. In fact, in order to distance themselves from the quasi-pathologizing associated with individual terms such as 'sadism', 'masochism' or 'submission', those within such sexual communities increasingly prefer to simply use the appropriate initials relevant to their sexual identities, such as SM or BDSM.

Like many other subcultures, those sharing sexual identities based on these pleasures and freedoms share a distinct style as regards both dress and behaviour. Leather, latex, rubber and 'uniforms' in general, are often accompanied by an array of sex toys. As BDSM is increasingly accepted within more 'open' societies, those sharing BDSM identities have created more organized subcultures, with their own vocabulary. The erosion of boundaries between the different sexual practices within BDSM is shown by the fact that abbreviations, such as 'S/M', are being abandoned, in favour of the more fluid 'grammar' of 'SM' or 'BDSM', indicating crossovers in practices.

However, while BDSM is a label of self-definition, there are many other 'sexual practitioners' who do not identify with the BDSM community, despite engaging in sexual practices, such as sadism and/or masochism. Beckmann (2001) has argued that this is an identity which has, in recent years, been normalized. In part, we can see this with mainstream films such as *Fifty Shades of Grey*. We can also see this through the relative proliferation of high street sex shops which sell handcuffs and other sex toys.

Discussion point

The mainstreaming of bondage?

If Beckmann (2001) is correct, and BDSM practices have become normalized, why do you think this is?

- You could perhaps list aspects of BDSM culture and identities which are mainstream; this might include the language of BDSM. You could read Airaksinen's (2018) 'The Language of Pain: A Philosophical Study of BDSM' to help you do this.

Bisexuality

Considering bisexuality is one of the most 'popular' forms of 'minority' sexual identities, in the US constituting forty percent of that group (Pew Research Centre, 2013), relatively little social scientific research has focused on bisexuals. Instead, as with BDSM identities, academic work has frequently been informed by psychology, placing bisexuality under a medical 'gaze'. In part, this is because of Freud's preoccupation with polymorphous sexuality. By this, Freud meant human sex drives in infancy, where before the family (and society) had imposed an 'order' upon children, they were bisexual or, more accurately, of neither sex. As children grew up, their infant pleasures became increasingly 'ordered' and, eventually, prepared the way for female and male development to diverge. When bisexuality is mentioned in contemporary parlance, it is often 'lumped' in with lesbian and gay sexuality, and considered as a practice rather than an identity (Esterberg, 2002).

Bisexual identities have been subject to a degree of stereotyping, often cast as the 'Snuffaluffagus of sexualities' (McAlister, 2003: 25), or they are believed to really be gay men or lesbians who have not yet plucked up the courage to come out. They are also frequently constructed as being more likely to engage in 'alternative' sexual practices, such as threesomes or swinging (Parrenas, 2007). Perhaps this is because it is an identity which challenges long-held either/or understandings of sexuality, indeed, the very label indicates the power of binary thinking. Some research suggests that their identity is less important to them than it is for gay men and lesbians (Pew Research Centre, 2013). Seidman (2010) argues that bisexuality came to the fore as a political and sexual identity, rather than just being read as a practice, in the 1970s, when, he suggests, the lesbian and gay movement cast it as an ideal – at times – in part because of an assumed 'liberal' approach to sexuality. The 1970s also saw a few prominent celebrities, such as David Bowie, 'come out' as bisexual (though he later went back 'in'). Bisexuals very often found themselves on the margins of the lesbian and gay community, viewed with suspicion or assumed to be hanging on the coattails of heterosexual privilege. Seidman argues that bisexuality is still often misunderstood. Whilst it can refer to sexual attraction to both men and women, he points out that for some, it's 'less about gender preference than about *sexual and gender openness and fluidity*' (2010: 94). Monro et al. (2017) have traced the ways in which bisexuality has been relatively ignored in social scientific research, a trend which seems to continue. Perhaps, as Yoshino (2000) has suggested, this is because lesbians, gay men and heterosexuals have a vested interest in ignoring bisexuality in order to maintain rigid sexual and gender binaries. Fields et al. (2016) conducted research with young black bisexual men, a group at the intersection of a variety of stigmatized identities. Some of the tensions these men experienced, they argued, came from the fact they identified 'first' with their ethnicity. As such, many had families involved in religious communities and they feared rejection or ridicule because of expectations around a performance of a particular kind of hegemonic masculinity and religiosity. Some countered this by adopting a hyper-masculinity, others resisted adopting a perceived racialized and gendered stereotyped.

As a non-binary sexuality then, where many resist any labels, bisexuality sits on the sexual margins but it also has the power to disrupt conventional ways of thinking about sexuality and gender (Callis, 2014).

Pansexuality

Pansexualism, sometimes also referred to as 'pomosexualism', seems to be an increasingly popular sexual identity, especially with younger generations, with celebrities such as Miley Cyrus identifying in this way (Staufenberg, 2015). As such, there is scant academic research on this identity to date. It would appear from mentions in popular culture more generally, that it is frequently conflated with bisexuality, however, it can be differentiated from bisexuality as a sexual identity in that it encompasses more than sexual attraction to and/or loving of both women and men. Thus, in some respects, pansexualism is sometimes associated with BDSM. According to David Cauldwell, a pioneer of sexuality theory, a **pansexual** is someone 'who indulges, to a greater or lesser degree, in all discovered forms of sexual expression' (2001 [1950]: 2). The term originates from the Ancient Greek word *pan*, meaning 'all' or 'every'. Therefore, as well as being sexually attracted to both cis women and men, pansexuals are also attracted to trans people. In essence, pansexuality is an expression of a sexuality with maximum fluidity. Many define 'pansexual' as being attracted to all genders (Fontanella et al., 2014), however it has been argued that this is a sexual identity which challenges any notions of gender or sex as essential aspects of sexuality, and fundamentally subverts hegemonic, dichotomous thinking. In this view, it is argued that pansexuality is anti-label, it cannot be pinned down like a butterfly. As a result, comparisons could be made between pansexuality and queer as an identity.

Discussion point

Three's a crowd?

Polamory

Another sexual identity which is arguably on the rise, or has more cultural presence, is that of polyamory, an identity which resists traditional monogamy, indicating, perhaps, a significant shift in attitudes towards monogamy. Like swinging, polyamory is a form of Consensual Non-Monogamy (CNM). The emphasis for polyamory, however, is on the emotional as well as sexual connections between more than two people. Swinging, on the other hand, usually involves an exclusive couple, in terms of emotions, with non-exclusive sexual encounters with others. Some studies have suggested that white, middle-class people are more likely to identify as polyamorous.

- How many cultural representations of polyamory can you think of? And in what ways is it represented? Why do you think that this might be an identity which appears to be growing in popularity?

Summary

Sexual identities can clearly provide an important sense of community for many people. This might be expressed in shared styles, practices or vocabulary. When looking at the relationship between sexuality and identity, a common theme seems to be that of the intersections between the body and sexuality in society, whereby the body becomes a site where 'good' citizens are made or unmade. There is a close relationship between practices and identity, so sexual practices seem to be connected to clear, often politicized, identities and others are left simply as practices. Had we more space, it would be interesting to explore this a little further. For instance, one aspect of sexual behaviour which receives little attention in social scientific theory, arguably because it's considered a taboo practice, is necrophilia. This is despite there being a rich seam of fascination for necrophilia through history. From the Greek hero Achilles, to Oscar Wilde's *Salomé*, death has been eroticized and necrophilia hinted at.

We might ask why the necrophiliac is an identity rarely talked about. Perhaps this is due to concerns of consent (though someone could write in their will that they wish to give their body up, not for medical purposes but for sexual services). Perhaps it is because corpses are raised to levels of sacredness in society and thus have greater 'zones of inviolability' (Shilling and Mellor, 2014), or that sex with the dead removes traditional ties of emotion.

Key questions

- What are the dominant forces involved in forming sexual identities today?

- Which groups are currently struggling to have their identity recognized as legitimate in society?

FURTHER READING

In order to start thinking a little more about heterosexual subcultures and identities, you could read David Bell's (2006) article 'Bodies, technologies, spaces: on "dogging"' (https://doi.org/10.1177%2F1363460706068040).

Gayle Rubin's collection of her essays, *Deviations: A Gayle Rubin Reader* (Duke UP, 2011), provides a fascinating ethnography of the 'kinky' sexual community.

If you are interested in the lost language of Polari, have a look at Paul Baker's (2002) 'The construction of gay identity via Polari in the Julian and Sandy radio sketches' (*Lesbian and Gay Review*, 3 (3): 75–83).

10

YOUNG PEOPLE AND SEXUALITY

―――――――――――― **Learning outcomes** ――――――――

By the end of this chapter you should be able to:

- Understand the ways in which the meanings of adolescent sexuality are constructed in society
- Explore some of the key social structures and sexual cultures which impact on young people's lives
- Consider the ways in which ideas of 'normality' are produced, experienced and contested

Introduction

In this chapter we will consider young people and sexuality, looking at the ways in which young people develop their own sexual identities. We will examine the ways in which not only is 'sexuality' socially constructed but so too are categories such as 'childhood' or 'youth'. As with previous chapters, the impact of social divisions on experiences of sexuality will be a focus. Adults are often troubled by young people's sexuality and it is often framed as a problem which needs to be regulated and controlled. Moral panics concerning teenage promiscuity and pregnancy frequently emerge in newspapers and on television and in government policy. Debates about when young people should first learn about sex and what kinds of sex they can know about are ongoing.

As you progress through this chapter, reflect on your own experiences, e.g. what sort of education did you receive at school about sexuality and relationships, and how did messages you received from the media, home or elsewhere shape your experience?

However, before we attempt to understand the social constructions, and experiences, of young people's sexuality, it might be worth looking briefly at the period they are understood to be leaving (childhood) in order to establish its legacy for young people.

Childhood sexuality

Childhood sexuality is often left out of textbooks on sexuality and the reasons are clear; it is, as we shall see, a highly controversial and sensitive subject. Many have noted a distinct tension between a desire to protect children from sexuality altogether and a need to deal with the realities and consequences of childhood sexuality (Robinson, 2017). Such tensions are, in part, a result of social and historical ideas of childhood and what it means.

Discussion point

Childhood and sexuality

- When does sexuality 'begin'?
- What is it about ideas of childhood that means thinking about sexuality is difficult and perhaps taboo?

One of the key texts still influencing current academic thinking concerning the nature of childhood is a work of social history by Philippe Ariès (1962). In it, he makes a bold statement that 'in medieval society the idea of childhood did not exist … it corresponds to an awareness of the particular nature of childhood, that particular nature which distinguishes the child from the adult, even the young adult. In medieval society, this awareness was lacking' (1962: 125). Using evidence from art, diaries and accounts of the time, he argued that they were viewed as mini-adults and as such were expected to participate in all aspects of social life alongside their parents. Foul language, sexual acts, death, and so on were all permitted in their presence.

Neil Postman (1994), influenced by Ariès and also sharing ideas with Norbert Elias (1994 [1939]), argues that the developing notion of 'shame' was at the heart of a shift in attitudes towards children. Gradually, with an increasing conceptual separation of the mind and body, spread by growing literacy rates and pamphlets on etiquette, adults were encouraged to exert more self-control over their bodily functions in order to seem more **civilized**. This included being more secretive around children about adult sexual relations. This culminated in the idealized Victorian notion of the innocent, dependent child who needed to be shielded against adult knowledge and corruption. Childhood, in other words, came to be seen as a state in need of protection. The boundary between childhood and adulthood, for Ariès a socially constructed boundary, needed to be kept distinct and preserved. Children were often viewed as pure and asexual, in much the same ways as women were often viewed. However, such a view of both women and children was hypocritical and drawn along lines of class. This was a time when many working-class women and children were working as prostitutes and:

> A Royal Commission in 1871 found that in London hospitals there were 2,700 cases of venereal disease among girls between the ages of 11 and 16 years. The sexual use of young girls was directly sanctioned as 12 was the age of consent. Girls of this age could be procured for the (substantial) price of £20, a valuation which gave some clue as to the social class of the purchasers. (Hawkes, 1996: 47)

FACT FILE

'The Maiden Tribute of Modern Babylon'

In 1885, W.T. Stead, a journalist for a London magazine, went undercover to show just how easy it was to 'purchase' a child's virginity, in an attempt to expose the extent of child trafficking and prostitution. He paid a mother £5 for her 13-year-old daughter; the cost included a medical examination to 'prove' she was a virgin. Stead wrote in his article how the doctor who performed the examination recommended he drug her with chloroform so that she didn't struggle when he raped her. As a result of widespread public outrage (some of this was genuine horror at what happened to young girls – others were perhaps more angered that the truth had been revealed), the government introduced the Criminal Law Amendment Act of 1885 which raised the age of consent to 16. Nevertheless, many children both under and over the age of consent continue to experience rape and abuse.

Despite the fact that an ideal of innocent childhood developed culturally, in many ways it was something which both state and society felt had to be inscribed and enforced by rules, e.g. the 'solitary vice', or masturbation, especially among children, was seen as a threat to society and became the focus of Victorian moral campaigns (see Chapter 2). One doctor invented a device which gave an electric shock to the penis of any boy with an erection – surely something which would give a child a complex if they didn't already have one! Gradually, however, with the influence of Freud's theories, childhood sexuality came to be understood as natural, if complicated, and masturbation was viewed as an expression of children's curiosity and exploration. This is not to suggest, however, that childhood sexuality holds the same meanings as adult sexuality.

Discussion point

On Sexuality

- Read Sigmund Freud's On Sexuality: Three Essays on the Theory of Sexuality and Other Works (Penguin, 2011 [1905]).
- Critically reflect on his ideas – how valid do you think they are?

Child sex abuse

By the 1980s, as a result of over a century of feminist campaigning, new understandings of children's sexuality were set alongside a growing awareness of their vulnerability to sexual abuse. However, frequently, hegemonic discourse about child sex abuse, as with rape more generally, has relied on myths which mask the extent and nature of the problem. One myth is that of the risk of 'stranger danger', which has recently shifted from the danger of the dirty old man on a park bench, to the dangerous predator behind a computer screen, when we are aware that most victims of child abuse know their abuser (Jewkes and Wykes, 2012). In fact, of the one in six children in the UK who will be sexually abused, over ninety percent will know their abuser (Radford et al., 2011). Liz Kelly (1996) and others have also highlighted problems with legal and media use of terms like 'paedophile', which construct abusers as something 'other', a biological anomaly, when in fact the majority of child sex abusers are 'normal', everyday men who have jobs, relationships with adults, friends and so on. They are 'normal' in as much as so many men perpetrate such abominable harms. The construction of the monstrous 'paedophile' lets the many fathers, uncles, grandfathers, teachers and friends who abuse children 'off the hook'. We live in a society which, arguably, normalizes and eroticizes abuse and 'power over', particularly male power over women and children. Jewkes and Wykes (2012) have also argued that ongoing moral panics about child sex abuse in contemporary society have led to greater sexual objectification of children.

Sexualization of childhood

Awareness of child sex abuse has led to intense deliberation about issues such as the sexualization of culture (see Chapter 4 and 6), and sex education for children and young people – is knowledge important or putting children at risk, just when is it 'safe' for them to start to learn about sex, and what are the appropriate kinds of sex they are allowed to learn about and where should they learn it from? Beauty pageants for children where, it's argued, girls are encouraged to perform a particularly sexualized and commercialized version of femininity, have sparked heated debate (Tamer, 2011), an example, for instance, of compulsory heterosexuality (Rich, 1980). One has to ask why these girls are paraded in this way and for whose visual pleasure (Mulvey, 1975). Some social scientists point to how images or symbols of childhood, such as ponytails, or school uniforms, have been sexualized in culture – as can be seen with the number of 'sexy schoolgirl' outfits worn on hen nights (Ringrose, 2012). Others suggest that adult modes of dress, such as short skirts or even padded bra tops, have been targeted at increasingly young children (Webster, 2012), leading to girls internalizing a move to sexualization at a progressively young age (McKenney and Bigler, 2016). It is also worth noting that much of the debate is focused on the sexuality of girls rather than boys, but we must not forget that one in six boys are estimated to have been sexually abused. Bragg (2015) reminds us to think carefully about dominant discourses which construct particular images of girls as hypersexualized, whilst equivalent depictions of boys are often cast as hypermasculinized, potentially masking the pressures young boys experience in contemporary culture.

Such issues shape the landscape in which young people experience sexuality. It is a site forged from contradictory, and often simultaneous, views of childhood sexuality as at risk and risky, as problematic or non-existent (Shucksmith, 2004). It is a terrain which has shifted considerably since the 'first' teenagers of the 1950s (see Fowler, 1995; Osgarby, 1998): more young people are staying in education for longer; they are living at home for longer; people are waiting until they are older before they marry and/or have children; women have better access (though still not equal) to paid employment. In other words, many of those traditional rites of passage for western youth into adulthood have changed and become more fragmented.

The social construction of young people's sexuality

Defining youth

What do we mean by 'young people'? Using chronological age to define a group is problematic (as we shall see in the following chapter), thus defining a group who are called variously 'youths', 'teenagers', 'adolescents', 'young people' is tricky. Many textbooks side-step definitions of youth altogether. It should be remembered that terms such as 'teenager' or 'young people', whilst often used by social science researchers, are frequently not to be found in the legal and policy documents which help shape and determine their lives. Such discourse often only distinguishes between the child and the adult.

A variety of social and cultural factors influence the process and perceptions of ageing. For instance, the concept of 'adolescence' typically used the biological marker of puberty to establish the shift away from childhood. The usefulness of puberty as a marker for the beginning of adolescence is rather questionable however, as social scientists have shown how this varies significantly between individuals and social groups. Children who are socially and economically disadvantaged, for instance, tend to experience early onset puberty (Sun et al., 2017). And, as Hunt (2005) has argued, the period of 'youth' is becoming increasingly protracted in the west not just because of the earlier onset of puberty but also the extended number of years spent in education. Many theorists define young people as being between the ages of 11 and 18, for the United Nations it is 15–24, and within the African Charter people between the ages of 15 and 34 are included. In other words, there is no clear agreement as to when youth ends, and adulthood begins in capitalist countries. Often, in non-capitalist cultures where there are clear rites of passage which delineate between childhood and adulthood, adolescence as a concept is rather meaningless, whilst it perhaps has more cultural cachet in the west (Whiting et al., 1986).

Youth is, however, widely understood as a transitional phase between childhood and adulthood; many social theorists see this period as a time of negotiating relationships with adults, friends and peers. It is a stage at which many nations have decided that young people are mature enough to form sexual relationships and have sex legally. In the UK, for instance, 16 is the legal age of consent. The age of consent is the legal age at which an individual or groups are deemed sufficiently mature to agree to engage in sexual activity with another person. The notion of consent is an important one, which will be explored elsewhere but it has received particular prominence in the light of #MeToo and awareness of the prevalence of abuse in schools and university campuses (Coy et al., 2013). Such laws in the UK have their history in Victorian drives to control child prostitution (Kinkaid, 1993). However, what

169

is considered 'sexual' varies significantly between nations and within them too. Some nations will enforce a different age for same-sex acts (always higher and usually only applicable to men). In some states of the US male-male sodomy is always illegal, whatever their age, and in other countries, such as Japan, same-sex is not mentioned in law at all (McLelland, 2000: 38).

Discussion point

Age of consent

- Have a look at a current Global Age of Consent Map online (for instance www.ageofconsent.net/world).
- Do any of the ages surprise you? Why?
- In what ways does this help us to assert that sexuality is socially constructed?
- You could also have a look at the various age-based legal restraints for issues such as drinking, smoking, working, voting, getting married and so on, across the globe. Are these coherent?

Jens Qvortrup has argued that the western understandings of young people tend to frame them as 'waiting' for adulthood: 'they are waiting to become adults; to mature; to become competent; to get capabilities; to acquire rights; to become useful; to have a say in societal matters; to share resources' (2004: 267). They are, in other words, seen as 'not quite' – not quite adults, not quite ready, not quite responsible. It is a shifting and uncertain transitional period in a person's life, when they are excluded from some adult rights and responsibilities, whilst being expected to behave like 'grown ups' in other ways. Yet often, when they do engage in 'adult' behaviour, such as with sexual activity, it can prompt outrage and panic.

Sex and drugs and rock and roll? The rise of the teenager

The emergence of youth cultures in the post-war west has been linked to economic changes. The relative affluence of young people in this period, compared to older generations, it is argued, led to a new social group – teenagers – who formed a specific market niche. Teenagers had distinct patterns of consumption (Davis, 1990), and teenage earnings rose by fifty percent in this period, so many young people had relatively high wages to spend on non-essentials such as alcohol, music and fashion. Such patterns of consumption were central to the construction of gendered and sexual identities (Miles, 1996). In turn, these shifts led to a greater focus on young people's sex lives – as Philip Larkin, in his poem

Annus Mirabilis, claimed 'sexual intercourse began in nineteen sixty-three'! A protracted youth, with more leisure time and greater financial freedoms, resulted in ongoing panics about drug and alcohol abuse, smoking, lack of exercise, obesity, eating disorders and sexual health. Viewed as the children they no longer are and the adults they have yet to become, there was, in short, an increased atmosphere of (often not so new) risk and vulnerability – fears which were often exaggerated by key social institutions.

With increasing commercial leisure, and the commodification of young lives, social scientists started to look at how the development of youth culture – cinema, pubs and clubs and so on – led to young people spending more time in mixed gender environments. Time which Clarke and Critcher state is 'charged with sexual promise' (1985: 162).

Many of the constraints on sexuality which we have considered in this textbook may particularly impact on young people, e.g. relatively speaking, young people are still restricted in terms of their economic and personal freedoms (Thomson, 2009). As with older people, however, there can be a tendency to talk about young people as if they are an homogeneous group. Stereotypes abound about adolescence being a turbulent time, with young people being particularly rebellious, but research actually suggests otherwise (Browne, 2011; Offer and Schonert-Reichl, 1992). Simultaneously we are told that young people are at risk and need to be protected. We need to be mindful of the ways in which intersections of differing forms of social stratification, such as gender, ethnicity, disability, social class and sexual identity, mean that young people experience sexuality in very different ways. We will now consider some of the ways in which those constraints are felt, starting with education.

Discussion point

Learning about sex

From your own experience as a young person, however long ago that may have been, consider what influenced your own sexual attitudes and behaviours.

When was sexuality discussed? What was the context for such discussions? What aspects of sexuality were discussed? What, if anything, was considered taboo? What was left out of those discussions?

Education, education, education

Sex education is a hotly contested and highly politicized area of social policy (Hockey and James, 2003: 144). The tensions caused by the transition from childhood into adulthood are perhaps part of the reason why adults seem to be so protective of young people's sexuality; it is seen as a departure from notions of childhood 'innocence'. Young people are constructed as a group in need of protection from risks such as exploitation. Many have argued that knowledge is a dangerous thing where sex and young people are concerned. Thomson (1994) has shown how fears about whether sex education encourages 'promiscuity' or is the cause of pregnancy have resulted in a distinct lack of detailed, informative sex education. As such, many have argued that there is a dearth of material and guidance for young people on how to have safe sexual relationships (Batchelor and Raymond, 2004).

UK Conservative minister Andrea Leadsom got herself into political hot water in early 2019 when debating sex education. In reference to new legislation on mandatory sex education in primary schools, which includes information on the rights of LGBT+ people, she argued that parents should be able to choose when children are 'exposed to that kind of information'. Many conservative Christian, Jewish and Muslim parents have protested against such education, demonstrating outside schools, and often bearing homophobic slogans. As LGBT+ rights activist Peter Tatchell has noted, what is currently happening is very reminiscent of events in the 1980s. Under Conservative Prime Minister Margaret Thatcher's leadership, Section 28, part of the Local Government Act 1988, prohibited Local Authorities (LA) in England and Wales from 'promoting homosexuality'. It also labelled same-sex family relationships as 'pretend'. Any LA worker, such as a teacher, found to be 'promoting' same-sex relationships – and just talking about LGBT+ issues could constitute this – ran the risk of losing their job. Council-run libraries were forbidden to stock literature or films containing lesbian or gay content, so young LGBT+ people were forced to seek information and cultural validation about themselves elsewhere. In effect it prevented teachers from being able to respond to the needs of the adolescents in their care, and the emerging awareness of their sexuality and that of others. It also sent out particular messages about heterosexuality (as 'normal', 'appropriate', 'desirable') and other forms of sexuality (as 'dangerous', 'predatory' and 'abnormal'). Heterosexuality thus dominated the curriculum. Section 28 was not repealed in England and Wales until 2003, under the Labour government (see Chapter 7 for more on this).

Heteronormativity and parental assumptions

Sociologist Karin Martin (2009) studied what parents say to their children about sexuality and reproduction, and found that with children as young as three and five years old, parents routinely assumed their children were heterosexual, told them they would get (heterosexually) married, and interpreted cross-gender interactions between children as 'signs' of heterosexuality. With this kind of socialization is an additional element of normative sexuality, i.e. the idea of compulsory monogamy, where exclusive romantic and sexual relationships and marriage are expected and valued over other kinds of relationship (Willey, 2016). Therefore, **heteronormativity** surrounds us at a very young age, teaching us that there are only two genders and that we should desire and partner with one person of the opposite gender, who we will likely marry.

Discussion point

Inclusive education?

What do you think some of the consequences are for young people if the sex education they receive is heteronormative?

Promiscuity, pregnancy and celibacy – time to panic?

You may well be familiar with the term 'moral panic', used to describe social responses to perceived problems. It is a concept coined by sociologist Stan Cohen and refers to the role the media plays in creating a panicked or frenzied moral outrage:

> Societies appear to be subject, every now and then, to periods of moral panic. A condition, episode, person or group of persons emerges to become defined as a threat to social values and interests; its nature is presented in a stylised and stereotypical fashion by mass media; the moral barricades are manned by editors, bishops, politicians and other right-thinking people. (Cohen, 1972: 9)

In short, a problem is identified, its causes simplified, and the groups perceived to be the source of the problem, known as 'folk devils', are stigmatized. The media, often using emotive language and powerful imagery, call for something to be done and the relevant authorities will then respond, often in a knee-jerk and harsh fashion. Children and young people are frequently the subjects of such panics, with issues relating to young people's sexuality being an almost permanent fixture in the news.

Discussion point

Don't panic!

Research news articles from a previous decade about a perceived 'problem' relating to young people's sexuality.

- In what ways does Cohen's notion of a moral panic fit?
- Is this still a concern in contemporary news? If so, is it reported in the same way? Is the same language used to describe young people's sexuality?
- If not, what is the current moral panic surrounding young people's sexuality?

Between a rock and a hard place: girls' negotiation of sexuality

Despite a raft of policy changes in support of equal rights (see Chapter 7), it would seem that young women and girls still face a sexual double standard. Tolman and McLelland's (2011) research in the US, for instance, highlights the ways in which adolescent girls walk a very difficult line between, on the one hand having to look 'sexy' in order to be popular, whilst risking being labelled a 'slut' – a label which Sue Lees (1993) showed us was very difficult to shake off. Research by Hockey and James (2003) adds to this: they argue that young women's sexuality is controlled by the sexual reputations that are constructed for them by their male peers, who label them as 'easy', for instance, if they did have sex. Girls' sexual subjectivity, it is argued, is supressed – they are expected to be sexy but they must not be sexual! Whilst many young women are aware of, and challenge, sexual double standards, and realize that female sexual desire is 'normal', these stereotypes are difficult to dispel (Allen, 2003). Tolman and McLelland's (2011) research, for instance, suggests that gendered stereotypes persist which construct girls as having little, if any sexual desire, but instead their aspiration is supposed to be for a steady boyfriend. By the same stroke, boys are cast having an active (heterosexual) sexual desire which, as we shall see, comes with its own problems.

The first decade of the twenty-first century saw several nations taking seriously the issue of the pressure that young people, and girls in particular, face to appear attractive in the context of a new 'sexualized' society. In Australia, the government funded research into the sexualization of children (Rush and La Nauze, 2006), the US saw the American Psychological Association Taskforce produce findings on the sexualization of girls (APA, 2007), and in the UK the Home Office released 'The Sexualisation of Young People

174

Review' (2010). A sexualized society, it is argued, is one that has increasingly permissive sexual values and behaviours, is obsessed with sexual identities and practices, with an ongoing media appetite for sexual stories and moral panics, has more and more public forms of sexual discourses, and finds new ways to experience sex with developing technologies (Attwood, 2006). Whilst there have been critics of the sexualization thesis (see Murch, 2010), it would appear that in a context of increasing social preoccupation with the 'sexy', it can be hard for girls to assert their sexual subjectivity or agency (Tolman, 2002).

Teenage pregnancy and the sexual double burden

Such pressure, it is suggested, can have significant sexual health consequences for young women. Thomson's (2004) research has shown that in order to protect their 'reputation', girls feel unable to either carry condoms, or insist on their use, for fear of seeming to be 'easy'. This can then put them at serious risk of sexually transmitted infections and pregnancy.

Ongoing moral panics about teenage pregnancy have been part of US and British culture for decades. Government legislation and the media have focused on it as part of moral campaigns about protecting 'family values' and 'outing' so-called welfare scroungers. The political dominance of Reagan and Thatcher in the 1980s saw much legislation focused on ways to tackle the 'problem', which continued into the 1990s with programmes such as the National Campaign to Prevent Teen Pregnancy (1999). Stereotypes of young people as irresponsible, dependent on welfare and promiscuous abound (SmithBattle, 2013). The language may have changed over the years from 'single mothers' to 'young mothers' and then 'teenage pregnancy', but the targets – perhaps even scapegoats – of such fears are overwhelmingly young women. In effect, blame is shifted onto those who are pregnant and away from the State. The consequence is that we accept teenage mothers as a social problem; rarely, are we encouraged to recognize that pregnancy at a younger age may be an active and positive decision (McNulty, 2010).

FACT FILE

Chav mums?

UK sociologists Bev Skeggs (2004) and Steph Lawler (2005) have both argued that the media frequently represent working-class femininity as lacking 'respectability'. Such representations are, they suggest, so that a

(Continued)

> middle-class readership can revel in their judgement of the poor. Imogen Tyler (2008) has suggested that this is typified by press constructions of working-class teenage mothers.
>
> • Can you think of any positive representations of young parenthood?

Under pressure: young men, masculinity and sexuality

Hegemonic social constructions of masculinity have a profound influence on young men's sexuality. Sexuality is often seen as important to confirm young men's gender identity; being (hetero)sexually active is a valued way of demonstrating masculine identity (Hockey and James, 2003). Some have argued that changes in the labour market – which have seen more women enter paid work and a decline in work traditionally seen as masculine, such as the steel, coal and shipbuilding industries – have led to changing routes for achieving masculinity for working-class youth. Mac an Ghaill (1994), for instance, argued that 'laddish' attitudes and behaviours are adopted, which include anti-school values. Such 'macho' school cultures also impact on young men's experience of their sexuality.

Research with boys in US high schools by Pascoe (2011) showed that young men use homophobic comments, teasing and 'jokes' as a way to develop and assert their sense of masculinity. Pascoe argues that such taunting has a significant impact not just on the mental health of those who are the object of such harassment, who may or may not be gay, but that ninety percent of random high school shootings in the US have been perpetrated by straight boys who were subject to homophobic harassment. False stereotypes of masculinity – lack of emotion, toughness, heterosexuality, power and dominance – mean that boys reject that which is considered unmasculine. Dominant and false ideas of gay men as effeminate feed into this discourse. For those young men caught on the intersection of gender, sexuality, class and ethnicity, adopting hypermasculine behaviour can be an uncomfortable but compulsory recourse to safety (Fields et al., 2016). In effect, homophobic taunts and bullying are part of a process of policing gendered identities and reinforcing the norm of hegemonic masculinity (Connell, 1995).

Because a boy's masculine identity is fragile, and constantly having to be re-produced, they carry an ongoing burden to 'prove' and assert that they are 'normal' males. In addition to homophobic behaviours, this involves boys feeling the need to assert their heterosexuality. This might be not only having a girlfriend in order to protect against being a target of homophobic teasing, but also the pursuit of girls and as many as possible, in order to display power and virility. Richardson (2010) has argued that such expectations can place a great deal of pressure on young heterosexual men. Many, she argues, feel compelled to behave in ways that do not sit comfortably with them. Many felt they were expected to have sex with as many partners as possible, when they might prefer to have a longer-term relationship, or wait to have sex with the 'right' person.

There are, however, possibilities for resisting dominant understandings of gender and sexuality. A study by Frosh et al. (2002), for instance, revealed a more positive outlook for young men's (hetero)sexuality, evidencing many who felt able to avoid the pressures and demands of hegemonic masculinity, and instead were able to be seen to be sensitive to the needs of women. Research by Maxwell (2007) with young men showed that they were keen to explore their emotional 'needs' not just in their sexual relationships but in their other relationships as well.

Discussion point

Compulsory heterosexuality

Adrienne Rich (1980) argued that heterosexuality is compulsory, i.e. people in society are assumed to be heterosexual, and social institutions support or enforce heterosexuality and often punish anything 'other'. Heterosexuality, in other words, is an institution.

- In what ways does compulsory heterosexuality impact on the lives of contemporary young men?

Sexual health information, the media and young people

Perhaps given some of the issues discussed above, it is not surprising that there has been an increase in reported sexually transmitted infections (STIs) among young people. Public Health England (2018) states that there is a new case reported every four minutes. This is a concern because if left untreated, they can cause a range of significant health problems, including infertility and swollen or painful testicles. For pregnant women, they also mean a higher risk of miscarriage. Whilst the UK teenage pregnancy rate has dropped significantly in Britain in recent years, we still have the highest in Western Europe – Bulgaria is the highest in Europe overall (Eastern Europe). Changes, it is argued, are closely linked to the quality of sex and relationship education. Whilst some of this happens in compulsory classes in schools, researchers point to the increasing role the media plays in educating young people about sex.

177

A study conducted by Batchelor et al. (2004) looked at UK magazines and television across the course of a week. The majority of the focus from newspapers was on risk and danger, while for television news programmes it was about criminal sex acts and pregnancy. Dominant, 'traditional' myths about attitudes to sex were reinforced and reproduced: girls were portrayed as being interested in emotion and relationships, boys were shown to only be interested in sex; girls were overwhelmingly depicted as being responsible for contraception. Within the media analyzed, there were very limited discussions of sexuality and disability. Only gay (male) issues were addressed (and not often) and only ever as a source of anxiety or abuse; lesbian, bisexual and transgender young people were not represented at all.

Discussion point

Media and sexuality

Conduct your own research into media output on sexuality over the course of a week, or just one day. How much has changed since Batchelor et al.'s (2004) study?

- Is sexuality presented as risky?
- How are LGBT+ youths represented? Are BAME youths included?

Social media, sexuality and young people

Among the general youth population, the internet has become a mainstream mode of access to information about aspects of health and sexuality, as well as anonymous support for personal issues such as drug use, depression and relationship problems (Borzekowski, 2006). The internet can be a useful way for young people to access sensitive health information, gather the courage to access offline resources, and find available information on offline services (Gray et al., 2005). However, increased access to technologies such as computers and mobile phones, coupled together with a growing commodification of youth culture and a rise in the popularity of a variety of social media platforms such as YouTube, Twitter, Instagram and Snapchat, has led to a rise in fears and anxieties about the associated risks posed for the young people who use such technologies. Such fears exist despite there being relatively little evidence-based research into the issue, according to Goodyear and Armour (2019).

Some research has shown, for instance, that contrary to popular opinion, social media offers new, positive, ways for young people to make sense of their sexualities. We tend to think of young people and the new technologies and social media in terms of risk – the risk of stranger danger, the consumption of sexually explicit material such as porn, sexting and so on (Livingstone, 2011). Research by Marijke Naezer (2019) of Radboud University, with young people between the ages of 12 and 18, suggests that social media can actually be a useful tool for young people. She found that they use the internet in four ways: to build sexual knowledge; develop and play with their identities; engage in romantic intimacies; to gain a sense of adventure. Young people, she argues, are very aware of the consequences of online behaviours and the potential risks. Rather than being reckless, they are actually very cautious. Other research supports this view. For instance, looking into the ways in which young LGBT+ people use the internet, Hillier and Harrison (2007) found that it provided a space for young people to develop their sense of identity and 'come out' and also develop a sense of community and make friends, in addition to meeting potential sexual partners. In general, adolescence is a sensitive period in which many young people begin to explore their sexuality and engage in close peer and romantic relationships. For those who identify as LGBT+, this period presents some unique challenges. When exploring their sexual identity, LGBT+ youth may fear being judged, are secluded, or victimized due to their sexual orientations (Mustanski et al., 2011). Some conceal their sexual identity, thereby limiting their offline opportunities for support (Detrie and Lease, 2007). This lack of support, along with the limited availability of LGBT+ peers and potential romantic partners, leads many LGBT+ youth to seek online relationships.

Conversely, a piece of research conducted in Belgium argues that social media spaces produce particular values and norms about sexuality which reflect a conservatism that impacts on young people's perceptions of sexuality. The result is a hierarchy of supposed 'good' and 'bad' sexual practices (De Ridder, 2017). Mulholland (2015) also points to the impact of porn which has been mainstreamed online – in many respects porn is normalized, as are dominant notions of heterosex (see Chapter 13 for more on the impact of online porn). The statistics vary but it would seem that as much as thirty percent of internet traffic is pornography (Optenet 2010), with over eighty percent of top-rated porn being violent, and over ninety percent of that violence directed at women (Bridges et al., 2010). There is a suggestion that after viewing, men display less empathy for rape victims (see Todd, 2017). Boys aged 12–17 are among the largest consumers of internet porn and the first images they may see of sex often involve violence against women (Ybarra et al., 2011). Such figures cannot be considered as anything other than worrying. Walker et al. (2015) have shown that such viewings lead to young men having particular sexual expectations which in turn put pressure on young women to conform to what is being viewed.

Reports also indicate that cyberabuse/bullying has increased exponentially as technologies have become more accessible and as new and advanced technologies continually emerge (Hinduja and Patchin, 2010). Cyberabuse can manifest itself in many ways, but it can include young people feeling pressured to send sexual or naked pictures of themselves, and sending partners sexual or naked pictures of themselves that they knew their partner did not want. According to Blumenfeld and Cooper (2010), almost twice as many LGBT+ youth experience cyberbullying compared to their heterosexual peers. In particular, perhaps because of their reliance on online spaces as discussed above, LGBT+ youth showed significantly higher rates of all types of cyber-dating abuse and sexual coercion than heterosexual youth. Few transgender young people are included in the samples, but where they are, they report the highest rates of victimization with regard to all forms of dating violence, including cyberabuse (Dank et al., 2013).

Given the ubiquity of the internet in the lives of youth today (Madden et al., 2013), arguably we need to better understand the relationships young people form online, and whether those relationships confer protective benefits or something more sinister.

Let's talk about (no) sex …

Despite continued fears about teenage pregnancy, the trend in recent years has actually been one of decline. From having the highest teenage pregnancy rates by far in Western Europe, statistics for the UK are now marginally higher (ONS, 2018). Many have argued this is because of the rise of 'generation sensible' – young people who are more risk averse, less likely to drink, smoke or take drugs, and are more aware of the need to focus on their studies rather than their sex lives (Schrager, 2019). It would seem that whilst some studies (and statistics should always be treated with caution) suggest young people, if they are having sex, are doing so at a younger age and are more experimental in terms of the kinds of sexual activities they engage in (NATSAL, 2000), overall, they are having less sex (YRBSS, 2017). Although the age when young people first have sex – their 'sexual debut', as many researchers are now referring to it – has dropped considerably from the 1950s onwards, it has tailed off. Sexual debut is, on average, at age 16–17, and first intercourse is at 18, on average, in the UK. There is a suggestion that so-called millennials are having sex later than their parents were, with one in eight still a virgin aged 26. This is mirrored by research in US, where both genders were, on average, still virgins in their twenties. Young people are perhaps a little more conservative than the media may suggest. This trend, however, has placed young people in something of a paradox, i.e. society panics when they are having sex, but it also panics when they aren't!

Research in the UK, the US and beyond suggests that more and more young people are having no sex (Twenge et al., 2017). Referred to variously as 'celibacy syndrome' and a 'sex recession', the majority of discussions position no or less sex amongst the young as a problem. What is less talked about is the fact that this seems to be a trend across the age groups, and is something we talk about in Chapter 6 in relation to new technologies. Less sex is often automatically interpreted as a bad thing, but what if we are having less, but better, sex (Carlson, 2016)?

Nevertheless, in some nations, such as Japan, the state has felt the need to step in and play cupid, in order to encourage its younger population to couple-up. According to one poll, almost a third of young people aged between 18 and 34 were virgins (National Fertility Survey, 2015), more than in many other nations, and the fear is that if this trend continues, there will be a population crisis. Quite simply there will not be enough young people to support the older generations. A raft of explanations has been put forward for this *sekkusu-banare*, or 'drifting away from sex', from a lack of confidence, and increased pressure to study or long working hours, to the prevalence of online porn and digital relationships. In response to such shifts, the government has invested in state-sponsored dating services. Encouraging young people to engage in the practice of *konkatsu*, or 'marriage hunting' (Yamada, 2007), local government marriage-promotion committees have organized music events, and given tickets to get youngsters to drink and eat in bars and restaurants and attend speed-dating events.

Summary

Given the fears surrounding children's and young people's sexuality, research into their practices is particularly fraught with ethical considerations. Nevertheless, in recent years, research has revealed some trends in young people's sexual lives. It would appear, for instance, that people are having their first sexual encounter at a younger age, there has been a rise in the number of sexual partners, and that there is an increased diversity in sexual practices (Lewis et al., 2017). This, of course, is if they are having sex, and there would seem to be a trend in many nations of young people abstaining from sex altogether. However, regulation and resistance still feature heavily in the lives of young people. Very often, their sexualities are either constructed as being non-existent (which, ironically, has frequently been enforced by rules) or are framed within a discourse of risk. This sense of risk is never very far away from rhetoric about young people; moral panics about their vulnerability to sexual abuse are seemingly ongoing. Concerns to preserve the sexual innocence of young people are reflected in the tensions surrounding their education.

The western world is preoccupied with the question of sex education for young people; what is deemed 'appropriate' knowledge is hotly contested. In this chapter, we have considered whether it is important for children's and young people's education to be placed within a context of their own experiences. We have also looked at the ways in which young people's sexualities are shaped through cultural norms around gender. We have begun to consider some of the mixed messages young people receive about their sexuality. Sexuality and identity is not something which begins or ends in this period – in many respects this is something which begins before we are even born, with choices and assumptions being made for us about our gender and sexual identity – it is something which is in transition, is fluid. Young people face many obstacles during this part of the life cycle, having to balance who they feel they are with what they think is expected of them. This is a group who are so often 'spoken for' (Alcoff, 1991) that we must remember to try and listen to their voice.

Key questions

- In what ways do social norms of sexuality create restrictions for young people's sexuality?

- What are the key ways in which young people's sexuality is restricted in your society?

- Are there examples of resistance to such restrictions?

FURTHER READING

For an in-depth consideration of young people's experience of parenthood, read Ann McNulty's (2010) chapter 'Great Expectations: teenage pregnancy and intergenerational transmission'. In S. Duncan, R. Edwards and C. Alexander (eds), *Teenage Parenthood: What's the Problem?* London: Tuffnell.

Louisa Allen's (2003) empirical research with 17–19 year olds provides some interesting examples of resistance to gendered sexual norms ('Girls want sex, boys want love: resisting dominant discourses of (hetero)sexuality', *Sexuality*, 6: 215–36.

A much under-researched area relates to the sexuality of disabled young people. You can read Ruth Garbutt et al.'s (2010) report, based on their work with young people with learning disabilities: 'Talking about Sex and Relationships: The views of young people with learning disabilities' (Leeds: CHANGE).

11

SEXUALITY AND OLDER PEOPLE

Learning outcomes

By the end of this chapter you should be able to:

- Define ageism
- Explain the ways that ageism impacts on understandings of older people's sexuality
- Understand some of the issues around ageing and sexuality for different social groups
- Discuss theoretical approaches which help explain social constructions of sexuality in later life

---

Ha! have you eyes

You cannot call it love; for at your age

The heyday in the blood is tame, it's humble,

And waits upon the judgment

(Hamlet, Act III Scene 4)

Introduction

That we live on a socially ageing globe has been well documented. Societal ageing has been happening across Europe and other world populations for a significant amount of time. In 1880 in the UK, fewer than five percent of the population was over 65. In 2001 this was sixteen percent. By 2005, the proportion of people under 16 had fallen to nineteen percent of the population, whereas those over 65 had risen to nineteen percent. According to the Office for National Statistics (ONS) by 2066, a quarter of the population will be 65 and over, exceeding those aged 16 and under. Similar patterns are to be found across Europe and beyond. Thanks to a fall in mortality rates in the last fifty years, technological advances in medicine and improved healthcare, life expectancy has gone up. This means that many people can expect longer, more productive lives in which they can continue (or begin) to enjoy sexual intimacy.

However, this social ageing has often been framed as a serious social 'problem', with concerns about how, with a declining working age population, society can afford to adequately care for its ageing population. It is certainly true that material deprivation, which is structured by gender, class and ethnicity, becomes exaggerated in later life. Austerity measures in the UK and countries like Greece, for instance, have impacted on the elderly too (see Papanastasiou and Papatheodorou, 2018). Yet, such 'moral panics' point to a key issue in regard to ageing, i.e. **ageism** and stereotypes. Such concerns result from an underlying assumption that older people are financially unproductive and constitute, instead, a dependent burden. Ageism reflects the fact that older people are culturally devalued, and old age is viewed as a pitiable state of decline and vulnerability. There are, of course, all sorts of problems with such views: ageing, in relation to biological deterioration, begins quite early in our lives, being a life-long process, and nor is an older age per se an indicator of physical or mental decline. Such popularized ideas of old age are constructed and reconstructed in society through, for instance, medical models of ageing and media portrayals of older age.

As Hamlet's words to his mother Gertrude at the start of this chapter suggest, there is a tendency, still, to see sexuality as the prerogative of the young, and something which is incompatible with ageing. It is vital, therefore, that we study old age and consider the issues which affect older people in relation to sexuality – after all, hopefully many of us will be part of this social group in the future! This chapter will explore the problems associated with ageing in a society that is arguably increasingly sex obsessed, but where we are told older sexuality is distasteful, and older bodies unattractive – a paradox that has the potential to render many older people marginalized but perhaps also offers up a site for resistance. Slowly this, along with the silence surrounding the issues of sexuality in relation to older people, is being challenged. This chapter will be an introduction to the main debates and discussions. As an ageing society, it is imperative that we consider some of the challenges and joys associated with growing older. Firstly, we will consider how later life has been categorized by social scientists. We then move on to a definition of ageism, and explore its impact on both research into the sexual lives of older people and older people's experience of sex.

Conceptualizing later life

First, it is perhaps useful to consider how older people have been defined in research. Research into old age suggests that the diversity of the elderly is much greater than any other age group, yet there is a tendency to stereotype the elderly and lump all the 'old' together as a homogeneous group with similar needs. Within the later stages of the life course, experience is hugely varied, more so than the category 'old age' would suggest (Hockey and James, 1993). This is a large group of people, from 50 years old to 100 plus. At the very least there are many different cultural and social subgroups, based on aspects such as religion, class, gender and sexuality, some of which we will be looking at in greater depth later in this chapter, in addition to significant age variations. These forms of social stratification and social division certainly persist into old age.

Many academic researchers and charities for older people, classify anyone over 50 as older (see Heaphy, 2009). Age UK, for instance, produces information and support for those of 50 and beyond. In addition, social scientific research has tended to make several broad distinctions between the elderly: one is the distinction between the third age – a period of life often free from parenting and paid work when a more active, independent life is achieved – and a fourth age – an age of eventual dependence (Laslett, 1996).

In addition, another distinction is often made between a very large group – the young old (65–75) who enjoy good health and financial security, are typically autonomous, and are likely to be living as couples (this group currently includes the so-called baby-boomers, who grew up in the 1960s, a time of social change impacted by the civil rights movement and feminism), and the older old (75–85) who become increasingly dependent on others because of both health and money problems. Finally, there is the group of the very old.

These ways of seeing the elderly suggest a move from periods of activity and autonomy to one of growing dependence – a negative assumption frequently compounded by the media, those who provide care services and both younger and older people's attitudes to sexuality (though as we shall see later, more recent research is beginning to challenge this assumption of inactivity and dependency).

It is also interesting to note that, whilst both old age and sexuality are socially constructed (what any given society at any time defines as 'old' is subjective and based on a range of assumptions), unlike thinking about sexuality – where we have terms such as 'sex' to denote biology (though this is contested) and 'gender' to reflect the social aspects of identity – Wilson (2000) has noted that there is no word to differentiate between biological ageing and social ageing.

The problems of ageism

Sexuality and sexual activity in later life has often been the subject of cultural humour, ridicule and disgust. (Butler and Lewis, 1986: 178)

Discussion point

Make a list of the stereotypes of 'old age' and 'ageing'.

Consider the impact these have on older people and on wider society.

If, as we shall see, older people are having sex, indeed having good sex, why do we live in a society which sees sex for the elderly as surprising or disgusting? Many argue that this is a result of ageism. Ageism was first defined in 1969 by Robert Butler, a psychiatrist, as 'prejudice by one age group toward other age groups' (1969: 243). He later expanded on this description by referring to it as stereotyping and discrimination against people because they are old. Whilst it can be experienced at any age, social scientists frequently use the term 'ageism' to designate prejudice and discrimination against the elderly.

Although it operates like sexism and racism, being based on discrimination and prejudice, in another respect it is slightly different as it tends to happen to us in later life and not so obviously when we're young (although young people are discriminated in the labour market, alongside women, being amongst the first to either lose their job or not be able to find employment in times of economic recession). It is also different in that, excepting an early death, it is something we can all potentially experience.

It can be blatant, as when individuals deny elderly women or men a job simply because of their age, or subtle, such as when people speak to the elderly in a condescending tone as if they were children. Ageism builds physical traits into stereotypes – people consider greying hair, wrinkled skin or a stooped posture as signs of personal incompetence. Older people and older age tend to be viewed negatively; our language is suffused with phrases which construct later life as unpleasant, e.g. 'past it', 'one foot in the grave', 'coffin dodgers' and so on. Negative stereotypes picture the aged as helpless, confused, resistant to change, and generally unhappy. Even seemingly positive, sentimental notions of sweet little old ladies and eccentric old gentlemen gloss over older people's individuality and accomplishments. It is ageist to assume that experience is determined by chronological age and points to the fact that we have no word to distinguish between this and the social construction of ageing (unlike the sex/gender distinction). Such attitudes serve to marginalize older people.

Another issue associated with later life is that of invisibility. We live in a youth-orientated society: to be old is not desirable in our culture, and rather than being perceived as a (potentially) wise and valued member of the community, older people are more likely to be viewed as a burden and unattractive. Andrew Blaikie (1999) has argued that we ignore, and in fact deliberately look away from, old people because they are a reminder of our own mortality, and thus become constructed as unsavoury.

A common form of discrimination against older people is infantilization. This is a process whereby individual, or groups of, adults are treated as though they were a child. This is an established way of thinking about the elderly: Shakespeare in *As You Like It* describes this stage of life as a 'second childishness and mere oblivion, sans teeth, sans eyes, sans taste, sans everything' – hardly a positive outlook! Thompson (2005) has argued that such views demean the targeted group because it constructs them as being fundamentally different from other adults and therefore less worthy of respect. Feminists, for example, have long pointed out how women are infantilized in a patriarchal society; calling women 'girls' denotes a lesser status.

If old age is viewed as a second childhood, it is easy to see why old-age sexuality has come to be viewed as inappropriate and older people seen as asexual (Gott, 2005). These dominant discourses about sexuality in later life can have serious consequences for older people's quality of life. In fact, these stereotypes are so entrenched, they have become part of the social fabric and create a limited view of older people. In turn, this impacts on how older people are treated.

Research into older people's lives

Perhaps because we live in a youth-orientated society, the lives of older people have been, until relatively recently, under-researched. Social prejudice against old age has been so entrenched and normalized that this has also impacted on academics' attitudes to it.

When it has been dealt with, there was the assumption that there is a natural decline in the individual's sexual functioning in later life (Gewirtz-Meydan and Ayalon, 2017). Furthermore, Irvine (2014), for instance, found that researchers who worked in this area found it harder to get published, funding or a promotion, as it was considered a form of 'dirty research'. In other words, there are very real barriers to research from an academic perspective, based on sexual stereotyping.

The silence around older people's sexuality, and a general perception of sex in older people as being non-existent, are further enshrined in many areas of social policy and practice in relation to ageing in policy. Key documents often mirror the invisibility found in other areas of society, e.g. the UK government's Department for Health's *Framework for Sexual Health Improvement in England*, informed by the 2010 Health Survey for England, despite talking about sex through the life course, only considers sex up to the age of 69 (Department of Health and Social Care, 2013).

Still doing 'it'

Whilst these ageist stereotypes persist, presenting later life as an asexual state, or sexual desire and activity at this age as inappropriate, growing research shows us that in fact sexual intimacy for older people not only happens but it is also socially, mentally and physically beneficial. *Sexual Health and Wellbeing Among Older Men and Women in England* – a piece of collaborative research conducted by Age UK and the University of Manchester in 2015 – showed that over half of men, and more than a third of women over 70 were regularly sexually active.

Research from the US confirms similar degrees of sexual and romantic engagement at older ages (Schwartz and Velotta, 2018). According to a 2009 AARP survey on midlife and older adults, nearly forty percent of married older adults were having sex more than once a week, and sixty percent of older people in relationships were having sex over once a month (Fisher et al., 2010). In addition, almost fifty percent of single older people who were dating had sex once a week. Where some research suggests that sexual frequency may reduce over time, it appears that what determines sexual activity is largely to do with factors like internalized ageism, stigma, poor body image, or absence of a partner (these last two impact on women in particular). Thus, possible reduction in sexual frequency is not as closely linked to the biological effects of ageing as is often suggested.

Studies indicate that as well as having sex regularly, older people also experience a high degree of sexual satisfaction – the degree of satisfaction does not appear to be age dependent (Penhollow et al., 2009). In a study with older people in relationships, Gillespie (2016) found that sexual communication (partners speaking about their needs) and more variety in sexual encounters (trying new positions, locations, or sex toys) were significant in terms of high sexual satisfaction and frequency

And doing 'it' differently?

Discussion point

Look at how online dating websites for older people advertise.

- How do they present sexually active (or inactive) older people?
- Is there a difference between men and women?
- Are diverse groups of older people represented?

Recent research into older people who embark on new relationships, suggests that older people seem to be challenging conventional ways of 'doing' love and intimacy. Rather than starting relationships with the intention of marriage and cohabitation, many are seeking companionship and sex, whilst maintaining independence. Increasingly, research such as Benson et al.'s (2017) in the US has shown the popularity of 'living apart together' (LAT). This is a challenge to those negative stereotypes society often has of 'sad', lonely widows or elderly men who have maintained a 'bachelor' life because they never found a partner, where both scenarios are often regarded as unfortunate and pitiable. We are becoming more aware, through such research, that many older people live this way through choice rather than necessity, as a way of maintaining independence and separate resources. Whilst current baby-boomers are still committed to the institution of marriage, in that many of them re-marry, we know too that the majority of divorces (over sixty percent) that occur after age 40 are initiated by women (Schwartz and Kempner, 2015).

In fact, older age seems to offer news ways of 'doing' sexuality for women in particular in some respects. Some research suggests that heterosexual women feel emboldened to remain sexually and romantically satisfied throughout their entire life cycle, and may even find that old age is a time to enjoy more sex. Partly this is because later life can bring a sense of relief because the fear of an unwanted pregnancy is usually removed, plus any children are likely to be grown up and taking care of themselves. Older people may well have more self-awareness and self-confidence, and feel released from some of the unrealistic ideals of youth, and as such become more liberated about their bodies than younger people (Gott and Hinchliffe, 2003).

New research is also revealing that online dating is becoming an increasingly common way for older people to meet new partners. Many dating sites have large numbers of people – 'silver surfers' as they are sometimes known – over 60 in their membership, with some sites such as *OurTime* and *HowAboutWe* actively recruiting older men and women as their clientele. There are also niche sites such as *MuddyPatches* … for people who love the countryside! McWilliams and Barrett's (2014) research into the online dating habits of heterosexual men and women, suggests that both men and women seek youthful characteristics in their potential partners, and both attempt to present themselves as youthful. Gendered norms are at play in the creation of profiles: men's profiles tend to emphasize their occupational and financial achievements, whereas women's profiles accentuate their attractiveness. Heteronormative tendencies are also reproduced in the seeking of partners, with men's search criteria focusing on the physical appeal of prospective dates and women looking for practical capabilities. Thus, whilst online platforms offer new ways to find partners – something which older people are evidently embracing – in many respects they simply reinforce existing norms.

Media representations

Arguably, such norms are strengthened in key institutions such as the media. We live in a culture which places a high value on youthfulness, where signs of ageing – loose skin, grey hair, wrinkles – are unwelcome. In addition, it is argued that western culture is preoccupied by sex but finds the thought of sexual activity amongst the elderly repulsive. As we have seen in Chapter 4, the media is a powerful shaping force, which helps to reproduce dominant ways of thinking about particular social groups (Hall, 1977). It has an important role in shaping the public image of later life and sexuality – and TV and film often perpetuate such norms about old age, presenting older people as sexually unattractive.

Media portrayals of older people frequently reflect negative cultural stereotypes of ageing. Youth is esteemed and associated with attractiveness and sexiness. Where older people are represented, it is often as a grump (Jack Nicholson and Clint Eastwood have played several between them). And when the subject is the sexuality of elderly people, it is often presented as something either farcical or shocking.

Discussion point

Harold and Maude

Hal Ashby's cult film depicts a romantic relationship between a 20-year-old man and a 79-year-old woman. In it, a priest states, *'I would be remiss in my duties if I did not tell you that the idea of [pause] intercourse [pause] the fact of your young, firm [pause] body commingling with the withered flesh, sagging breasts, and flabby buttocks [pause] makes me [pause] want to vomit'.*

Watch either *Harold and Maude* (Ashby, 1971), or *The Mother* (Michell, 2003).

- What does the film tell us about social attitudes to older women's sexuality?
- What was your own reaction to this?

Would reactions be similar if the film portrayed a younger woman with an older man? Or is this more to do with 'age-gap' sex?

Whilst the media undoubtedly celebrates youthfulness, there is a suggestion that it is beginning to produce more films and television programmes which present older actors as both having sex and possibly being sexually desirable. The Chilean film *Gloria* (with Paulina Garcia), the US's *It's Complicated* (with Meryl Streep, Alec Baldwin and Steve Martin) and *Book Club* (with Diane Keaton, Jane Fonda, Mary Steenburgen and Candice Bergen), and the BBC's *Last Tango in Halifax*, are among a growing number of films and television programmes which present sex and romance for the over 60s in a more positive light. Interestingly, though, the sex scenes in such films are rarely explicit; *45 Years*, with Charlotte Rampling and Tom Courtney, is an exception.

Discussion point

When I'm 64?

Whilst Hollywood might be mirroring research showing that sexually-active older people is not just a fantasy, can you think of any songs about 'sexy' older people?

It's a man's world...

Recent research into the representation of older women on television shows how this is something which arguably impacts more on women, with older women deemed less attractive and less acceptable than older men (Cochrane, 2011). Heterosexuality, and reproduction, is seen as the norm in relation to sexuality. Thus, in many ways in the west, old age impacts particularly on women – their sexuality is most closely related to reproduction – rather than on men. Sex for older women represents a disjuncture therefore; it is out of place as, usually, they can't reproduce (Bildtgard, 2000). As such, older women become viewed as sexually unattractive, impacting negatively on many women's sense of self, and research has revealed how it leads them to feel somehow less feminine (Hinchliffe and Gott, 2004). DeLamater et al. (2017), for instance, found that whilst older women still have the same frequency of sexual activity, many have experienced a decline in sexual desire, and they put this down to feeling less attractive or 'frumpy'. This is perhaps hardly surprising when, as the French feminist and philosopher Simone de Beauvoir argued, 'it is the fate of woman to be the object of eroticism in the eyes of man, once she has become old and ugly she forfeits her assigned place in society; she is a monster that arouses aversion and even fear' (1972: 104).

FACT FILE

The double standard of ageing?

In 1972, US activist Susan Sontag argued that society is more accepting of older men's faces, and indeed they can be read as attractive, unlike those of older women, who are seen as unattractive:

> Happily, men are able to accept themselves under another standard of good looks – heavier, rougher, more thickly built. A man does not grieve when he loses the smooth, unlined, hairless skin of a boy. For he has only exchanged one form of attractiveness for another: the darker skin of a man's face, roughened by daily shaving, showing the marks of emotion and the normal lines of age.

> There is no equivalent of this second standard for women. The single standard of beauty for women dictates that they must go on having clear skin. Every wrinkle, every line, every grey hair, is a defeat. (Sontag, 1972: 291–2)

- Is this still true today? Can you think of examples which either confirm or challenge Sontag's assertion?

Oldies but goldies?

Many argue that such representations are in actual fact reproducing ideas of youth as desirable and ageing as undesirable. Notions such as the 'sexy senior' might be said to be replacing stereotypes of 'mutton dressed as lamb' or the 'dirty old man' (Marshall, 2011; Vares, 2009). However, those older people considered 'sexy' (celebrities such as Helen Mirren, Susan Sarandon, Pierce Brosnan, Harrison Ford) are, arguably, deemed attractive because they are still considered 'youthful for their age'. 'Successful' ageing is, perhaps, driven by notions of 'youthfulness'.

Arguably, older people who remain sexually active are still stereotyped by the popular media. Heterosexist concepts such as 'cougar', or pornography's 'MILF' and 'GILF' (acronyms for 'Mother/Grandmother, I'd like to fuck'), reproduce ageist attitudes about older people's sexuality and about older women particularly (Alarie and Carmichael, 2015). Thus, whilst these labels may show sexual desire in older persons, do they also perhaps reinforce the idea that most older people are asexual (Montemurro and Siefken, 2014)?

Reconstructing ageing? Consumerism and medicine

Increasing numbers of people, perhaps under pressure from the increased visibility of the 'sexy older celebrity', are attempting to fight off the signs of ageing with cosmetic surgery. Despite the fact that many older people feel positive about ageing, they are clearly still subject to cultural attitudes that make them feel invisible and devalued. The challenges of ageing are, as we have already seen, gendered in many ways. Cultural standards of female beauty are largely youthful; women, in particular, are framed in relation to their deteriorating reproductive system. Thus, after the menopause, women are desexualized by society, unlike men. As a result of this double standard of ageing, many women resort to surgical interventions to combat the signs of ageing; women constitute the largest growing market for cosmetic surgery. Clarke and Griffin's (2008) interviews with 44 women between 50 and 70 showed the pressures placed on them by our cultural obsession with youth, with many using cosmetic surgery and a variety of non-surgical cosmetic procedures in an attempt to fight invisibility. As Andrew Blaikie (1999) has argued, consumer society has successfully capitalized on such fears. Current baby-boomers who were raised in a period of relative prosperity have, overall, more disposable income to spend on leisure pursuits and beauty products.

Discussion point

Collect some adverts for anti-ageing moisturisers. How do the images used reveal views on sexuality and ageing? Do they show people dating, in long-term partnerships or single?

Biomedical professionals have been quick to exploit fears of ageing in a youth-orientated society, encouraging older people to use pharmaceutical and medical interventions, such as Viagra, to 'boost' sexual performance or 'fix problems' (Wada et al., 2015). Older men, whose criteria for ageing successfully are sexual performance and the ability to accomplish penile-vaginal penetration, are often pushed into using such products. As Gott (2005) has suggested, heterosexual penetration is still presented as the 'gold standard' of sexuality. This has served to reinforce a narrow definition of 'normal' sexuality and shores up ageism by privileging penetration, orgasm and retaining one's youth (Loe, 2004). The dominant narrative here is that successful sexuality through the life course should remain unchanged and youthfully defined. Though interestingly, the biological effects of ageing for older women (such as drier vaginas and thinner skin), in addition to increased confidence in some respects, has resulted in many women finding it easier to express their sexuality in a non-penetrative way. Indeed, Katz and Marshall (2003) have argued that sex becomes the way older people are told they can defy old age, so perhaps there are increased pressures on older men and women to have sex in later life compared with their earlier years.

Pharmaceutical companies have also capitalized on the intersection of ageism and sexism, offering women 'cures' to certain symptoms to delay the impact of the menopause and post-menopause. Interestingly, not all cultures view life stages such as the menopause in such a negative way. What has become a 'truth' about ageing in the west is not experienced globally. Lambley (1995) noted that for Japanese women the menopause did not have quite the same negative implications, and neither were the symptoms experienced in the same way, hot flushes being relatively rare. Komesaroff et al. (1997) also noted that German women did not find the menopause and beyond as distressing as French or British women did.

Health and STIs

Positioning sexuality in later life as unnatural, shameful or disgusting can have the effect of rendering it invisible. Thus, of course, not only affecting older people's sense of self, but also excluding them from the services and resources available to them. Such isolation and silencing of sexuality can have dangerous consequences for older people, both heterosexual and LGBT+, in terms of their mental and physical health.

Certain groups in society are particularly at risk of contracting sexually transmitted infections (STIs). Often, these groups are at risk because of misleading dominant discourses, e.g. there has been a rise in STIs amongst the older heterosexual community.

In addition, figures also suggest that HIV is rising among older people, the signs of which can be mistaken for the aches and pains of ageing more generally. Age Concern (2007) has shown that more than ten percent of those men who are HIV positive are over 50, and in 2017 eighteen percent of people living with HIV were 50 and over. Partly, this is because many older people feel too ashamed to be asked to be tested, due to the perceived stigma around being sexually active. Medical practitioners are also not putting older people forward for tests because they often don't conceptualize older people as having a sex life. Older people are less likely to use condoms because they don't perceive themselves as being at risk. In addition, post-menopausal women also have thinner vaginal tissue and less natural lubrication, which means their skin is more likely to tear during penetrative intercourse. When they are eventually diagnosed, the disease is often at an advanced level, and therefore older people diagnosed with HIV have higher morbidity and mortality levels.

As a result, many NHS Trusts, such as the University Hospitals Trust in Birmingham, have started to add new sections to their websites in an attempt to educate older people about the risks of having intercourse without using protection. Dr Kaveh Manavi, Consultant Physician and HIV Service Lead for the University Hospitals Birmingham NHS Foundation Trust, which runs the Whittall Street Clinic in Birmingham city centre, said 'many older adults believe that they are not at risk of STI. The common mis-belief that older adults do not engage in sexual activities adds to the stigma and means people do not seek help early enough.'

Over the rainbow: LGBT+ experiences in later life

Discussion point

- Do you think that older LGBT+ have different needs from those who are heterosexual?
- Write down what you anticipate will be the key issues for older LGBT+ people.
- What issues are related to sampling minority groups of older people?

Until relatively recently, little effort had been made to explore the lives of older LGBT+ people. There is, however, a small but growing body of research which allows us to look at the LGBT+ experience of growing older in relation to the heterosexual experience, though it is important to recognize that there is no unitary experience of ageing as an LGBT+ person, and arguably most of the research has focused on the lesbian and gay experience (Ward et al., 2012). It is also important to remember that a minority sexuality is not the only, or necessarily most significant, determining factor of later life.

Research has revealed that older LGBT+ individuals are, for instance, more likely to live alone, to age as a single person, and to not have children. This means that, compared to their heterosexual peers, many lack traditional social support networks, though this is not always a disadvantage. From the existing research, we know that lesbians remain sexually active into their old age (Adelman, 1991). As Richardson (1992) has pointed out, definitions of what counts as 'sex' for lesbians may well challenge heterosexist assumptions. There is also a suggestion that ageing outside of the heterosexual 'norm' can be a liberating aspect for some older lesbians. It is argued that the privileging of youth in society affects lesbian communities less than it does for their heterosexual counterparts (Blasius, 1994).

Whilst the twenty-first century has, in many ways, seen a raft of positive legislative and social change for LGBT+ people (the UK alone has seen the Civil Partnership Act (December 2004), Equality Act (Sexual Orientation) Regulations 2007, and the Same-Sex Marriage Act, which came into force in 2014), many older lesbians and gay men have lived through less liberal times. They will have experienced both informal and formal discrimination. In many respects, this means that older lesbians and gay men can find ageing less problematic than their heterosexual counterparts because, it is argued, negotiating non-heterosexual identities in adverse conditions provides skills in 'crisis competence' (see Fredriksen-Goldsen and Muraco, 2010. However, it can have a profound effect both on their preparedness to 'come out' as LGBT+, and impact on their use, and experience, of a range of services, including health services. In fact, older LGBT+ people are five time less likely to access services for older people than is the case in the wider older population, because they fear discrimination and homophobia, and feel that they will have to hide their sexuality (Todd, 2011).

Older LGBT+ people also experience the paradox of ageing experienced by the general older population, in that they live in a time of increasing sexuality, yet it is within a society where they are told older sexuality is distasteful. But it is also a time when arguably it is easier to be gay. However, as older members of the LGBT+ community – a commercialized youth-orientated community – many feel marginalized (Todd, 2013). The stigma of ageing may hit gay men particularly hard (Heaphy et al., 2004). This sense of isolation, marginalization and invisibility is something which impacts on many aspects of older LGBT+ lives.

Bisexuals

One of the most unstudied sexual minority groups, in relation to sexuality in old age, is bisexual men and women. What little research has been done suggests that older bisexual men are very likely to have had their last sexual encounter with an acquaintance rather than a partner (Rosenberger et al., 2011), and may be more generally cut off from positive social or intimate relationships. Some indication that this is true, is that research has shown higher rates of internalized stigma and smaller social networks for male bisexuals, and a higher likelihood for them to live alone (Fredriksen-Goldsen et al., 2013). Additionally, because bisexual men and women experience biphobia – being seen as emotionally or sexually untrustworthy – by both heterosexuals and lesbians and gay men, they are more likely to keep their sexual lives private, undiscussed or remain 'in the closet'.

Transgender ageing

We know even less about how transgender people experience their sexuality in later life; there is a distinct paucity of research which looks at this. There are growing numbers of older trans people, both those who transitioned many years ago and those who decided on **transitioning** later in life, and due to improved medical care and the growth of the trans population, this is a demographic set to rise. One piece of research of interest by Witten (2016) looks at the experiences of bisexual transgender individuals. Given the impact of **transphobia** and **biphobia**, coupled with ageism and possibly sexism, many go under the 'research radar' due to fears of stigma. Witten (2015) has also looked at the intersection of ageing and sexuality for older lesbian trans women. However, neither study focuses on their sexual lives per se. Notably, both trans-bisexuals and trans-lesbians experienced similar fears about expected discrimination from service providers. As a group who statistically are most likely to experience hate crime, in addition to increased levels of poverty and isolation, this is perhaps understandable (Bailey and Bramley, 2012). An added worry was how they would be able to maintain self-actualization of their gender identity if they had to live in a care home. They also had significant concerns about late-life events (dementia, death) and legal difficulties (Witten, 2015).

Home is where the heart is? Care homes and sexuality

A significant decision that many older people must make, is whether or not to move into a residential care home. Whilst we know that many people continue to engage in sexual activity into later life, sadly, many nursing homes have a very negative attitude toward sex in later life (Hinrichs and Vacha-Haase, 2010). The stereotype of the asexual elderly perhaps offers a convenient excuse for not addressing a topic which many care workers are either too embarrassed to broach or feel unqualified to discuss. Many older people, both gay and straight, have reported experiencing negative attitudes to their sexual relationships, with many being prevented from sharing beds (Bouman et al., 2007).

As we have seen, this may be especially so for LGBT+ older people who may feel unable to express their sexuality in an environment which they perceive, rightly or wrongly, to be heterosexist and homophobic (Hinrichs and Vacha-Haase, 2010). Research has shown that older LGBT+ residents might not 'come out' in such settings, and they also might not reveal important information (such as HIV status) in an attempt to avoid discrimination (Griebling, 2016). Residential and care home workers may also be unaware of the particular needs and identities of their residents. Maes and Louis (2011), for instance, conducting a random sample of US nursing practitioners, found that very few – only two percent – conducted a sexual history assessment with patients, and over twenty-three percent never did. Workers who may express a positive approach to minority sexualities, are often ignoring the issue at work and not dealing with sexuality adequately. In part, this could be related to a tendency to view sexuality as 'private', rather than recognizing the myriad ways it is produced in the so-called 'public' sphere. Simpson et al. (2016) found a common response was 'we don't have any [LGBT+ residents] here', or 'we treat them all the same'. Further, as Weeks et al. (2001) have shown, LGBT+ people often rely on 'families of choice' for social support (a chosen rather than a biological family). In such situations, depending on laws at any given time, if judgements must be made on whether someone can give sexual consent (if they had dementia), it may be difficult for those closest to the client to prove their relationship and thereby be allowed to make decisions in their best interest. Fears and anxieties around such issues have led to many LGBT+ people requesting LGBT+-specific residential and care homes (Simpson et al., 2016).

Summary: 'Don't come a-knocking…'

We have seen that western culture still stigmatizes and/or ignores sexual desire and sexual relationships among older men and women. Despite a lack of empirical evidence, society still associates old age with unattractiveness and an absence of sexual desire, and considers sex for older people as something shameful. A review of the literatures available indicates that there is a lack of recognition of older people's sexuality, and that professionals who work with older people, as their carers or medical professionals, might not be affording them the same sexual recognition and rights as they do for younger people. This may be especially true for older gay, lesbian, bisexual, and transgender people.

Whilst ageing is still, frequently, constructed as an unavoidable misfortune, and sexual activity for older people viewed as incompatible with ageing, there are challenges to this stereotype. Overwhelmingly, we have seen from the literature available, that sexual interest and activity are sustained throughout the life course, into older age – though sexual expression may take different forms. Some studies have revealed the importance of sexual expression for boosting self-esteem and general wellbeing in later life, when other sources of support might be reduced. However, we need to be cautious about how positive all these new messages are, as ageing (sexualized) celebrities and the biomedicalization of sex and ageing through medicines such as Viagra, may well be putting older people under new pressures.

Ignoring the issue of sexuality in later life, means we fail to acknowledge the role that sexuality plays in many people's relationships, health, wellbeing and quality of life. We have seen that the invisibility of, and taboos around, sexuality amongst the elderly place them in a potentially vulnerable position emotionally, as well as physically. It is vital, therefore, that research into older age continues, in order to help us further challenge the ongoing stereotype of the 'asexual older person'.

Key questions

- Think about how culture shapes ideas about older age and sexuality. Where does this happen? Can you find examples from the media, government policies, religion, medicine?

- In what ways are these messages gendered? For instance, you might want to think about social, and your own, opinions on the latest age men should be when they become fathers. What age is too old for a woman to become a mother?

FURTHER READING

Andrew King et al.'s *Older Lesbian, Gay, Bisexual and Trans People: Minding the Knowledge Gaps* (Routledge, 2018) offers a useful exploration of the ways in which aspects such as ethnicity and class impact on later life for LGBT people.

For some cross-cultural analysis, have a look at Traeen et al.'s (2018) 'Attitudes towards sexuality in older men and women across Europe: similarities, differences, and associations with their sex lives' (www.researchgate.net/deref/http%3A%2F%2Fdx.doi.org%2F10.1007%2Fs12119-018-9564-9).

You could also explore the issue of older people in care homes in more depth by looking at the Royal College of Nursing's (2018) report, 'Older people in care homes: Sex, sexuality and intimate relationships'.

12

HEALTH

By the end of this chapter you should be able to:

- Have an understanding of the ways in which sexuality has been theorized in relation to health
- Recognize the ways in which hierarchical social ordering of sexuality gives rise to a number of health inequalities
- Identify the structural inequalities that lead to differential experiences, and treatment, of service users along lines of sexuality

Introduction

The topic of sexualities in relation to health remains a relatively neglected, and perhaps even taboo, area for discussion. Arguably, sexuality has often been secondary to other important issues such as class, gender and ethnicity. As we shall see, this can have potentially serious consequences for the wellbeing of many groups in society, not least potential service users. In this chapter, we will be looking at the ways in which certain bodies have been subject to a medicalized 'gaze' which has had a lasting impact on how they are treated both within health services and in the wider community. Feminists, for instance, have pointed to the ways in which women's bodies and their bodily experiences, in particular, have been routinely subject to medical surveillance – pregnancy, menstruation and the menopause for instance, are frequently conceptualized as conditions which need to be monitored closely (Tiefer, 2001). Conversely, the male body and self is positioned as being one of containment and control: bounded in time and space, rational and autonomous and closed off from other bodies and the world, the majoritarian norm in the west against which all others are judged (Grosz, 1994).

Medicalized approaches to the body also frequently neglect to see the social aspects of our relationships with, and experiences of, our bodies, and instead tend to focus solely on the biological aspects of, those bodies. For instance, of particular concern for the medical establishment since the 1990s has been so-called 'female sexual dysfunction'. Women who don't want sex, don't enjoy sex or can't reach orgasm, are frequently presented as having a biologically-based 'problem' which can be cured by a pill (Drew, 2003). Rarely considered are the ways in which sexual satisfaction/enjoyment might be based on social factors such as experiences of abuse and fear, the impact of poverty or over-working, or a poor lover! Sex in this context is understood in terms of the phallocentric belief that all 'normal' women should want and enjoy penetra-tive sex (Smart, 1989). In fact, many studies suggest that the majority of women, indeed up to eighty percent according to some studies, cannot achieve orgasm through penetrative sex alone (Herbenick et al., 2017).

This chapter aims to provide you with a deeper understanding of the impli-cations for us both socially and culturally more generally, but also as potential service users. And, of course, for those who may go on to work in field of health and social care, this might help raise awareness when working with a range of service users. We begin with a brief consideration of how our understandings of sexualities, health and bodies have been gendered and polarized, before considering how this has impacted on attitudes to sexualities with regard to health historically. However, we also look at the ways its legacy remains with us. In order to do this, we will consider a few cases studies which might not be the ones you'd necessarily expect in a chapter on sexualities and health. Rather than look only at those issues you might expect to see in a chapter on sexual health specifically (such as contraception, sexually transmitted infections (STIs) and so on), we will take a slightly broader conceptual approach to think about sexualities and health.

Divided again: mind/body, male/female

During the Enlightenment period, the philosophical tradition of seeing the body as outside, or indeed in opposition to, the body, was popular among its thinkers. The familiar dictum 'I think, therefore I am', was translated from Latin (*cogito ergo sum*) by the French philosopher René Descartes in his *Discourse on the Method of Rightly Conducting One's Reason and Seeking Truth in the Sciences* (1637). The ideal, in this view, was someone who was a rational, and independent subject, in control of their body, emotions and desires. The separation of mind and body was, therefore, hierarchical, with the mind being valued above bodies. While this philosophical separation has a long history which, like many other strains of thought that impact on us today, goes back to Ancient Greek philosophers, it is strongly associated with Descartes, and therefore it has come to be known as Cartesian dualism. This mind/body dualism is also, arguably, gendered. The philosopher Hélène Cixous (1981) has looked at how dualistic binary ways of thinking are central, determining characteristics of western thought (see Table 12.1). Arguably, we can see that when we consider contemporary medical and moral considerations of the relationship between bodies, sexualities and health.

Table 12.1   Gendered mind/body dualism

Male	Female
Public	Private
Rational	Emotional
Active	Passive
Strong	Weak
Subject	Object
Controlled	Messy

Women's bodies, from this perspective, are considered weaker and inferior to men's. Their bodies are seen as messy, leaky and uncontrolled, and therefore more primitive and closer to nature. Such a view explains why menstruation and menstrual blood are still considered a taboo, shameful or dirty in many societies. Whilst increasingly this mind/body dualistic thought is being eroded, and we no longer see the body as separate from the mind, the gendered divisions remain. Indeed, the reading of disordered, messy bodies as feminine has also been a pathologizing lens through which disabled, LGBT+ and BAME bodies have been seen. This, in conjunction with structural racism, explains the abhorrent practice of forced sterilization which so many black women have been subjected to across the globe (Eichelberger et al., 2016). Bev Skeggs (1997) has also argued that working-class bodies are placed within this moralizing frame too, and often seen as out of control or excessive. Television programmes frequently focus on working-class lives in relation to excess consumption of food, alcohol or cigarettes for instance. Their bodies are also presented as having excess sexuality (too sexual, too fertile) – notions of hypermasculinity/femininity or hypersexuality are, she posits, frequently classed. Thus, moral panics about sex or pregnancy frequently are about working-class bodies.

Discussion point

Dualism and contemporary sexual health

Consider an issue related to sexual health which features regularly in the media or government discourse, e.g. pregnancy or STIs.

- Can we see evidence of dualistic ways of thinking?
- Is it possible to argue still that the masculine, heterosexual, white, middle-class body/mind is still read as the default norm against which all others fail?

An approach to thinking about health and sexualities which relies on these binaries can be dangerous for members of the assumed normative group and those left on the margins.

Prostitution and the gendering of sexual health

Dualistic thought has meant that issues related to the body, and particularly those bodies belonging to minority groups, have long been considered distasteful. Despite being a taboo topic, however, sexual health is something which has been subject to considerable scrutiny at all levels of society, from the individual and communities right through to state interest. As we have seen in previous chapters, alongside the new 'science' of sexology, the nineteenth century saw anxieties about sex and sexuality increase as a result of the rapid changes stemming from industrialization. As a consequence of both of these developments, sexuality became inextricably bound up with medicine in the west and arguably has remained so ever since. Between 1812 and 1851, Britain's population doubled and had done so again by the beginning of the twentieth century. Many middle-class Victorians, who were faced with living in close proximity to the working classes for the first time, began to see the city as a place of vice and depravity. It is oft cited that during this time prostitution rose rapidly; we do not have an accurate estimation for the number of women, and indeed young men, who were prostitutes at the time, but irrespective of numbers, their presence, 'the Great Social Evil', was a source of concern for several moralists, such as Dr William Action, and social campaigners. Though poverty was understood to be a factor in prostitution, often the fault was constructed by those in privileged positions as being a problem of the 'lower orders' – unemployment led to boredom, which in turn led to vice in those 'unfettered' by morals. One such moralist asked 'who can wonder that young girls wander off into a life of immorality, which promises release from such conditions' (Mearns, 1883: 11). In addition to fears about prostitution, pornographic materials were made more readily available as a result of improved printing technologies, thus society's new medical 'sexperts' produced literature focusing on the dangers which accompany sex, in particular the proliferation of sexually transmitted diseases. Such literature also reproduced sexual double standards by suggesting the problem stemmed from the prostitutes themselves and not the men who used them. From the 1850s, rubber condoms became available as a form of protection against venereal disease transmitted by prostitutes. Prostitution and prostitutes were seen as the main source of the contamination of men and venereal disease was seen to be the very embodiment of dangerous female sexuality; the French, for instance, had the euphemism 'Dame Syphilis'. As we have seen in other chapters, States are often concerned with the health of the citizens for a variety of reasons, and at this time many nations across Europe began to regulate prostitutes who were seen as a threat to the health of potential young military men. As a threat to the health of the nation who 'contaminates the very air, like a deadly upas tree, and poisoning the blood of the nation, with most audacious recklessness… The woman was nothing better than a paid murderess, committing crime with impunity' (Hemyng, 1862: 235), prostitutes were subject to severe medical inspections.

The 1864 Contagious Diseases Act meant that those women who were suspected of being 'common prostitutes' had to endure fortnightly, painful, internal examinations; later acts in 1864, 1866, 1868 and 1869 further extended the legislation, despite their debatable medical efficacy. Many at the time were angered by these acts which were thought to encourage the double standard further, being directed against women and not the men who funded the trade (Garrett, 1870: 3). In addition to fears about venereal disease, prostitutes were also linked to the dangers of an increased heart-rate and excessive emission of semen. Such fears were also levelled at masturbation, which was understood to be responsible for a host of ailments from gout to gonorrhoea, blindness and madness (see Chapter 10).

Whereas once, we sought explanations for people's unusual or perhaps unacceptable sexual activities from religion, Foucault has argued that in the west we now seek explanations from medicine and psychiatry, although often we have not lost those ideas of morality. This western model for thinking about sexuality has also had profound global implications for the ways in which people experience their sexual relationships and relate to their bodies. We will now move on to consider some of the ways in which sexuality bears important relation to health, medicine and social care in contemporary society.

Disabled bodies and the medicalized gaze

As we have already seen, minority groups have often been neglected in the existing sexualities literature (Caldwell, 2010). Gordon and Rosenblum (2001: 16) highlighted how, unlike many other areas of enquiry, research into disabled people's experiences of sexuality has been 'peculiarly un-sociological'. Historically, studies of disability have been firmly grounded in the medical model. In other words, this is research which constructs disability as an impairment which needs a solution, i.e. treatment or a cure. A medical model of disability frequently marginalizes disabled people (particularly those who are physically disabled) by constructing them as asexual and heterosexual (Milligan and Neufeldt, 2001). Conversely, they can often find themselves depicted as hyper-sexual and sexually 'deviant', especially if they are cognitively disabled. Disability and sexuality, in other words, are seen as incompatible concepts (O'Toole and Bregante, 1992). Gradually, as Shakespeare (2013) has acknowledged, there has been shift to a social model, where disability is framed as not located in the body but rather something which comes from social exclusion and disadvantages. Many have pointed out problems with this view too. One argument is that it has a tendency to minimize the very real impact of impairment (Crow, 1996). There is also still a tendency to present disabled people as a homogeneous group, whereas it is important to note that there is a range of cognitive and physical disabilities – disabilities which require medical interventions, others which are congenital, and those which have come as a result of trauma or accident. These have to be considered alongside cross-cutting aspects of identity such as sexuality, gender, ethnicity, and class position. However, arguably, even research from this perspective has still largely focused on medicalization. Kim (2011) has suggested that there is a tendency within recent scholarship on disability, to place so much emphasis on the sexuality of disabled people, that it places those who do identify as asexual further into the margins, and therefore some have felt accused of reinforcing stereotypes the movement has worked so hard to denounce. The study of the intersections of health, disability and sexuality, from a social science perspective, is therefore in its infancy.

A significant development in terms of sexual health and disability came from a World Health Organization's (2006) agenda which included a definition of the sexual health rights which have been applied to disabled people. This included an assertion that all people have a right to enjoy sexual health and express their sexuality. Despite this, many argue that there are still many social and cultural barriers preventing disabled people from being able to exercise those rights. One area which is subject to ongoing campaigns is around the availability (or lack) of appropriate sexual health education. A UK charity, Leonard Cheshire, for example, conducted a survey in 2010 and found that fifty percent of disabled people had not received any sexual health education; in an attempt to counter this, the government started initiatives such as Undressing Disability. Stereotypes of disabled people as asexual feed into this – many studies argue that teachers and other professionals often assume sex education just isn't necessary. There is also a perceived sense of heightened risk associated with sex and disabled people. For instance, Maguire et al. (2019) have identified a tension for care workers between trying to enable positive relationships and also trying to protect the person with a learning disability from abuse or exploitation. Whilst it is important to be mindful of these risks for any group, this becomes problematic when it infringes on human rights. There is plenty of evidence to show that people with learning disabilities, for instance, are able to engage in safe sexual relationships (Sinclair et al., 2015). A lack of appropriate sexual health education has been shown to put disabled people at more risk of contracting sexually transmitted infections or unwanted pregnancies (Baines et al., 2018). Another barrier to sexual health is access to potential partners and a private space. As Shakespeare (2000) has argued, being a sexual being requires a degree of self-esteem, but systematic social exclusion and devaluing negates this. Penny Pepper, who writes about disability and sex, has observed that 'when you're dealing with disability or chronic illness, there's a sense that sex isn't something you should be worrying about. You seem to be expected to exist in a shadow world of sadness and struggle' (quoted in Fixter, 2019). Attitudes to disabled people tell us something more generally about hegemonic notions of what are deemed appropriate 'sexual' bodies.

Discussion point

Disability is normal

Have a look through some statistics either for your country or on a global level. Make note of the following:

- How many people are registered disabled?
- How many people have a chronic health condition?
- How many people have a condition which affects their sex life, such as erectile dysfunction?

What does this tell us about how we define disability?

Impairment is an everyday experience. Many people are having to adjust to changes in their bodies (such as ageing) which impact on how they might 'do' sex.

For those disabled people whose disability involves a degree of physical impairment, phallocentric and heteronormative definitions of sex frequently have a negative impact on how their sexuality is viewed (Tilley, 1996). There is often an assumption, for instance, that 'sex' only ever involves penile penetration. More recently, there has been some interesting research which takes a more nuanced approach to thinking about disability and sexuality, e.g. research which considers the intersections of deafness and queer identitites and communities (Leigh and O'Brien, 2019).

Medicalization of trans bodies

Another group who have been subject to a medicalized 'gaze' are trans and **intersex** people. As we have seen, sexualities involve understandings of both bodies and genders. Many people may challenge expected gendered norms, or feel uncomfortable with the roles expected of them, by having sexual identities which perhaps don't map neatly onto their gender identity. For trans and intersex people, who may well have bodies which have non-standard sex characteristics, or bodies which do not align with typical gender categories, this can be even more complicated (Schilt and Windsor, 2014). As Reicherzer (2008) has shown, as medicine became the 'expert' knowledge we turned to in the nineteenth century, many medical researchers focused on non-normative expressions of sexuality. Their approach was to conflate sex, gender and sexuality, and any behavioural or physical variance was seen as pathological (see Chapters 1 and 2). So rigid were their binary ways of thinking around male-female and heterosexuality-homosexuality, that intersex people, or hermaphrodites as they were known then, were believed to have a true sex which medicine could reveal (Dreger, 2000). It was in 1949 that 'sexologist' David Cauldwell used the term 'transsexual' to describe the wish to be the 'other' gender, a condition he argued was linked to 'homosexuality' and psychiatric problems (Heath and Wynne, 2019). Later, in the 1960s, scientists such as Harry Benjamin saw transsexualism as a separate 'condition', one needing to be treated with hormones and surgery. From his work, has come the stereotype that all trans people feel that they are in the 'wrong' body and desire surgery, an assumption that some trans activists have challenged. Arguably, the medical model has been as hard to shake off for trans people as it has for disabled people.

There are, according to Devor and Dominic (2016), three main areas of concern for the sexual health of trans people, namely sexual satisfaction, the health of sexual organs (including the storage of viable eggs, or sperm) and sexually transmitted infections. Another key issue is that of access to health care provided by informed professionals. Living in a society which regulates bodies along rigid binary lines means that many trans people experience shame in relation to their bodies, particularly if they have not yet had any of the procedures they are waiting for. Such feelings, in addition to living in a transphobic society, mean that many people will be reluctant to access health services if they need them. We know, for instance, that transwomen are less likely to have their prostrate and testicular checks, and transmen are less likely to have cervical smear tests and breast examinations. Of real concern is the relatively high rates of HIV infection amongst this group. This seems to be a particular problem for BAME trans people and transwomen more generally (Hwang and Nuttbrock, 2014).

In recent years, transmen's bodies have come under the media, and medical, spotlight. Most notably, this was in relation to Thomas Beatie, a transman who shared his pregnancy with the media in 2007. In sharing his stories and pictures of his pregnant body, Halberstam (2010: 77) argued that he had created the first public image of a 'queer pregnancy'. Halberstam's discussion shows the ways in which Beatie's body became medicalized and sexualized in the same breath. Members of the public, as well as the medical profession, felt able to ask Thomas a range of intimate questions about his transition and genital surgeries, whilst images of a bare-chested Beatie saturated television screens, his body becoming an eroticized site of potential resistance. More recently, research into pregnancy and trans people has tended to revert to a slightly medicalized gaze but they do ask some important questions. Charter et al. (2018), for instance, have argued that many pregnant transmen experience body dysphoria as a result of having to stop taking testosterone. Their changing, increasingly fecund, body could also present other problems. For those who had had breasts removed, for instance, changes to the chest were a real concern. They conclude that social exclusion, isolation, and loneliness were common to transmen's experiences of pregnancy.

Amputated sexuality? Mental health patients and sexuality

A sense of dislocation from one's own sexuality was something shared by the participants in a study looking at the experiences of inmates in a UK forensic medium secure unit. These men had entered the criminal justice system but had also been 'sectioned' under the Mental Health Act (1983). Many would spend between two and twenty years in the facility, and at the time of interview ranged in age from 20 to 40. During their 'stay', they were neither allowed to spend any time alone with their partners, nor were they encouraged to talk about their sexuality. Based on semi-structured interviews with the inmates (Duke et al., 2018), the conclusion was that the men experienced a sectioned-off or amputated sexuality. Senior members of teams within the units, it's argued, held the view that expressions of sexuality hinder recovery and that most men won't be interested in sex when they're ill anyway. Arguably, a pervasive discourse of risk, predation and vulnerability frames how sexuality is viewed in such an institution, in terms not only of their own safety but also in relation to others within the unit. This is interesting in and of itself, however arguably this study also sheds light on the experiences of others who live within an institution. Older people, for instance, who live within a care home setting are frequently denied sexual autonomy. The same can be said for those with long-term health conditions or disabled people who are in the looked-after population.

Here, we must turn once more to Foucault, whose work on sexualities and power can help us think through some of these issues. In both *The Birth of the Clinic* (1973) and *The History of Sexuality* (1979), he traces the ways in which power is exercised through the body – not by violence or physical coercion (though this does happen) but through self-discipline and surveillance. Medical and moral discourses on health, hygiene and sexuality proliferate, providing guidelines on how 'suspect' populations should live. Concern for an ordered social body can be found in institutional settings such as prisons, hospitals and nursing homes. Here we see preoccupations with the disciplining of the body.

The next few sections will look at the legacy of such ways of thinking for LGBT+ people in a range of health-related areas.

LGBT+ Health

Mental health and LGBT+ communities

For decades 'homosexuality' itself was considered a mental illness. Despite the fact that research findings have effectively collapsed any evidence for this belief, there are still a significant number of psychiatrists and clinicians who maintain that same-sex desire is an illness per se or symptomatic of mental ill health. Research findings do suggest that LGBT+ people have a higher instance of mental health problems than the wider population (King and McKeowan, 2003), with anxiety, depression, self-harm and suicidal behaviour being the main expressions of this ill health. Arguably, it is homophobia, rather than being gay, which is the cause of such anxiety, with rejection, discrimination, exclusion and victimization being identified as primary reasons (Stonewall, 2018). A lack of appropriate social spaces, as discussed elsewhere, has also been cited as an additional source of stress for young LGBT+ people, particularly in rural areas. Studies into sexuality and mental health have shown consistently that the majority of those interviewed do not have faith in current health care providers and have stated they would prefer to see an LGBT+-specific counsellor (Chakraborty et al., 2011).

Drug and alcohol abuse in the LGBT+ community

Use and misuse of tobacco, alcohol and other drugs appears to be higher among LGBT+ people (Age Concern, 2007). One explanation may be related to the stress linked to living with prejudice and homophobia. Another reason may be that it is difficult for LGBT+ people to enjoy taking part in the leisure activities that many heterosexual men and women take for granted. Recent studies, for example, have pointed to the difficulties and anxieties related to being LGBT+ and becoming part of an (unquestionably heterosexual) sports team, with individuals being reliant on the goodwill and 'tolerance' of hetero-sexual team members (Baiocco et al., 2018). As a result, in many towns and cities, gay areas or bars have developed which offer a degree of safety and security. Such gay spaces tend to be heavily commercialized and revolve around pubs, bars and clubs, where alcohol becomes difficult to avoid. This might also be an issue related to research recruitment. The LGBT+ popula-tion, despite recent social and legal shifts, is also a stigmatized population, and therefore a relatively marginalized and hidden one. Hence many studies into LGBT+ lives recruit from 'gay villages', so a study into alcohol consumption is likely to encounter some heavy drinkers if the sample is taken largely from bars and clubs.

Breast and other cancers

One health issue which appears to be a particular problem in the lesbian com-munity is breast cancer (Breast Cancer Care, 2011; Meads and Moore, 2013): 'Over 1 in 12 lesbian and bisexual women aged between 50–79 have been diagnosed with breast cancer, compared with 1 in 20 of women in general' (Hunt and Fish, 2008). It is important, however, to unpick the problem here. Lesbians are not at higher risk of breast cancer because they are lesbians. Rather, it is because there are certain characteristics associated with lesbian communities and lifestyles which place lesbian women at greater risk. These include childlessness (thus, crucially, not breast feeding), obesity and excess consumption of alcohol. Figures are extrapolated from small-scale studies, and, as discussed above, populations may well be drawn from bars and clubs given the relative 'hard to reach' nature of the population. We do not know how many lesbians have breast cancer, as the NHS does not routinely make a note of sexual identity. Neither do we know how many lesbians have children. Much research (see Hunt and Fish., 2008) has found that lesbians continue to have negative experiences in health services despite anti-discriminatory legis-lation, hence there is a very real chance that those suffering ill health do not seek medical advice, or if they do, do not wish to add to the stress with the additional hurdle of coming out (Fish, 2010).

There is also a suggestion that lesbians are falling off the radar when it comes to cervical cancer. Many lesbians either believe, or have been told by medical practitioners, that they do not need to have smear tests. Certainly, it would appear that women who have never had sex with a man are at less risk of developing cervical cancer. Firstly, however, many lesbians have had sex with men, either before they came out or after (despite neat labels, many people do not conform to rigid boundaries of 'gay' or 'straight'). New evidence also suggests that the Human Papillomavirus (HPV), a cause of cervical cancer passed by sexual contact, can be transmitted by female-to-female sexual contact. In addition, it is thought that smoking is another risk, and as discussed above, it is thought that lesbians are more likely to smoke or have smoked than heterosexual women.

Discussion point

Collect the annual reports of as many health and social care service providers as you can. Do they make reference to heterosexual, lesbian, gay, bi or trans identities?

Ageing

As discussed in Chapter 11, ageing in general is increasingly becoming an issue of importance partly because we are an ageing population. In addition, with recent government austerity measures, pressures on older people have increased and are likely to continue to do so.

Domestic abuse

Domestic abuse among LGBT+ people is a significant social problem (Donovan and Hester, 2014) and older same-sex couples suffer both direct and indirect discrimination in relation to this (ACE, 2002). Arguably, the image of the older LGBT+ person as depressed, isolated, desperate, and sexless is still prevalent (Ginn and Arber, 1995). We also know that many older people feel there are risks associated with an 'out' identity in certain circumstances, whether that be in their local community, work or family environment, for instance. There is also evidence that there is little sense of support from LGBT+ communities. Many feel excluded from LGBT+ spaces which are conceptualized as being youth-orientated (Todd, 2013). If you believe that your values are derided or you are just 'too old' to enjoy yourself, it may mean that there are few safe spaces in which to discuss same-sex domestic violence and seek support. Many from the baby-boomer generation and beyond, depending on what point in the life course they came out, will have been involved in political communities and had access to social spaces beyond LGBT+ bars and clubs (see Chapter 7). Several of these spaces, a source of support and solidarity, have now gone – perhaps because the internet has meant they are less needed (Rosser et al., 2008). Views of older LGBT+ people as isolated, desperate and perhaps vulnerable, may also render potential perpetrators of domestic violence, in particular, invisible.

Elder abuse

Societal reluctance to acknowledge that older people engage in sexual activities results in the invisibility of their relationships. This means that when domestic violence happens in relationships involving older people, any abuse tends to fall under the umbrella term 'elder abuse'. This is especially so for older LGBT+ people who are more likely to keep their sexuality hidden.

Bereavement

The death of a loved one is a difficult time for anyone. Being an older LGBT+ person at such a time can also present additional anxieties. Many of the issues discussed previously about 'coming out' apply here, as experiencing a bereavement may require a constant 'coming out'. This may be especially problematic for many, especially older LGBT+ individuals who are less comfortable in disclosing their sexuality to service providers. Despite recent formal recognition of same-sex partnerships, many LGBT+ people experience a lack of recognition of their relationships by families, and in some cases, agencies. Again, many have felt that LGBT+-specific counselling would be desirable.

Care and the older LGBT+ person

For many of us, 'home' represents a sanctuary, a safe place to retreat; somewhere we can 'be ourselves'. Home can also be seen as important site for constructing our identity, so that it becomes not just a space but also somewhere with social meaning. As we have already seen, many LGBT+ people experience a constrained sense of self in the public sphere, so their home may well have additional resonance. Asking for and accepting help in the home may therefore be especially hard for older LGBT+ people. Research has highlighted that older LGBT+ people receiving care in the home experience many difficulties (Pugh, 2005). Many older gay men and lesbians have expressed concern that they would be subject to a disapproving or policing 'gaze', and subsequently have had to de-gay or de-dyke their flat before a visit, by hiding 'incriminating' CDs, books or pictures. Other studies have begun to look into the issue of residential care homes. Heaphy et al. (2004) found that many lesbians and gay men feared getting older and having to enter care homes because they believed their sexuality would not be understood. There is evidence, for example, that many LGBT+ couples in care homes find their relationships are not recognized. As a result, LGBT+-specific care is something desired by many older LGBT+ individuals.

Such examples point to the fact that perhaps generic providers for older people need to make specific efforts to ensure older LGBT+ people feel included, able to access services on their own terms, without fear of discrimination, and that the information and services they receive are relevant and responsive to their circumstances and needs.

Discussion point

Health, sexuality and diverse bodies

The examples above have focused on research on LGBT+ people, but arguably many of the issues relate to other minority groups in society. Take each of the issues in turn and think about the ways in which they may impact on other groups in society.

Masculinities, health and sexuality

As mentioned elsewhere, in texts on sexuality, there is a tendency to focus on minority groups for understandable reasons, and this is something I have been guilty of thus far in the chapter. However, it is always important to scrutinize the unmarked category too, and various theorists have shown the ways in which hegemonic heterosexuality impacts on all (Connell and Messerschmidt, 2005). We know, for instance, that those dominant, binary ways of thinking about gender we looked at towards the start of this chapter, have a significant impact on men's health. Stereotypes about masculinity being synonymous with strength, for instance, mean they are less likely to seek help from their GP if they are ill than women are, who have been brought up with a sense of their bodies as weak and vulnerable. However Wang et al. (2013) has shown that the age of men impacts on this too, with those younger than 16 and older than 60 showing less resistance to visiting health workers. Social norms are incredibly powerful. So pervasive was the view that boys should be circumcised in the US, that a significant number of paerents thought the procedure was a legal requirement, thus it became a common practice (Waldeck, 2003). We are only just beginning to acknowledge the significant emotional, sexual and psychological impact that childhood circumcision has on men (Boyle et al., 2002).

There is a range of areas which could be focused on in relation to masculinity and health, but we are going to look briefly at unsafe sex to provide a case study. Much research has focused on the ways in which gay and bisexual men engage in risky sexual behaviours (Brennan et al., 2015; Jacobs et al., 2010; Starks et al., 2013), but perhaps less focus has been placed on men who identify as heterosexual and their sexual practices.

One useful study by Apostolopoulos et al. (2011) looked at the risky sexual behaviours of truckers in the US. It would appear that a small but determined percentage of this group engage in a range of sexual encounters which might be considered risky. These include 'bridging', which means having unprotected casual sex when on the road and away from long-term partners, and 'sex-cruising', which is using the internet to hook up with people at toilets on the road. Some of the men who identify as heterosexual will have sex with other men when on the road. Despite misleading stereotypes of AIDS/HIV being a gay problem, these men, or the men who had sex with them, sometimes assumed that 'heterosexualness', especially if they had a wife, was protection enough from STIs of any kind.

Discussion point

'Doing' masculinity and health

Despite men (in general) enjoying more opportunities and privileges than women, research suggests these don't translate into better health outcomes (WHO, 2014).

How else might stereotypes of masculinity impact on men's sexual health?

Summary

Clearly, the relationship between sexualities and health is not only a complicated one but also an important one. It covers a huge arena, including abortion, birth control, cancer, contraception, pregnancy, STIs, mental health, body integrity, sexual safety, eroticism, gender, emotional attachment, and reproduction. Sexual health is political in that the right to good sexual health is not evenly distributed but clearly linked to issues of social equity. We have only just begun to touch on some of these, and hopefully, in your reading, you will explore other related areas. Crucially, we have started to understand how particular bodies have been medicalized – in other words, they have become objects for scrutiny. We have started to explore the processes of medicalizing particular practices, bodies or acts as healthy or unhealthy, normal or deviant, productive or unproductive. Heterosexual (masculine, white, middle-class) bodies are naturalized in relation to non-normative bodies and sexualities. Such processes can have serious consequences for those deemed 'unhealthy', 'deviant' or 'unproductive'. Social and cultural norms impact on the sexual health of all of us, young or old, black or white, LGBT+ or straight and being mindful of the impact of structural violence in the form of racism, sexism, ageism or homophobia can help us idenitify communities at risk at any given point.

The historical stigmatizing of LGBT+ sexualities and the promotion of a particular expression of heterosexuality have served to regulate and police intimate lives. This has led to problematic health and social care provision for many LGBT+ and heterosexual service users, challenges which can only be countered by thinking critically, and troubling notions of 'normality' and 'acceptability'.

In addition to being judged in terms of productivity, and despite being subjected to heavy scrutiny or a medical gaze, we are increasingly expected to be responsible for the health of our (sexual) bodies. The language of lifestyle, choice and responsibility abounds. In an age of austerity measures in many nations, and an attendant reduction in state welfare and health services, this responsibility becomes increasingly harder for some people – the tragic and devastating pandemic of Coronavirus being a case in point. We need to be mindful of the social, political and cultural forces which frame people's lives and impact on their relationship with their sexual identity and health. Sexual health relates to the media we consume, the identities we invest in, the policies of our rulers.

Key questions

- In what ways can we argue that our sexual bodies, health and personhood are historically and culturally interrelated?

- How are bodies constituted through medical discourse? What are the prevailing norms?

- How do our views of social norms and our cultural, political or religious beliefs about sex impact on our health and wellbeing?

FURTHER READING

Richard Parker's analysis of sexual health in relation to human rights in *Sexuality, Health, and Human Rights* (Routledge, 2007) is a useful starting point and provides some references to interesting related research.

Tamsin Wilton's *Sexualities in Health and Social Care* (OUP, 2000) provides an excellent and humorous overview of how certain bodies have been shaped through history, and the impact that has on the health care services received.

13

VIOLENCE AND SEXUALITY

Learning outcomes

By the end of the chapter, you should be able to:

- Identify structures which support ongoing sexual violence in societies
- Recognize patterns between forms of violence
- Interpret and evaluate key explanations for sexual violence
- Discuss a range of strategies for resistance to violence

Introduction

... if the allegations made by these two women were true, 100% true, and even if a camera in the room captured them, they don't constitute rape. At least not rape as anyone with any sense can possibly recognise it ... 'Woman A' met Julian Assange, invited him back to her flat, gave him dinner, went to bed with him, had consensual sex with him, claims that she woke up to him having sex with her again ... I mean, not everybody needs to be asked prior to each insertion ... It might be really bad manners not to have tapped her on the shoulder and said: 'Do you mind if I do it again?' It might be really sordid and bad sexual etiquette, but whatever else it is, it is not rape ... (George Galloway, 18 August 2012)

The issue of violence or, more specifically, of violence related to and surrounding sexuality is one of the most controversial topics. This was graphically illustrated by the heated debates which arose from the comments made by George Galloway via his weekly online broadcast *Goodnight with George Galloway*, about the allegations of rape against the WikiLeaks founder, Julian Assange. In particular, anti-rape campaigners accused Galloway of a 'deeply disturbing and disappointing' attitude towards sexual violence, after he claimed that the allegation against Assange had no basis because having sex with a woman when she is asleep is not rape. Lawyers, as well as anti-rape campaigners, were quick to point out that Galloway was wrong, for the simple reason that the law is clear: consent is required *every time* someone has sex.

Although this particular issue focused on sexual violence against women, it also has relevance for sexual violence against men. As a general point of departure, it is important to recognize that sexual violence, in its many forms, poses a broad threat to both men's and women's sense of safety and wellbeing, in both the public and private spheres. Other chapters consider related issues of sex robots and domestic abuse (see Chapter 6) – their treatment in chapters outside of this does not mean that they are unrelated. It should also be added that this chapter is focusing on sexual violence as harm. Ideas of consensual violence in the context of BDSM are looked at elsewhere (see Chapter 9). This chapter will examine women's and men's experiences of sexual violence, but it will primarily focus on the violence experienced by women because this is the group who overwhelmingly experience sexual/gendered violence in its many forms. Drawing on feminist theories, it will look at the prevalence and impact of such violence on different social groups, highlighting the pervasiveness of the problem and the degree to which responses deal with those impacts. Forms of sexual violence are many, ranging from bullying and sexual harassment to rape and murder. Using Kelly's (1988) notion of the continuum of violence, we will consider whether and how pornography, prostitution and so-called 'gentlemen's clubs' fit into the debate. The chapter examines recently conducted research into sexual violence, as well as discussing recent policy developments in the area.

What's in a name? The problem of definitions

As Kelly (1988) points out, much of the debate surrounding the Julian Assange case was to do with what counts as rape/sexual assault in law and life: in particular, whether it has to be 'violent' in order to qualify. In fact, few commentators used Kelly's definition of, and ideas related to, her concept of a continuum (see below). In addition, there was little or no awareness of the fact that one aspect of the recent reforms of sexual offences law in Sweden – passed in 2018, it states that sex with no consent is rape and passivity is not a sign of consent – was to establish the underlying principle of violation of women's bodily integrity, rather than force, as a definition of rape/sexual assault.

Many feminists have argued that for too many years, therefore, laws and practices relating to all crimes have reflected male viewpoints and do not adequately represent the experiences of women. With specific regard to acts of sexual violence, scholars such as Sylvia Walby (2005) have argued that narrow, legal definitions do not include experiences which many women regard as violent. Defining an act as violent is a political issue. Certain behaviours may count as violent, or sexual, in one culture or context but not in another; an act may be seen as abhorrent when commissioned by one particular social group but not another (the difference between what counts as legitimate state violence and an act of terrorism for instance). Definitions are an issue of power, reflecting the power some social groupings have to make their perspective count as to what is, or is not, violence. Violence may be narrowly defined, as in the legal sense of it being the unlawful use of physical force by an individual against others. A broader approach defines violence as behaviour which harms others, either physically or emotionally (Pilcher and Whelehan, 2004). Depending on the definition, an act may or may not be included in prevalence studies, and it will also mean some people are more or less likely to be recognized as perpetrators or victims. Terms such as domestic violence, for instance, might place a focus unintentionally on physical violence, or infer that it can only happen in the home. The notion of 'wife beating' again emphasizes physical aspects of abuse, and also suggests that in order to be a victim of such abuse you have to be female and married. Potentially, many people are left outside of such narrow definitions, which can have an impact on recognition of abuse and how it is dealt with.

It is also important to consider the impact of labelling individuals or groups as 'victims' or 'perpetrators'. These terms imply particular identities with which some may be unhappy (Dobash and Dobash, 1992; Kelly, 1988). The use of the term 'victim' in particular, has posed conceptual problems for many years. For example, as Kelly suggests, the category 'victim' may render women as passive, whereas 'survivor' has (for her) more positive and active connotations (Kelly, 1988: 163). Barry (1979) has argued that it is a form of objectification which obscures the person who has endured violation. 'Victim' then becomes a stereotype either for all women, or particular groups of women along the lines of ethnicity or class for instance (Murray, 1998). This then means that it becomes difficult for society to conceive of men as victims of abuse, and we know that this impacts severely on men's reporting of the abuse they suffer (Wallace et al., 2018). However, 'victim' remains the most used term and perhaps, rather than do away with it, we need to do away with the often false connotations associated with the word (see Alcoff, 2018). Likewise, we must be cautious and critical about our use of a term like 'perpetrator'. As with 'victim', if 'perpetrator' connotes false, fixed ideas along lines of gender, for instance, we cannot then accept that women can be violent (Wallace et al., 2018). Just as the legal system often fails black and Asian women in particular (either not seeing them as victims or being too quick to render them as passive victims respectively, see Finoh and Sankofa, 2019), it is often more ready to label black men as perpetrators of sexual violence than it is white men (Wriggins, 1983). Victim/perpetrator can also become another false binary, obscuring the fact that people can be both these things (McAlinden, 2014).

FACT FILE

Discursive manoeuvres

Adrian Howe (2009) uses Hilary Allen's (1987) concept of discursive manoeuvres to think about how sexual violence is defined and talked about. She argues that they are techniques of neutralizing behaviour, deflecting blame. She analyzes the way language is used to distort people's perception of sexual violence. Media (and legal) texts use, in effect, code words to eliminate the gender and identity of the perpetrators of men's violence against women (MVAW) (Phillips and Henderson, 1999: 118). We hear about *'the attacker'*, *'the abuser'*, or attacks by a woman's *'spouse'*, *'partner'*, for instance. Terms like *'domestic violence'* or *'marital violence'* don't reveal who is being violent. Drawing on Foucault's ideas, she suggests that dominant discourses around 'domestic violence' serve to 'degender the problem' and 'gender the blame' (Berns, 2001). Any identifying agency goes only as far as marking women as the victim; it becomes a problem of women, and men disappear from view. Media and criminal justice references to 'just a domestic' also serve to minimize the problem and make it sound cosy. Clark (1998), for instance, looked at how the *Sun* reported instances of MVAW. Women are referred to in a variety of ways – as *daughter, wife, brunette, mother* – rather than actual individuals, while men are defined in two ways – as *husbands* ('hubby'), *'spurned lover/ husband'*, *'sex-starved'*, *'tormented'*, or as *'monsters'*, *'fiends'*. In other words, they are pathologized through the use of medical discourse and 'expert truths', they become not like 'normal' men. Both framings have the effect of reducing/removing blame from men. The 'fiends' are dehumanized and located outside society – they are not responsible (and not men in any 'normal' meaning of the word).

Prevalence of sexual violence

Kelly (1987) has pointed out the importance of feminism in exposing the extent of sexual violence. As she argues, much of what feminists came to know about the prevalence of sexual violence was voiced by consciousness-raising groups and those who worked in refuges and rape crisis centres, as these provided a space to safely talk about experiences. Decades of feminist campaigning and activism have meant that there is much we do know about sexual violence in society. Female victims of violence are more likely than men to know the perpetrator, who is usually a current or former partner. Female homicide victims are also more likely than male victims to be killed by their present or former partner. Studies over time and across the globe reveal similar patterns, allowing us to state that one in three women on the planet will be raped or beaten in her lifetime (One Billion Rising.org), that on average two women a week in the UK are killed by a male partner or former partner (Department of Health, 2005; Povey, 2005), that women are much more likely than men to be the victim of multiple incidents of abuse, and of sexual violence (Walby and Allen, 2004), and one in four women in the UK will suffer rape or attempted rape. These are shocking statistics and yet still, only in exceptional cases, do they make headline news. Sexual violence is clearly a significant 'everyday' social problem (Stanko, 2001); Amnesty International described global violence against women as 'the greatest human rights scandal of our times'. Connell (1995) sees such violence as a resource available to men, based on the cultural acceptance of domination over women, in pursuit of sexual gratification. Given that we know abuse happens in same-sex relationships, and that men can be victims of women's violence, do we need to see violence as a resource available to all? We also know that the majority of victims of sexual violence, male and female, will never report their experiences, and that if they do, the chances of successful criminal convictions for their abusers are slim.

Rape: a case study

> The core stereotype for women in the courts is that of victim, and blaming the victim is the classic courtroom response to crime in the private arena. (Kennedy, 2005:117)

The example of rape can be used to exemplify and illustrate some key themes and issues relating to sexual violence more broadly. Over eighty percent of rapes are committed by someone known to the victim. Whilst the number of rapes reported to the police has gone up in recent years, the number of convictions is dropping. To explain such statistics, scholars have looked closely at key social institutions. One key factor which has been revealed is that society very often blames the victim for what happens to her (or him). Amnesty International, for instance, have shown that significant numbers of the public blame women for being raped if they had been drinking, flirtatious or had more than one sexual partner. In effect, we can see those binary constructions of men's and women's sexuality, and related double standards, discussed in Chapters 1 and 2 coming into force.

Rape culture

Blaming victims and normalizing and minimizing what happens are part of what is often referred to as rape culture.

Discussion point

Rape culture?

- Are women taught to do specific things to protect themselves from being raped? Create a list. What does this list tell us about the expectations of men's behaviour? In what ways is this problematic?
- Are men taught to do anything to protect themselves from being raped? Create a list. Compare this list with the one you created for women. What does this tell us about cultural gender expectations and rape?
- Create a list to give to men of how to not rape or one for men and women on how to not perpetuate a rape culture.
- What is your response to preparing such a list? Explore.

Adur and Jha (2018) have developed ideas on rape culture in their study of sexual harassment in Delhi. They consider the ways in which the use of public spaces can legitimize sexual aggression. Using the example of the gang rape on a Delhi bus and the subsequent activism and debate it provoked, they argue that sexual harassment in India is organized around hierarchies of femininity, where those at the bottom of the hierarchy, lower caste women, are considered 'indecent' and easy prey. Victim-blaming here centres around discourses of 'honour' and culpability; women are constructed as 'leaving themselves' open to abuse. They assess the UN 'Safe Cities Initiative' in Delhi, seeing it as an important development because it shifts understanding such abuse as a crime towards identifying the need for it to be recognized as an issue of human rights and social justice. The initiative challenges ideas of public space being 'male' and the private sphere as 'female', arguing that everyone has a 'right to the city'. Nevertheless, they note it still has its problems, neglecting to challenge, for instance, the role of masculinity in violence against LGBT+ people.

In the UK, Horvarth et al. (2011) found that members of the public could not differentiate between the language used by 'lads' magazines and that of convicted sex offenders. A key characteristic of such, laddism, they argue, is the inbuilt defence of 'irony', which is used to deflect any criticism and instead accuses detractors of having no sense of humour. Such language is a key part of rape culture.

Discussion point

Men's sexuality – unproblematic?

Horvath et al. (2011) contend that men's magazines normalize and legitimize (the language of) sexual violence. Their study shows an overlap in the content of convicted rapists' speech and the content of contemporary 'lads' mags'. They suggest that the framing of such content within these mags may normalize it for young men.

Read some copies of 'lad's mags':

- Is there evidence of apparently misogynistic (and homophobic) content? If so, is it *ironic*?
- Do they help insecure men find their place in the world (c.f. Gauntlett, 2008)?
- Do men's magazines reinforce the idea of a constant ('natural') male sexuality? If so, how?

Rape myths

Many researchers have shown the ways in which society has constructed particular stories, or myths, about what rape is and why it happens. Payne and colleagues (1999), for instance, identified seven rape myths, including 'rape is a trivial event', 'he didn't mean to', 'she wanted it', 'she asked for it', 'she lied about it', 'not really rape', and 'rape is a deviant event'. If similar myths were applied to other crimes, such as car theft – for instance, the victim was asking for it because he had a BMW – we could hazard a guess that there would be widespread outrage. Smart (1989) traces the ways in which rape myths find their way into the courtroom and are also constructed and reconstructed there, the result being that the law has the power to turn the victim into the prime suspect – what did she do to 'provoke' him? Feminists have pointed out that law is not the only discourse which serves to construct such ideas of male and female sexuality; media, religious and other discourses constantly re-present such ideas. However, in this instance, we will draw on Smart's work to look at the power of law in framing this issue.

Understanding the power of law

In conceptualizing power, Smart went back to Foucault's notions of truth and power. Certain discourses, as we have seen, claim to speak the truth and can thus exercize power in a society that values the notion of truth. For instance, as we saw in Chapter 2 a claim to science is a claim to truth, and thus has the effect of subordinating or silencing non-scientific knowledges. For Smart there are very close parallels between this process and the process by which law has a claim to power, setting itself apart from other discourses in the same way that science does. It has a claim to truth that is grounded in the ideal of law – society operates as if the legal system does dispense justice. Law is taken to be outside the social body – it transcends it and acts upon it. Crucially, it is viewed as impartial. Law is seen as a 'unified discipline' that responds only to its own 'internal logic', and the more this idea is reinforced the more powerful the law becomes. The fact that the evolution of law in relation to 'progressive' reforms has come through political struggle is denied – law is again presented as being above and beyond the social and political order. Its power is not confined to the courtroom, it has the ability to make claims about other areas of social life, and the legitimacy law claims within the field of law extends to every issue in social life.

Phallocentric culture

From a feminist standpoint law needs to be understood as a site of struggle and not simply as a tool. Understanding law's response to women and to feminist challenges requires an understanding of the idea of phallocentrism – basically a culture which meets masculine 'needs'. This concept helps us understand how patriarchy is 'part of women's (and men's) unconscious rather than a superficial system imposed from outside' (Smart, 1995: 78). It helps to construct subjectivities and meanings within a phallocentric culture. Smart argues that law constructs ideas of maleness and femaleness, and contributes to long-held commonsense understandings of sexual difference between men and women. In a phallocentric culture, sexuality is always assumed to be heterosexuality. Law constructs the category of woman; it constantly (re)produces the sexed body which can rarely be escaped. As such it reproduces the notions of women as sexualized and subjugated and men as powerful and 'straightforward', which impacts on the shaping, expressing and maintaining of power relations. Law, therefore, has the power to dictate social and moral discourse; it is a central legitimating and ordering mechanism, which encroaches on everyday life.

Setting the parameters

Smart argues that law also sets and re-sets the parameters within which rape is dealt with more generally in society; it reflects cultural values about female sexuality but goes beyond simply re-producing these norms. Within law, the heterosexual couple is presented as devoid of history: power relations and possessive relations are omitted. Women are constructed as 'either selfish and unloving, or that their libido deteriorates, hence demonstrating the problematic nature of female sexuality (which contrasts with the virile straightforwardness of male sexuality)' (Smart, 1989: 29). Men are constructed as sexually virile but potentially vulnerable to women's sly and vindictive sexuality. In a rape trial, rape is treated as an isolated event; any context (apart from the sexual history of the victim!) is removed. Smart is attempting to show that law reflects but also produces cultural values and norms about female (and male) sexuality. Thus, whilst it sets itself up as being objective, it in fact represents the interests of men (see Connell, 1994, quoted in Ballinger, 2009: 23). Victim-blaming views are hegemonic – the current law reinforces this – and are 'expressed by lawyers and judges (Temkin and Krahe, 2008). The law, of course, shapes who can rape and who can be raped. In England and Wales, for instance, rape in marriage was not a crime until 1991, and men could not legally be victims of rape until 1994. As a result, the voices of those men who have been raped by other men have gone unheard for too long (Javaid, 2018). Women still cannot legally be considered as rapists; only the penis is viewed as a weapon capable of rape – this has a significant impact on those men and boys who are sexually assaulted by women. Smart's work therefore goes someway to explain why, whilst more people are perhaps willing to report rape, conviction rates in many countries are falling. Many cases, around eighty percent, are lost at the investigation stage, but even for those that do find their way into the courtroom, a successful result is not guaranteed (Kelly, 2016).

A continuum of sexual violence

Many of the issues raised by rape, are also relevant for other forms of sexual violence, some of which will be discussed briefly below. Liz Kelly (1987) argued that it was important for us to recognize that these various forms of violence are connected. This concept, which emerged from her PhD research, has since been used by many researchers and academics around the world. Her original (1987) formulation of the 'continuum concept' was based on two dictionary definitions:

- 'a basic common character that underlies many different events';
- 'a continuous series of elements or events that pass into one another and cannot be readily distinguished'.

The first definition, that the many forms of intimate intrusion, coercion, abuse and assault were connected, has perhaps been the definition most often used subsequently. The second definition, that the categories used to name and distinguish forms of violence, whether in research, law or policy, shade into and out of one another, has arguably been less understood and/or used. However, as Kelly points out, this second meaning 'remains a challenge at both the level of women's experience – that they may name the similar experiences differently – and with respect to legal reform' (Kelly, 1987: xviii). Legal practice, and some research, has a tendency to treat violent events as distinct and separate, but Kelly emphasized the importance of recognizing the commonalities across a range of harms. Rape, domestic violence and sexual harassment may all be used to constrain and limit the lives of women and children. They are a means by which men gain social power. Kelly was also quick to assert that a spectrum or continuum of violence is not meant to be used to form a hierarchy of harm. The consequences and meanings of violence, such as feelings of shame or impacts on careers and status, are, she argues, remarkably consistent across the continuum.

Discussion point

Joined-up thinking

Before we progress through the chapter, it might be useful to read more about Kelly's concept of a violence continuum, and then consider the ways in which the various forms of violence and abuse discussed here can be understood as being on a continuum.

- What is the impact of seeing the connections between the many different forms of abuse?
- Why do you think we might not be encouraged to view sexual violence in this way?
- Kelly focused on violence in the lives of girls and women, but do you think her concept could be a useful tool for thinking about sexual violence aimed at men and boys?

Sexual assault on campus

In recent years, there has been a considerable amount of research investigating the issue of sexual assault on university campuses. Research conducted online suggested that over half of students at UK universities, for instance, have experienced some form of sexual assault or unwanted sexual advances, although a small proportion of those had reported it; the vast majority of victims were women (Brook and Dig-In, 2019). Equally worrying, was the fact that many of the victims did not realize that what they had experienced constituted assault. Experiences of sexual assault on campus reflect findings from The Everyday Sexism project in the UK, which began in 2012 and received a variety of posts about the problem. This has led to academic analyses of so-called 'lad culture' on campus, the sexual pursuit of freshers, which one institution named 'seal clubbing'. This led the National Union of Students (NUS) to commission a report, *That's What She Said*, into this problem (Phipps and Young, 2012). The concept 'lad culture' referred to a particular group mentality, characterized by heavy consumption of alcohol and sporting activities, which featured sexist and homophobic 'banter'. Many have linked this to earlier feminist accounts of rape culture, a culture which normalizes violence against women, viewing it as inevitable and 'natural' – male sexuality is active, competitive and aggressive and female sexuality is passive – and which tends to blame the victim (Suarez and Gadalla, 2010). Such cultures subscribe to a variety of rape myths, as outlined above, and are indicative of Smart's phallocentric culture which constructs particular ideas about women's sexuality and serves to disqualify them, perpetuating ideas about men's natural and powerful sex drive and women as untrustworthy and sly. Documentaries, such as *The Hunting Ground* (Dick, 2015), which included a public service video by Lady Gaga to accompany a song the documentary used, highlighted the problem on US college campuses, with a particular focus on the problem of sports cultures. Arguably, the documentary, in addition to an open letter signed by many prominent figures, led to new legislation, referred to as 'Enough is Enough', to help combat the problem on New York campuses. There have been some interesting studies which suggest such cultures are hidden by higher education institutions in order to remain competitive in education's neoliberal market culture (see Phipps and Young, 2014). Nevertheless, in the UK too, there have been attempts to combat 'lad' culture and sexual assault through Student Union (SU) campaigns such as *I Heart Consent* and education about consent. Many have argued, however, that rapists are quite clear on what consent is – they just don't care.

Pornography

Placing pornography in a chapter on sexual violence, is a contentious decision and one you might want to resist. Porn, both its message and its impact on men and women, has been a concern of feminists for decades, and there has been a resurgence of interest in pornography in recent years. In part, this can be explained by what has been described by Linda Williams (2004) as a mainstreaming of pornography. While Hollywood makes approximately 400 films a year, Williams points out that 'the porn industry makes ten to eleven thousand a year and there are 700 million porn rentals annually. Yearly pornography revenues – which in one estimation include magazines, websites, cable, in-room hotel movies, and sex toys – total between $10 to $50 billion' (2004: 74). Advances in technology mean that soft and hard-core pornography can be accessed more easily via a variety of platforms. Karen Boyle (2010) has also highlighted the ways in which mainstream film, television and reality TV have borrowed from pornography, thus society has become increasingly sexualized and pornified (Paasonen, 2016).

One complexity is that pornography is difficult to define, for some it refers to hardcore imagery, for others it is simply signposted by nudity. Most pornography portrays heterosexual dynamics and is consumed mainly by men. Many feminists have focused on pornography because they view it as a source of degradation for women, contributing to their position in society by perpetuating images of violence and domination (Dines, 1998; MacKinnon, 1993). Other feminists have downplayed the levels of violence against women portrayed in pornography (McKee et al., 2008; Rubin, 1993), arguing there is less than in previous decades. It should perhaps be noted, however, that academics such as McKee, when mapping out the violence in pornography, argued that BDSM didn't count as there was 'no intent to harm', and if the actors seemed to be enjoying whatever was being done to them, that didn't count either. One could argue that a significant aspect is missed from such a view, i.e. that even if these individual performers were actually enjoying what was being done to them, the issue is one of representation (arguments which have been made in relation to lap dancing and prostitution as well) – women are being portrayed as enjoying and asking for humiliation and abuse and we have to consider the wider social impact of such a message. Dworkin (1994), for instance, has stated that this is one of the places where we learn that, in relation to women, 'no' means 'yes' (see the discussion on rape). Perhaps not surprisingly, other recent research, such as Meagan Tyler's (2010) work, has revealed that levels of violence in pornography remain consistently high, and that the majority of this violence is directed at women. The pornography industry has acknowledged that sexually violent content has become both more common and popular with consumers of porn, and that performers are increasingly being pushed to their physical and emotional limits (Ramone and Kernes, 2003). Annette Ballinger argues that if society repeatedly sees sex as synonymous with subordination, it fosters an understanding 'in which the putting-down of women, and ultimately, the brutalization of women, is what sex is taken to be' (cited in Power, 2009: 47).

Others have paid attention to shifts in the porn industry, including porn produced by women, for their visual pleasure. Bakehorn (2010), for instance, has highlighted how feminist porn encourages collaborations across lesbian, bisexual, trans and straight porn. There is also an argument that porn provides an opportunity for sexual validation for many women and sex information. Sex instructive porn, created by Nina Hartley, for instance, as been cited by Heffernan (2013) as facilitating greater sex knowledge for the viewers. Similar debates are to be found regarding gay porn. Some have argued that it is democratic and an important part of gay culture (Stein et al., 2012). Others suggest that it reasserts racist and heteronormative stereotypes and has a negative impact on men's body image (Morrison, 2004). Perhaps it is more useful to think about a continuum of pornography from the harmful to the empowering.

Prostitution

> The images so often portrayed in pornographic films not surprisingly impact on those sex workers who sell sex. As one sex worker (Angela) noted when interviewed by Anette Ballinger 'What was extreme five years ago is commonplace now. I get enquiries about being tied up, being gagged, they want to tie you up, they want threesomes ... Basically, you've consented to being raped ... for money'. (cited in Walter, 2010: 61)

The notion of violence against sex workers is not new, and indeed, in many ways, is familiar and expected – from Jack the Ripper to the five women murdered in Ipswich in 2006, the murdered prostitute has become something of a cultural trope. Yet arguably we haven't been encouraged to be outraged by such violence. Police attitudes to the women murdered by Peter Sutcliffe in the 1980s, who were either believed to be, or were, sex workers, shows us the ways in which sex workers have historically been understood as being undeserving victims, culpable for the violence which happens to them. It was only when Sutcliffe killed women the police described as 'innocent' victims, that the murders were taken seriously (Boyle, 2005). A key issue is that female sex workers are seen to be challenging rigid constructions of female sexuality (see the discussion of Smart earlier in this chapter). As such, their status as sex worker overrides their identity as sister, mother, worker etc. (O'Neill, 2008). Phoenix (2012) also adds that prostitution blurs rigid (and also false) distinctions between the private (sex) and the public (economics). From a radical feminist perspective, prostitution per se should be seen as a form of violence against women: as Dworkin has argued 'when men use women in prostitution, they are expressing a pure hatred for the female body' (1997 [1987]: 145).

229

Others, such as Sanders (2016), argue that sex work is not inherently violent, but that violence results from the interplay between factors such as the stigma of prostitution and the spaces in which it takes place. It is only in recent years however, again as a result of feminist campaigning, that society is perhaps ready to see prostitutes as potential victims of violence deserving of our sympathy (Richardson and May, 1999). Research shows that prostitutes are subject to exploitation, intimidation, assault, and harassment. Hart and Barnard's (2003) study, for instance, showed the ways in which violence is an ever-present threat in the lives of sex workers. Lowman (2000) has also highlighted the stark levels of violence that trans sex workers in particular experience.

Prostitution is currently subject to intense debate about the best ways to reduce the violence experienced by its workers. Some, such as organizations like Amnesty International, argue that decriminalization would reduce violence against the women who 'choose' to make money this way. However many, like Julie Bindel (2017), argue that that choice is more often than not a coerced choice, and that it would be better instead to shift the target of crime to the people who pay for sex, rather than the sex workers themselves (this in turn raises bigger questions about whether, if one can argue that some sex workers are coerced into the industry, every sexual encounter should be considered rape; see Group Sisterhood; 1998; Lloyd, 2011; Shrage, 1994). In fact, there is evidence to suggest that decriminalization leads to greater violence against women; legal mega-brothels, as depicted in a Channel Four documentary, for instance, offer their workers no contract, no security, but rather offer the clients license to do whatever they want with no fear of recrimination. However, it should be noted that many have argued that a focus on the vulnerability of sex workers has led to their further marginalization and stigmatization, with street sex workers in particular being brought further into the criminal justice system under the auspices of 'protection' (Carline, 2011). We should also not forget that men can be sex workers too and that they are vulnerable to the sexual double standard so often levelled at women (Marks and Fraley, 2006). Society is more likely to view a male escort positively because he is seen to be conforming to sexual norms; such a view means we are less likely to recognize the vulnerabilities and harms that many face (Baral et al., 2015; Spotose, 2013).

Lap dancing

Strip and lap dancing clubs are a familiar sight in cities across Europe, the UK and US. There has been a proliferation of so-called gentlemen's clubs in recent years – For Your Eyes Only, Wiggle, and Platinum Lace in the UK, to name but a few. However, the Scottish government has recently argued that lap dancing should be seen as an act of violence against women. In 2018, Holyrood passed legislation which means that councils can ban lap dancing and strip clubs. This follows decades of feminist campaigning along these lines. So, just what is it about this form of 'adult entertainment' that means it can be seen as an act of violence?

Many have argued that (mainly) men paying to watch (mainly) women strip, adds to the stereotype of women and girls being sex objects, there to meet the needs of men. When men strip, arguably there is a still a performance of hegemonic masculine sexuality; male strippers are subjects rather than objects (Scull, 2013). When women strip, their bodies effectively become commodities in such exchanges, and the spaces where they strip, serve to confirm ideas about masculine power and domination and women's lower social value (Banyard, 2010). To add to this, the conditions they work in and the poor pay they receive can themselves be viewed as a form of violence (Sanders and Hardy, 2012). These views have been countered by some, who suggest that lap dancing should be seen as something which can be both empowering and enjoyable, as well as potentially lucrative, for the women who do this work (see Colosi, 2010; Liepe-Levinson, 2002). Recent research has however revealed the extent to which women who work in the industry experience violence and abuse from the men who frequent the sexual entertainment venues (SEVs) (Bindel, 2004; Holsopple, 1998). Barton (2007), for instance, documented the 'toll' stripping took on dancers, which included having to fend off unwanted verbal and physical attention.

Of course, SEVs don't exist in vacuums and are part of a wider community. Therefore, it is argued, the ways in which the objectification of women is normalized within these spaces inevitably spill over onto the surrounding streets. Jackie Patiniotis and Kay Standing (2012) are among a number of scholars who have also argued that lap dancing clubs impact more widely by affecting women's sense of safety in public spaces, with women actively avoiding certain streets and areas due to fear of abuse. However, Hubbard and Colosi (2015) argue that something else might be at play; it may also be that women's aversion to such areas is related to feelings of disgust rather than fear. They argue that such spaces become seen as repositories for potential contamination. In part, women's and men's reaction to such spaces is formed by a devaluation of working-class cultures and identities. Nevertheless, in 2009, local authorities in England and Wales were given greater control over the licensing of SEVs. As a result, some local councils have refused permission, whereas in other areas, often larger urban city centres, there can be a greater proliferation of such clubs. One body of research by the Lilith project which looked at areas of London, found that there was a fifty percent increase in rapes and sexual assaults in areas near such clubs, more violence against local prostitutes, and an increase in perceptions of danger for women in the area (Eden, 2007). What is so often missing from these debates, however, are the voices of the women who work in these industries. In 2019, the dancers at the Spearmint Rhino club in Sheffield, UK, campaigned for their place of work to remain open, despite campaigns from local feminists for it to be closed down. In this instance, the workers were successful and the club kept its licence.

We also need to ask ourselves whether the issue of men who strip for men, or women, and women who strip for women should also be considered exploitative (Pilcher, 2008). Do women watching men strip, challenge the male gaze by subjecting men to a female gaze? Does society imbue the male stripper with the same levels of shame and disgust it confers on women?

Discussion point

Pole position?

The legally binding United Nations Convention to Eliminate Discrimination Against Women (CEDAW) has made a link between the objectification of women and discrimination and violence towards women.

- Read some of the literature referenced above. How strong is the argument that SEVs contribute to violence against women and girls in society?
- In what ways might Kelly's notion of a Continuum of Violence be relevant in thinking through potential links between rape, pornography and SEVs?

Homophobic and transphobic violence

Whilst LGBT+ people have long been depicted as objects of fear and hate (see Duggan, 2000), more recently, we have been able to recognize that they are subjects of fear (Moran et al., 2003). Victim surveys reveal that homophobic violence is an everyday occurrence for many LGBT+ people. Indeed, in recent years, it is argued that hate crime against gay men and lesbians has doubled, and trebled against trans people. In part, this might be explained by greater awareness that verbal and physical abuse constitutes a hate crime or incident which can now not only be reported to the police but which will also be taken seriously. However, many have argued that, since the Brexit referendum, there has been a sharp rise in racist and homophobic attacks in Britain. High-profile cases, such as the lesbian couple who were beaten for refusing to kiss on a London bus in 2019, have drawn attention to the levels of homophobic and transphobic violence in the UK and elsewhere. In 2018, 28 transgender people were killed in the US, over half of whom were black trans women.

In addition to the homophobic violence experienced by the adult LGBT+ community, we are increasingly aware of the ways in which school students are often vulnerable to a range of violent acts. Young LGBT+ girls are twice as likely to be touched sexually in an unwanted way and are four times as likely to experience sexual harassment according to Human Rights Watch (2001). Christine Pettett (2007) documented that US LGBT+ students have their clothing torn, are spat on, hit by broken bottles, slammed into lockers, cut, or dragged down stairwells. She argues that the derogatory LGBT+ terms that she heard in schools, often directed at heterosexual students too, and the violence young LGBT+ students experience, lead to them being further ostracized, and stripped of their agency and identity. The NMHA (National Mental Health Association) reports that a third of LGB students are physically harassed due to their sexual orientation, and for one in six it is severe enough to require medical attention. Pettett argues that this increases rates of depression, suicidal thoughts (and actions), and is also linked to poor attendance in school and poorer academic performance.

Meanwhile, in 2019 in the UK, as a result of pressure from various groups such as Level Up, the government agreed to introduce a non-optional Sex and Relationships education programme that will integrate LGBT+ issues. This is an historic victory, as the education programme is intended to work throughout the curriculum, for all genders and sexualities. In the words of campaigners, 'now young people in England will be taught pride, not shame' (Level Up, 2019).

Discussion point

- How might transphobia and/or homophobia affect a member of the LGBT+ community's decision about whether or not to report a sexual assault? Discuss.

However, and perhaps predictably, there has been a backlash against these plans by some more socially-conservative organizations and individuals – much of this opposition comes from various religious groups, some of which have been as accused of spreading hate and homophobia.

Summary: uncertain times

Force is all right to employ, and women like you to use it;

What they enjoy they pretend they were unwilling to give.

One who is overcome, and suddenly, forcefully taken,

Welcomes the wanton assault, takes it as proof of her charm.

But if you let her go untouched when you could have compelled her,

Though she pretends to be glad, she will be gloomy at heart.

(Ovid, *Ars Amatoria*)

That we live in violent times, is undisputed. Decades of research into sexual violence has established it as a significant social problem in many arenas – sport, war, homes, schools, prisons, the street – and the same research has also enabled societies to hear the voices of those whose stories of abuse and suffering had fallen on deaf ears for too long. A broadening of perspectives has meant that women, men, children and LGBT+ people have been included in the analysis in a range of contexts. Conceptual frameworks for understanding violence and sexuality have provided possibilities for change and hope. The examples outlined above indicate that male sexual violence against women is the result of social and cultural processes, not unalterable, problematic biology. Arguably, society is more able to hear the voices of those who have experienced abuse. Consequently, some powerful men have had to stand trial and subsequently faced punishment as a result of their abuse of (mostly) women. Nevertheless, a key theme in much theorizing on violence is its relationship to power and domination, and in particular, the continued use of violence by men against women. Violence in this sense can be understood as part of everyday life, happening in recurring ways as part of gendered social relations. This chapter has only just begun to touch on the many forms of sexual violence which exist (and there are many more which we have not been able to consider – rape as a weapon of war, sexual assault in prisons, sexual harassment in the workplace, sexual abuse of children – or which will be looked at elsewhere – domestic abuse, sex trafficking, upskirting, revenge porn). Many working in the field see storm clouds looming on the horizon. We haven't, it would seem, managed to move far beyond Ovid's misogynistic rendering of sexual relations between men and women. The rise of far-right politics in Europe, the success of Donald Trump despite allegations of sexual misconduct in the US, and the ongoing question mark over Brexit in the UK, all raise uncomfortable questions about the future for tackling sexual violence.

234

> ## Key questions
>
> - Who has the power to say what 'counts' as violence?
> - In what ways can we see violence, as well as sexuality, as a principle organizing structure in society?
> - How are we to successfully combat such violence?

FURTHER READING

It would be useful for any student of violence and sexualities to have a look at Liz Kelly's 'continuum of violence' as set out in *Surviving Sexual Violence* (Polity, 1988). Then they could read Jo Phoenix's critique of Kelly's concept, 'Violence and prostitution: beyond the notion of a "continuum of sexual violence"' (chapter in Brown and Walklate (eds), *Handbook on Sexual Violence*, Routledge, 2012).

Carol Smart's work on the law and its response to sexual violence is still very relevant and also offers students the chance to compare the approaches of other key social institutions. *Feminism and the Power of Law* (Routledge, 1989) is a good place to start.

There's also a growing body of research into sexual assault on campus, which may interest students studying sexualities at university. A valuable addition to the field is *Gender Based Violence in University Communities: Policy, Prevention and Educational Initiatives*, edited by Sundari Anitha and Ruth Lewis (Policy, 2018).

Martha Nussbaum's development of Sen's capability approach, is also worth looking at. Framed around human rights, she argues that bodily integrity, including freedom from sexual violence, is central to justice, dignity and equality. See *Creating Capabilities: The Human Development Approach* (Harvard UP, 2011).

CONCLUSION

From the sexual norms of the Ancient Greeks and Romans, early Christian values to the Enlightenment period and beyond, we can trace ways of thinking about sex and sexuality which are still with us today. There remain strong messages which construct sex as sin, as dangerous and harmful, as something which needs to be regulated and restricted. At the same time, we are told sex is pleasure, is freedom, is liberating, is a basic human right. These tensions – between repression and liberation, pleasure and danger, right and wrong, normal and unnatural, nature or nurture – may wax and wane over time but they are never far away.

We can take Kimberlé Crenshaw's (1989) concept of intersectionality and look at the ways in which sexuality can be considered in relation to gender, age, class, ethnicity, (dis)ability and religion – all of these cross-cutting aspects of our identities impacting on how we understand, respond to and experience sexuality. These differences are not just connected to present-day societies but are often also rooted in various historical pasts. Although sexuality is closely associated with biological and mental processes, it is essentially a phenomenon constructed by the cultural forms and social relations existing at various historical periods. Since the mid-twentieth century, there have been many studies focusing on topics related to sex and gender: pre-Christian and non-Christian moral codes; marriage and the family; women's bodies and health; sexual violence; the evolution of sexual identities; prostitution; and oppositional sexualities. Such sociological and anthropological studies have shown that there is a vast range of sexualities – not just in present-day western societies, but also in other cultures and in other historical periods. The existence of so many different sexualities, both past and present, not only shows that uniformity is not the norm, but also demonstrates that these different sexualities are often related to specific historical periods.

A key aim of this book has been to encourage you to approach a range of issues about sexuality in a critical way by adopting this social constructionist approach. It may be that the idea of a socially constructed sexuality was a novel one for you, and if that was the case, I hope your engagement with this notion has been exciting and challenging. Nothing to do with sexuality is 'normal', and all sexualities, both normative and transgressive, should be open to scrutiny. If this was a concept you were already familiar with, then hopefully this book has strengthened your existing knowledge and provided you with opportunities to think through some of its tensions and limitations.

Another aim has been to encourage you to think of sexuality as an issue for everyone; hopefully the various chapters have enabled you to recognize some of the complexities that people may face when trying to express their sexuality. Whilst much of the scholarship on sexuality has come from those with a vested interest in improving conditions and attitudes, feminists, lesbian and gay and more recently trans scholars, the result has been a focus on sexuality across the spectrum. The thirteen chapters, of which you may have read selected ones, or all of them, in the order presented, were designed to point you in as many different directions as possible, so as to allow you to develop your own ideas and to make your own connections between different issues. The main body of material in the book does raise a series of connected questions. What are the understandings of sexuality as experienced by groups of people across the globe, over time? In what ways can we see sexuality as a central organizing principle in society? Can we see heterosexual hegemony being challenged? Indeed, are we becoming more aware of a range of heterosexual ways of being which question the dominant, 'traditional' expression of heterosexuality? Conversely, are we seeing a normalizing of LGBT+ identities? As a result, are we nearing a time when we can do away with labels altogether and move back to a time when sexuality was something we 'did' rather than an identifying marker? What are the key inequalities of sexualities people are facing across the globe today? Can we predict future problems and tensions? By now, you will have already asked yourself at least some of these questions. A book like this cannot attempt to answer them, but hopefully it has given you some useful approaches to the problems.

We live in a time of shifting attitudes and must never be complacent. Sexuality is still deemed so significant or threatening as to be a cause for persecution across the globe – North and South – and in the time it has taken you to read this book, several people will have lost their lives, simply because of their sexual identity. But we must take heart from the fact that while society has always had difficulty in regulating sexuality, collectively, people have effectively challenged and changed the status quo.

At the start of this book, I asked you to write down a few ideas about what sexuality is and how it is shaped. I hope that reading it has broadened how you think about sexuality and perhaps it has answered a few questions, or even better, has prompted you to ask a few more.

This book has given you a very brief and partial overview of the field of sexualities studies. To gain a fuller understanding, I would encourage you to continue your exploration of this fascinating area – explore the suggested readings, talk to friends, quiz your tutors, examine your own attitudes.

Above all, keep thinking about sex and sexuality!

GLOSSARY

Ageism   Set of discriminatory beliefs and stereotypes stemming from the ageing process.

Agency   Self-determination or free will. The capacity social actors have to engage in their social world.

AIDS   AIDS, or acquired immune deficiency syndrome, refers to the infection(s) which attack someone with an immune system weakened by HIV. Recent drug treatments used in the west have meant that HIV is now seen as a chronic, rather than acute, condition.

Asexual   Someone who is not sexually attracted to men or women. It does not necessarily mean they do not experience romantic or aesthetic attraction, sexual arousal or that they do not want intimacy in their relationships. As such, asexual people can have heterosexual or same-sex preferences.

BDSM   Bondage, Domination, Sadism and Masochism. Sometimes referred to as S/M or S&M.

Binary tendency   To describe people in terms of two mutually exclusive categories which are presumed to be opposites, though these are socially constructed. Binary ideology is usually hierarchical, with one category having more power and privilege than the other, e.g. man/woman, black/white, heterosexual/homosexual etc.

Bisexual   A person sexually and/or emotionally attracted to both men and women.

Biphobia   The discrimination and oppression experienced by people who identify as bisexual.

Butch   An identity that draws from traditional ideas of masculinity. Often used to denote 'masculine' lesbian women.

Celibacy   The state of abstaining from sexual intimacy.

Cis(gender)   Someone whose gender identity is assumed to match their ascribed sex. Non-trans.

Citizenship   The legal status conferred on groups and individuals by a state, such as the right to vote. It also relates to relative degrees of agency in everyday life. Sexual citizenship can refer to the access of particular rights for particulate social groups based on sexuality.

Civilized body   Concept developed by Norbert Elias. Relates to the historical and cultural processes whereby bodies are subject to increasing restraints.

Coercion   Being made to do something through use of threat or intimidation. Sexual coercion is related to the issue of consent in that if sex occurs due to coercion, consent has not been given.

Coming out   The process of identifying and acknowledging oneself as lesbian, gay, bisexual or trans and disclosing this to others. The phrase is a metaphor, coming out of 'the closet', a political and personal journey from inside to outside, from (assumed) shame to pride. Coming out as anything other than heterosexual is necessary because of societal assumptions of heterosexuality.

Commodification   The process whereby something that previously did not have a monetary value becomes a commodity and is measured by its economic value.

Discourse Ways of describing and thinking about the world, a framework that provides a particular perspective and governs the way something is discussed or understood.

Discrimination   Behaving in a way that treats people unequally. Often this is based on ethnicity, gender, age, sexuality.

Drag   Exaggerated and theatrical performance of gender, often used to describe cross-dressing, i.e Drag Queen/Drag King.

Emancipatory research   Seeks to free or empower the subjects of research. Knowledge is produced with the intention of helping the disadvantaged.

Embodiment   The experience of living with the physical body and the meanings and values we attach to our bodies.

Enlightenment, the   A European intellectual movement of the eighteenth century, which challenged explanations of the world that relied on religion or superstition. Enlightenment thought was based on the principles of rationality and science.

Epistemology   The philosophy of knowledge – how do we 'know' what we know and do we actually 'know' anything. A consideration of social 'facts' versus social construction.

Equality   A state of individuals and groups being treated fairly in terms of things like legal and political rights, social status and pay. It does not mean treating everyone the same, rather it refers to access to the same standard of treatment, which may differ depending on need.

Essentialism The view that groups share certain traits and behaviours due to natural/biological attributes.

Femme An identity that draws from traditional ideas of femininity. Often used to denote 'feminine' lesbians.

Gay An acronym for 'Good As You'. Whilst this can refer to women who are attracted to other women, it is more often used to denote men attracted to other men.

Gender The socially and culturally produced characteristics of men and women, ideas of masculinity and femininity, which become the norms or 'rules' of behaviour: these vary between cultures and over time.

Globalization The increasing interconnectedness and interdependence of societies across the world, especially in relation to trade, industry, communications and culture.

Global north/south Relational terms which, rather than referring to geographical location per se, reflect historical and contemporary unequal power relations. There is a danger that these are used in such a way as to construct a reductive binary of the north (west) and the south (everywhere else).

Heteronormativity A system which promotes heterosexuality as the only 'natural' and normal sexuality, which presumes heterosexuality and uses a strict gender binary. Certain types of heterosexuality are privileged along lines of class, ethnicity, relationship status.

Heterosexism A system of beliefs which assume everyone is heterosexual. It also assumes that heterosexuality is superior.

Heterosexual Someone attracted to people of the opposite sex.

HIV HIV stands for human immunodeficiency virus, a retrovirus which infects and destroys the immune system, thus someone with HIV has reduced protection against infections and cancer. The disease can be transmitted in a variety of ways but the greatest risk is when semen is deposited in an anus or vagina.

Homonormativity Normativity and privilege among sexual minorities (especially gay men and lesbians) via the 'race', class, and gender systems inherent to heteronormativity.

Homophobia The oppression and discrimination experienced by LGBT people. Often, this is used to refer to acts of violence such as hate crime.

Homosexual A dated, medicalized term used to describe someone attracted to the same sex, usually used in relation to gay men. It is offensive because of its history.

Ideology   Framework of thought/ideas that is used in any given society to give meaning to the social world; it provides a viewpoint or set of beliefs. Often used to denote the way in which ideologies obscure or justify inequalities.

Intersectionality   Coined by Kimberlé Crenshaw, a theory which describes the ways people can experience multiple oppressions and discriminations (originally racism, sexism and classism but including ageism, homophobia etc.).

Intersex   A term used to denote those people whose sexual or reproductive anatomy does not appear to fit the standard definitions for male or female.

Lesbian   A woman attracted to other women.

LGBT+   Acronym used to denote sexual and gender minorities. L-lesbian, G-gay, B-bisexual, T-transgender. Often includes Q-queer and/or questioning, I-intersex, and other initials.

Life course   A way of conceptualizing the passage of life that includes a consideration of the typical culturally constructed circumstances they are likely to experience as they age.

Masochism   To experience sexual pleasure from being humiliated or receiving pain. Along with sadism, this was 'named' and pathologized by Krafft-Ebing.

Metropole   A colonial or imperial power, sometimes the capital city of said power.

Neoliberalism   'New' liberalism. Economic, social and political approach valuing free trade, competition and individualism. It promotes privatization of public assets and dislikes trade unions.

Non-binary   People who do not identify with the rigid categories of male or female. They may reject the identities or fluctuate between them. Some non-binary people identify as genderqueer.

Objectification   The reduction of a person to something with no agency, thought or feeling – in other words, they become an object in the eyes of the viewer. This often impacts on women, who are reduced to objects for sexual pleasure.

Ontology   The philosophical study of the nature of being. Can we talk about an objective reality?

Pansexual   Attracted to others regardless of their gender identity.

Paradigm   A distinct way of thinking; a systematic set of concepts or thought patterns.

Patriarchy   Originally an anthropological term for male-headed family or tribe. Feminists use it to describe a social system of male domination over women that operates both privately and publicly.

Phallocentric   A culture, society or institution structured to meet the needs of the phallus. The penis becomes a symbol of masculine power.

Polyamory   Having more than one sexual/emotional relationship at one time, with the consent of all involved.

Polymorphous   By this, Freud meant human sex drives in infancy – before the family (and society) had imposed an 'order' upon them – were bisexual or, more accurately, of neither sex. As children grew up, their infant pleasures became increasingly ordered and, eventually, prepared the way for female and male development to diverge.

Power   The capacity of groups and individuals to ensure their wishes are realized, or their point of view prevails.

Prejudice   Negative attitude toward someone from a different social group (ethnicity, gender, age, class, disability, sexuality etc.) based on perceived, usually false, characteristics.

Qualitative method   Generation or collection of non-numerical data – beliefs, attitudes, experiences – to understand a social phenomenon. Sometimes considered less 'scientific' and more discursive. Particularly useful if little is known about an issue.

Quantitative method   Generation or collection of numerical data – numbers, statistics – to understand a social phenomenon. Sometimes considered more 'scientific'. Useful to map the extent of an issue.

Queer   A term 'reclaimed' from its earlier discriminatory meaning. Used by many different groups and individuals as a self-defining term, in defiance of heteronormativity.

Queer Theory   Influenced by the work of Michel Foucault, this body of work challenges the heterosexual/homosexual model of sexuality. It sees identity as socially constructed and unstable. Key theorists include Judith Butler and Diana Fuss.

Reflexive   To be aware of how one's own social position may impact on research or interpretation. More broadly it is about acknowledging that our understanding of the world is part of the processes which create and reproduce that world.

Sadism   To gain sexual pleasure from causing pain or humiliation. The term originates from the French 'libertine' the Marquis de Sade who wrote about his sexual preferences in novels such as *Justine*.

Sex   One of two categories – male or female – dividing humans based on (presumed) biological differences including chromosomes, hormones and reproductive organs.

Sexism   Prejudice, stereotyping or discrimination against an individual/group because of their sex. Feminists argue that male assumption of authority over women happens in patriarchal societies.

Sexuality   Refers to beliefs, identity, desires, acts and relationships. Often simply refers to sexual attraction to others. Shaped by culture, history, politics and society.

Sexual orientation   A term used to describe the focus of someone's sexual attraction. Heterosexual, gay, bisexual and lesbian are common terms used to describe someone's sexual orientation. Sexual identity and sexual preference are also often used to mean sexual orientation.

Social constructionist   A theoretical approach which argues that the social reality we take for granted as natural or inevitable is actually socially produced, and thus may change through time or differ between cultures. Labels and identities such as 'heterosexual' and 'gay' are not universal concepts, for instance.

Trans   An inclusive term for the wider transgender, transsexual and sometimes transvestite community.

Transgender   Someone whose gender identity doesn't match the sex ascribed to them at birth and/or politically rejects society's rigid gender binary.

Transitioning   The process of undergoing alterations to physical appearance to adhere more closely to the norms associated with the gender identified with. It refers to any part, or the whole process, of changing gender – it may or may not involve surgery.

Transphobia   The discrimination and oppression experienced by trans people.

Transsexual   Someone who has undergone sex/gender reassignment using a range of medical interventions.

Transvestite   Someone who dresses in the clothes typically associated with the sex opposite to that ascribed at birth.

West, the   In the context of this book (and many other academic texts), this refers not to a geographical location but denotes a Eurocentric world and way of thinking.

REFERENCES

ACE (2002) *Opening doors … to the needs of older lesbians, gay men and bisexuals: Report of the one-day conference held in London April 2002.* London: Age Concern England.

Ackard, D., Kearney-Cooke, A. and Peterson, C. (2000) 'Effect of body image and self-image on women's sexual behaviors', *International Journal of Eating Disorders*, 28 (4): 422–29.

Acton, W. (2013 [1871]) *The Functions and Disorders of the Reproductive Organs in Childhood, Youth, Adult Age, and Advanced Life.* London: Forgotten Books.

Adam, B., Duyvendak, J.W. and Krouwel, A. (eds) (1999) *The Global Emergence of Gay and Lesbian Politics: National Imprints of a Worldwide Movement.* Philadelphia: Temple University Press.

Adams, C.J. (1990) *The Sexual Politics of Meat.* London: Bloomsbury Press.

Adelman, M. (1991) 'Stigma, gay lifestyles and adjustment to aging: a study of later-life gay men and lesbians', *Journal of Homosexuality*, 20 (3–4): 7–32.

Adur, S. and Jha, S. (2018) '(Re)centering street harassment – an appraisal of safe cities global initiative in Delhi, India', *Journal of Gender Studies*, 27 (1): 114–24.

AFSC (American Friends Services Committee) (2002) 'AFSC Hawai'i Gay Liberation Program: Activist Materials Addressing Tourism', *GLQ: A Journal of Lesbian and Gay Studies*, 8 (1–2): 207–26.

Age Concern (2007) *UK Inquiry into Mental Health and in Later Life, Improving Services and Support for Older People with Mental Health Problems: the second report from the UK Inquiry into mental health and well-being in later life.* London: Age Concern England.

Airaksinen, T. (2018) 'The language of pain: A philosophical study of BDSM', *Sage Open*, https://doi.org/10.1177%2F2158244018771730

Alarie, M. and Carmichael, J. (2015) 'The "cougar" phenomenon: an examination of the factors that influence age-hypogamous sexual relationships among middle-aged women', *Journal of Marriage and Family*, 77 (5): 1250–65.

Alcoff, L. (1991) 'The problem of speaking for others', *Cultural Critique*, 20: 5–32.

Alcoff, L. (2018) *Rape and Resistance: Understanding the Complexities of Sexual Violation.* Cambridge: Polity.

Aldrich, R. (2010) *Gay Life and Culture: A World History*. London: Thames & Hudson.

Alexander, J., Chesnay, M., Marshall, E., Campbell, A., Johnson, S. and Wright, R. (1989) 'Research note: parallel reactions in rape victims and rape researchers', *Violence and Victims*, 4 (1): 57–62.

Alexander, M.J. (2003) 'Not just (any) body can be a citizen: the politics of law, sexuality and postcoloniality in Trinidad and Tobago and the Bahamas', in J. Weeks, J. Holland and M. Waites (eds), *Sexualities and Society: A Reader*. Cambridge: Polity.

Alexander, M.J. and Mohanty, C.T. (eds) (1997) *Feminist Genealogies, Colonial Legacies, Democratic Failures*. New York: Routledge.

Allen, H. (1987) 'Rendering them harmless: the professional portrayal of women charged with serious violent crimes', in P. Carlen and A. Worrall (eds), *Gender, Crime and Justice*. Milton Keynes: Open University Press.

Allen, L. (2003) 'Girls want sex, boys want love: resisting dominant discourses of (hetero)sexuality', *Sexualities*, 6 (2): 215–36.

Altman, D. (1996) 'On Global Queering', *Australian Humanities Review 2*, http://australianhumanitiesreview.org/1996/07/01/on-global-queering/

Altman, D. (2001) *Global Sex*. Chicago: University of Chicago.

Anderson, E. (2011) 'Masculinities and sexualities in sport and physical cultures: Three decades of evolving research', *Journal of Homosexuality*, 58 (5): 565–78.

Anthias, F. and Yuval-Davis, N. (1992) *Racialized Boundaries: Race, Nation, Gender, Colour and Class and the Anti-racist Struggle*. London: Routledge.

APA (2007) *Report of the APA Task force on the Sexualization of Girls*. Washington, DC: American Psychological Association Taskforce.

Apostolopoulos, Y., Sönmez, S., Shattell, M., Kronenfeld, J., Smith, D. and Stanton, S. (2011) 'Cruising for truckers on highways and the Internet: Sexual networks and infection risk', *AIDS Education and Prevention*, 23: 249–66.

Appel, J. (2010) 'Sex rights for the disabled?', *Journal of Medical Ethics*, 36 (3): 152–4.

Ariès, P. (1962) *Centuries of Childhood*. New York: Vintage.

Arrizon, A. (2006) *Queering Mestizaje: Transculturation and Performance*. Ann Arbor: University of Michign Press.

Attwood, F. (2006) 'Sexed up: theorizing the sexualization of culture', *Sexualities*, 9 (1): 77–94.

Attwood, F. (2010) 'Dirty work: researching women and sexual representation', in R. Ryan-Flood and R. Gill (eds), *Secrecy and Silence in the Research Process*. London: Routledge, pp. 177–87.

245

Bacchus, L.J., Buller, A.M., Ferrari, G., Brzank, P. and Feder, G. (2016) '"It's always good to ask": a mixed methods study on the perceived role of sexual health practitioners asking gay and bisexual men about experiences of domestic violence and abuse', *Journal of Mixed Methods Research*, 12 (2): 221–43.

Badran, M. (2011) 'From Islamic feminism to a Muslim holistic feminism', *IDS Bulletin*, 42 (1): 78–87.

Bagshaw, D. and Chung, D. (2000) *Women, Men and Domestic Violence*. Department of the Prime Minister and Cabinet, University of South Australia Partnerships Against Domestic Violence. Canberra: Department of Prime Minister and Cabinet, University of South Australia.

Bailey, N. and Bramley, G. (2012) *The Poverty and Social Exclusion in the UK Survey 2012: Headline Results for Scotland*. Bristol: PSE-UK.

Baines, S., Emerson, E., Robertson, J. and Hatton, C. (2018) 'Sexual activity and sexual health among young adults with and without mild/moderate intellectual disability', *BMC Public Health*, 18 (1): 667.

Baiocco, R., Pistella, J., Salvati, M., Loverno, S. and Lucidi, L. (2018) 'Sports as a risk environment: Homophobia and bullying in a sample of gay and heterosexual men', *Journal of Gay and Lesbian Mental Health*, 22 (4): 385–411.

Baird, V. (2004) *Sex, Love and Homophobia: Lesbian, Gay, Bisexual and Transgender Lives*. London: Amnesty International.

Bakehorn, J. (2010) 'Women-made pornography', in R. Weitzer (ed.), *Sex For Sale: Prostitution, Pornography, and the Sex Industry*. London: Routledge.

Baker, P. (2002) 'Construction of gay identity via Polari in the Julian and Sandy radio sketches', *Lesbian and Gay Review*, 3 (3): 75–84.

Ballinger, A. (2009) 'Gender, power and the state: same as it ever was?', in R. Coleman, J. Sim, S. Tombs and D. Whyte (eds), *State, Power, Crime*. London: Sage.

Bamforth, N. (ed.) (2005) *Sex Rights: The Oxford Amnesty Lectures*. Oxford: Oxford University Press.

Banyard, K. (2010) *The Equality Illusion: The Truth about Women and Men Today*. London: Faber and Faber.

Baral, S., Friedman, F.R., Geibel, S., Rebe, K., Bozhinov, B., Diouf, D., Sabin, K., Holland, C., Chan, R. and Caceres, C. (2015) 'Male sex workers: practices, contexts, and vulnerabilities for HIV acquisition and transmission', *The Lancet*, 385: 260–73.

Barker, M., Gill, R. and Harvey, L. (2018) *Mediated Intimacy: Sex Advice in Media Culture*. Cambridge: Polity Press.

Barker, M., Richards, C. and Bowes-Catton, H. (2012) 'Visualizing experience: using creative research methods with members of sexual and gender communities', in C.N. Phellas (ed.), *Researching Non-Heterosexual Sexualities*. Farnham: Ashgate, pp. 57–80.

Barry, K. (1979) *Female Sexual Slavery*. New York: Prentice Hall.

Bartkowski, J., Xu, X. and Bartkowski, S. (2019) 'Mixed blessing: The beneficial and detrimental effects of religion on child development among third-graders', *Religions*, 10 (1): 37.

Bartolucci, C., Gómez-Gil, E., Salamero, M., Esteva, I., Guillamón, A., Zubiaurre, L., Molero, F. and Montejo, A. (2015) 'Sexual quality of life in gender-dysphoric adults before genital sex reassignment surgery', *Journal of Sexual Medicine*, 12 (1): 180–88.

Barton, B. (2007) 'Managing the toll of stripping: boundary setting among exotic dancers', *Journal of Contemporary Ethnography*, 36 (5): 571–96.

Batchelor, S. and Raymond, M. (2004) '"I slept with 40 boys in three months": teenage sex in the media, too much too young?', in E. Burtney and M. Duffy (eds), *Young People and Sexual Health: Individual, Social and Policy Contexts*. Basingstoke: Palgrave Macmillan.

Batchelor, S.A., Kitzinger, J. and Burtney, E. (2004) 'Representing young people's sexuality in the "youth" media', *Health Education Research*, 19 (6): 669–76.

Bates, S. (2004) *A Church at War: Anglicans and Homosexuality*. London: I.B. Tauris.

Bauer, I. (2013) 'Romance tourism or female sex tourism?', *Travel Medicine and Infectious Disease*, 12 (1): 20–8.

Bauman, Z. (1988) 'Sociology and postmodernity', *The Sociological Review*, 36 (4): 790–813.

Bauman, Z. (2013) *What Use is Sociology? Conversations with Michael Hviid Jacobsen and Keith Tester*. Cambridge: Polity.

Beck, U. (1992) *Risk Identity: Towards a New Modernity*. London: Sage.

Beck, U. (1994) 'The reinvention of politics: Towards a theory of reflexive modernization', in U. Beck, A. Giddens and S. Lash (eds), *Reflexive Modernization: Politics, Tradition and Aesthetics in the Modern Social Order*. Cambridge: Polity Press.

Beck-Gernsheim, E. (1998) 'On the way to a post-familial family: From a community of needs to elective affinities', *Theory, Culture & Society*, 15 (3–4): 53–70.

Beckmann, A. (2001) 'Deconstructing myths: the social construction of "sadomasochism" versus "subjugated knowledges" of practitioners of consensual "SM"', *Journal of Criminal Justice and Popular Culture*, 8 (2): 66–95.

Beckmann, A. (2009) *The Social Construction of Sexuality and Perversion*. Basingstoke: Palgrave Macmillan.

Benson, J., Kerr, S. and Ermer, A. (2017) 'Living apart together relationships in later life: constructing an account of relational maintenance', in C. Scott and S. Blair (eds), *Contemporary Perspectives in Family Research: Vol 11. Intimate Relationships and Social Change: The Dynamic Nature of Dating, Mating, and Coupling*. Bingley: Emerald, pp. 193–215.

Berger, J. (1972) *Ways of Seeing*. Harmondsworth: Penguin.

Berger, M. (2004) *Workable Sisterhood: The Political Journey of Stigmatized Women with HIV/AIDS*. Princeton: Princeton University Press.

Berger, M. and Guidroz, K. (eds) (2010) *The Intersectional Approach: Transforming the Academy through Race, Class, and Gender*. Chapel Hill: University of North Carolina Press.

Berger, P. and Berger, B. (1976) *Sociology: A Biographical Approach*. Harmondsworth: Penguin.

Bergmann, E.L. (2007) 'Queering transculturation', GLQ: *A Journal of Lesbian and Gay Studies*, 14 (2–3): 451–3.

Berns, N. (2001) 'Degendering the problem and gendering the blame: political discourse on women and violence', *Gender and Society*, 15 (2): 262–81.

Berry (2001) 'Asian values, family values', *Journal of Homosexuality*, 40 (3–4): 211–31.

Bhambra, G. (2007) *Rethinking Modernity: Postcolonialism and the Sociological Imagination*. London: Palgrave.

Bhambra, G. and Santos, B. de Sousa (2017) 'Introduction: global challenges for sociology', *Sociology*, 51 (1): 3–10.

Bhatt, C. (1997) *Liberation and Purity: Race, New Religious Movements and the Ethics of Postmodernity* (Race & Representation). London: Routledge.

Biale, R. (1984) *Women and Jewish Law*. New York: Schocken.

Bildtgard, T. (2000) 'The sexuality of elderly people on film – visual limitations', *Journal of Aging and Identity*, 5 (3): 169–83.

Bindel, J. (2004) 'Profitable Exploits: Lap Dancing in the UK', www.cwasu.org/publications

Bindel, J. (2017) *The Pimping of Prostitution: Abolishing the Sex Work Myth*. London: Palgrave Macmillan.

Binnie, J. (2004) *The Globalization of Sexuality*. London: Sage.

Bird, R. and Donaldson, R. (2009) '"Sex, sun, soccer": stakeholder-opinions on the sex industry in Cape Town in anticipation of the 2010 FIFA Soccer World Cup', *Urban Forum*, 20 (1): 33–46.

Blackwood, E. (2005) 'Transnational sexualities in one place – Indonesian readings', *Gender and Society*, 19 (2): 175–87.

Blaikie, A. (1999) *Ageing and Popular Culture*. Cambridge: Cambridge University Press.

Blaikie, N. (2000) *Designing Social Research*. Cambridge: Polity.

Blasius, M. (1994) *Gay and Lesbian Politics: Sexuality and the Emergence of a New Ethic*. Philadelphia: Temple University Press.

Blumenfeld, W.J. and Cooper, R.M. (2010) 'LGBT and allied youth responses to cyberbullying: policy implications', *International Journal of Critical Pedagogy*, 3 (1): 114–33.

Bockting, W., Benner, A. and Coleman, E. (2009) 'Gay and bisexual identity development among female-to-male transsexuals in North America: emergence of a transgender sexuality', *Archives of Sexual Behaviour*, 38: 688–701.

Boellstorff, T. (2006) *The Gay Archipelago: Sexuality and Nation in Indonesia.* Princeton: Princeton University Press.

Boister, N. and Cryer, R. (2008) *The Tokyo International Military Tribunal: A Reappraisal.* Oxford: Oxford University Press.

Bordo, S. (2004) *Unbearable Weight.* Berkeley: University of California Press.

Borzekowski, D.L.G. (2006) 'Adolescents' use of the Internet: a controversial, coming-of-age resource', *Adolescent Medicine Clinics*, 17 (1): 205–16.

Boswell, J. (1994) *Same-sex Unions in Premodern Europe.* New York: Random House.

Bouhdiba, A. (1985) *Sexuality in Islam.* London: Routledge.

Bouman, W.P., Arcelus, J. and Benbow, S.M. (2007) 'Nottingham Study of Sexuality and Ageing (NoSSA II). Attitudes of care staff regarding sexuality and residents: a study in residential and nursing homes', *Sexual and Relationship Therapy*, 22: 45–61.

Bourke, J. (1999) *An Intimate History of Killing: Face-to-Face Killing in Twentieth Century Warfare.* London: Granta.

Boyle, G.J., Goldman, R., Svoboda, J.S. and Fernandez, E. (2002) 'Male circumcision: Pain, trauma, and psychosexual sequelae', *Journal of Health Psychology*, 7: 329–43.

Boyle, K. (2005) *Media and Violence.* London: Sage.

Boyle, K. (2010) *Everyday Pornography.* London: Routledge.

Bragg, S. (2015) 'What about the boys? Sexualization, media and masculinities', in E. Renold, J. Ringrose and D. Egan (eds), *Children, Sexuality and Sexualization.* Basingstoke: Palgrave Macmillan.

Brandon, J. and Hafez, S. (2008) *Crimes of the Community: Honour Based Violence in the UK.* London: Centre for Social Cohesion.

Braun, V. (1999) 'Breaking a taboo? Talking (and laughing) about the vagina', *Feminism and Psychology*, 9: 367–72.

Breast Cancer Care (2011) *Lesbian and bisexual women and breast cancer.* London: Breast Cancer Care. (ESRC knowledge exchange programme, RES-192-22-0111.)

Brecher, E. (1969) *The Sex Researchers.* Boston, MA: Little, Brown.

Brennan, D.J., Souleymanov, R., George, C., Newman, P.A., Hart, T.A., Asakura, K. and Betancourt, G. (2015) 'Masculinity, muscularity, and HIV sexual risk among gay and bisexual men of color', *Psychology of Men and Masculinity*, 16 (4): 393–403.

Bridges, A.J., Wosnitzer, R., Scharrer, E., Feng Sun, C. and Liberman, R.A. (2010) 'Aggression and sexual behaviour in best-selling pornography videos: a content analysis update', *Violence Against Women*, 16 (10): 1065–85.

Brook and Dig-In (2019) 'New Research on Sexual Harassment and Violence at UK Universities', https://legacy.brook.org.uk/press-releases/sexual-violence-and-harassment-remains-rife-in-universities-according-to-ne

249

Brooten, B. (1996) *Love Between Women: Early Christian Responses to Female Homoeroticism*. Chicago: University of Chicago Press.

Browne, K. (2011) *An Introduction to Sociology*. Cambridge: Polity.

Brownmiller, S. (1975) *Against Our Will: Men, Women and Rape*. London: Secker & Warburg.

Buchanan, E.A. and Ess, C. (2008) 'Internet research ethics: the field and its critical issues', in K.E. Himma and H.T. Tavani (eds), *The Handbook of Computer and Information Ethics*. Hoboken, NJ: Wiley, pp. 273–92.

Butler, J. (1990) *Gender Trouble: Feminism and the Subversion of Identity*. New York: Routledge.

Butler, R. (1969) 'Age-ism: another form of bigotry', *The Gerontologist*, 9 (4): 243–46.

Butler, R.N. and Lewis, M.I. (1986) *Love and Sex After 40*. New York: Harper & Row.

Caldwell K. (2010) 'We exist: intersectional in/visibity in bisexuality and disability', *Disabilities Studies Quarterly*, 30 (3–4): 1273–303.

Califia, P. (1997) *Sex Changes: The Politics of Transgenderism*. San Francisco, CA: Cleis.

Callis, A. (2009) 'Playing with Butler and Foucault: bisexuality and queer theory', *Journal of Bisexuality*, 9 (3–4): 213–33.

Callis, A.S. (2014) 'Bisexual, pansexual, queer: non-binary identities and the sexual borderlands', *Sexualities*, 17 (1–2): 63–80.

Campbell, B. (1980) 'A feminist sexual politics: now you see it, now you don't', *Feminist Review*, 5: 1–18.

Campbell, B. (2013) *End of Equality: The Only Way is Women's Liberation*. London: Seagull Books.

Campbell, B., Nair, Y. and Maimane, S. (2006) 'AIDS stigma, sexual moralities and the policing of women and youth in South Africa', *Feminist Review*, 83: 132–8.

Carabine, J. (2009) 'Sexualities, personal lives and social policy', in J. Carabine (ed.), *Sexualities: Personal Lives and Social Policy*. Milton Keynes: Open University Press.

Carline, A. (2011) 'Criminal justice, extreme pornography and prostitution: protecting women or promoting morality?', *Sexualities*, 14 (3): 312–33.

Carlson, A. (2016) 'Sex, biological functions and social norms: a simple constructivist theory of sex', *Nordic Journal of Feminist and Gender Research*, 24 (1): 18–29.

Carrigan, M. (2012) 'How do you know you don't like it if you haven't tried it? Asexual agency and the sexual assumption', in T.G. Morrison, M.A. Morrison, M. Carrigan and D.T. McDermott (eds), *Sexual Minority Research in the New Millennium*. Hauppauge, NY: Nova Science.

Cauldwell, D. (2001[1950]) 'Questions and answers on the sex life and sexual problems of trans-sexuals', *International Journal of Transgenderism*, 5 (3): 1–37.

Cavanaugh, M. (2017) 'Ancient Greek Pederasty: Education or Exploitation?', https://stmuhistorymedia.org/ancient-greek-pederasty-education-or-exploitation/

Cerankowski, K. and Milks, M. (2010) 'New orientations: asexuality and its implications for theory and practice', *Feminist Studies*, 36 (3): 650–64.

Cervantes-Altamirano, E. (2013) 'Islamic feminism and the challenges of gender, sexuality and LGBTQ rights in contemporary Islam', *International Journal of Religion & Spirituality in Society*, 2 (3): 76–85.

Chakraborty, A., McManus, S., Brugha, T.S., Bebbington, P. and King, M. (2011) 'Mental health of the non-heterosexual population of England', *British Journal of Psychiatry*, 198 (2):143–8.

Charles, N., Aull Davies, C. and Harris, C. (2008) *Families in Transition: Social Change, Family Formation and Kin Relationships*. Bristol: The Policy Press.

Charter, R., Ussher, J.M., Perz, J. and Robinson, K. (2018) 'The transgender parent: experiences and constructions of pregnancy and parenthood for transgender men', *International Journal of Transgenderism*, 19 (1): 64–77.

Cixous, H. (1981) 'The laugh of the Medusa', in E. Marks and I. de Courtivron (eds), *New French Feminisms*. Brighton: Harvester.

Clark, K. (1998) 'The linguistics of blame: representations of women in The Sun's reporting of crimes of sexual violence', in D. Cameron (ed.), *The Feminist Critique of Language: A Reader*. London: Routledge.

Clarke, J. and Critcher, C. (1985) *The Devil Makes Work*. (Titles in the Crisis Points series.) London: Palgrave.

Clarke, L. and Griffin, M. (2008) 'Visible and invisible ageing: beauty work as a response to ageism', *Ageing & Society*, 28 (5): 653–74.

Clover, C. (1992) *Men, Women, and Chainsaws: Gender in the Modern Horror Film*. Princeton, NJ: Princeton University Press.

Cochrane, K. (2011) 'Standing Up to the BBC was the Right Thing To Do', *Guardian G2*, 12 January, pp. 6–9.

Cohen, C.J. (1997) *The Boundaries of Blackness: AIDS and the Breakdown of Black Politics*. Chicago: University of Chicago.

Cohen, S. (1972) *Folk Devils and Moral Panics*. St Albans: Paladin.

Collins, P.H. (2008) *Black Feminist Thought: Knowledge, Consciousness, and the Politics of Empowerment*. London: Routledge.

Colosi, R. (2010) *Dirty Dancing: An Ethnography of Lap Dancing*. London: Routledge.

Connell, R.W. (1987) *Gender and Power: Society, The Person and Sexual Politics*. Stanford: Stanford University Press.

Connell, R.W. (1994) *Masculinities*. Oxford: Blackwell.

Connell, R.W. (1995) *Masculinities*. Cambridge: Polity.

Connell, R.W. (2003) 'The big picture: masculinities in recent world history', in J. Weeks, J. Holland and M. Waites (eds), *Sexualities and Society: A Reader*. Cambridge: Polity.

Connell, R.W. (2015) 'Meeting at the edge of fear: theory on a world scale', *Feminist Theory*, 16 (1): 49–66.

Connell, R.W. and Dowsett, G.W. (1992) 'The unclean motion of the generative parts: frameworks in western thought on sexuality', in R.W. Connell and G.W. Dowsett (eds), *Rethinking Sex: Social Theory and Sexuality Research*. Melbourne: Melbourne University Press.

Connell, R.W. and Messerschmidt, J.W. (2005) 'Hegemonic masculinity: rethinking the concept', *Gender and Society*, 19 (6): 829–59.

Cookingham, L. and Ryan, L. (2014) 'The impact of social media on the sexual and social wellness of adolescents', *Journal of Pediatric and Adolescent Gynaecology*, 28 (1): 2–5.

Coontz, S. (2006) *Marriage, A History: How Love Conquered Marriage*. New York: Penguin.

Copestake, J. (2006) 'Gays Flee Iraq as Shia Death Squads Find a New Target', *Observer*, 6 August, p. 31.

Corrêa, S., Petchesky, R. and Parker, R. (2008) *Sexuality, Health and Human Rights*. New York: Routledge.

Corrin, C. (ed.) (1996) *Women in a Violent World: Feminist Analyses and Resistance Across 'Europe'*. Edinburgh: Edinburgh University Press.

Coy, M., Kelly, L., Elvines. F., Garner, M. and Kanyeredzi, A. (2013) *'Sex without consent, I suppose that is rape': How young people in England understand sexual consent*. London: Office of the Children's Commissioner.

Cranny-Francis, A., Waring, W., Stavropoulos, P. and Kirkby, J. (2003) *Gender Studies: Terms and Debates*. London: Red Globe.

Crenshaw, K. (1989) 'Demarginalizing the intersection of race and sex: a black feminist critique of antidiscrimination doctrine, feminist theory and anti-racist politics', University of Chicago, *Legal Forum*, 8: 138–67.

Cronin, A. and King, A. (2010) 'Power, inequality and identification: exploring diversity and intersectionality amongst older LGB adults', *Sociology*, 44: 876–92.

Crow, G. (2002) 'Families, moralities, rationalities and social change', in A. Carling, S. Duncan and R. Edwards (eds), *Analysing Families: Morality and Rationality in Policy and Practice*. London. Routledge.

Crow, L. (1996) 'Including all of our lives: renewing the social model of disability', in J. Morris (ed.), *Encounters with Strangers: Feminism and Disability*. London: Women's Press.

Cruz-Malave, A. and Manalansan, M.F. (eds) (2002) *Queer Globalizations: Citizenship and the Afterlife of Colonialism*. New York: New York University Press.

Curran, J. (2005) 'Cultural theory and market liberalism' in J. Curran and D. Morley (eds), *Media and Cultural Theory*. London: Routledge.

Daly, M. (1978) *Gyn/ecology@ The Metaethics of Radical Feminism*. Boston, MA: Beacon.

Dank, M., Zweig, J.M., Yahner, J. and Lachman, P. (2013) 'The rate of cyber abuse among teens and how it relates to other forms of teen dating violence', *Journal of Youth and Adolescence*, 42: 1063–77.

Davis, J. (1990) *Youth and the Condition of Britain: Images of Adolescent Conflict*. London: Athlone.

Davy, Z. and Steinbock, E. (2011) '"Sexing up" bodily aesthetics: notes towards theorizing trans sexuality', in S. Hines and Y. Taylor (eds), *Sexualities: Past Reflections, Future Directions*. London: Palgrave Macmillan.

de Beauvoir, S. (1972[1949]) *The Second Sex*. Harmondsworth: Penguin.

De Ridder, S. (2017) 'Social media and young people's sexualities: values, norms, and battlegrounds', *Social Media and Society*, 3 (4): 1–11.

De Ridder, S. and Van Bauwel, S. (2013) 'Commenting on pictures: teens negotiating gender and sexualities on social networking sites', *Sexualities*, 16 (5–6): 565–86.

DeLamater, J., Koepsel, E. and Johnson, T. (2017) 'Changes, changes? Women's experience of sexuality in later life', *Sexual and Relationship Therapy*, 34 (2): 211–27.

Delmar, R. (1976) 'Looking again at Engels's origin of the family, private property and the state', in J. Mitchell and A. Oakley (eds), *Rights and Wrongs of Women*. Harmondsworth: Penguin.

Denison, B. (1998) 'Sexuality and fertility', in W. Swatos (ed.), *Encyclopedia of Religion and Society*. Lanham, MD: AltaMira.

Department of Health (2005) *Responding to Domestic Abuse: A Resource for Health Professionals*, https://assets.publishing.service.gov.uk/government/uploads/system/uploads/attachment_data/file/597435/DometicAbuseGuidance.pdf

Department of Health and Social Care (2013) *A Framework for Sexual Health Improvement in England*, https://assets.publishing.service.gov.uk/government/uploads/system/uploads/attachment_data/file/142592/9287-2900714-TSO-SexualHealthPolicyNW_ACCESSIBLE.pdf

Derrida, J. (1991) 'La differance', in P. Kamuf (ed.), *A Derrida Reader*. New York: Columbia University Press.

Detrie, P.M. and Lease, S. (2007) 'The relation of social support, connectedness, and collective self-esteem to the psychological well-being of lesbian, gay and bisexual youth', *Journal of Homosexuality*, 53(4): 173–99.

Devor, A. and Dominic, K. (2016) 'Trans* Sexualities', in J. DeLamater and R.F. Plante (eds), *Handbook of the Sociology of Sexualities*. New York: Springer.

Di Nucci, E. (2017) 'Sexual rights and disability', *Journal of Medical Ethics*, 37 (3): 158–61.

Dines, G. (1998) *Pornography: The Production and Consumption of Inequality*. London: Routledge.

Dobash, R. and Dobash, R. (1992) *Women, Violence and Social Change*. London: Routledge.

Donovan, C. and Hester, M. (2014) *Domestic Violence and Sexuality: What's Love Got To Do With It?* Bristol: Bristol University Pres

Douglas, M. (1966) *Purity and Danger: An Analysis of Concepts of Pollution and Taboo*. London: Routledge and Keegan Paul.

Dreger, A. (2000) *Hermaphrodites and the Medical Invention of Sex*. Cambridge, MA: Harvard University Press.

Drew, J. (2003) 'The myth of female sexual dysfunction and its medicalization', *Sexualities, Evolution and Gender*, 5 (2): 89–96.

Duggan, L. (2000) *Sapphic Slashers: Sex, Violence, and American Modernity*. Durham, NC: Duke University Press.

Duke, L., Furtado, V., Guo, B. and Vollm, B. (2018) 'Long-stay in forensic-psychiatric care in the UK', *Social Psychiatry and Psychiatric Epidemiology*, 53: 313–21.

Duncan-Smith, I. (2006) 'Foreword', in Social Policy Justice Group *Fractured Families*, Centre for Social Justice.

Dworkin, A. (1997 [1987]) *Intercourse*. New York: Simon and Schuster.

Dworkin, D. (1994) *Woman Hating*. Harmondsworth: Penguin.

Eadie, J. (ed.) (2004) *Sexuality*. London: Arnold.

Eden, I. (2007) 'Inappropriate Behaviour: Adult Venues and Licensing in London', report for the Lilith Project, www.womenssupportproject.co.uk/userfiles/file/uploads/Inappropriate_Behaviour.pdf

Eder, F., Hall, L. and Hekma, G. (1999) *Sexual Cultures in Europe: Themes in Sexuality*. Manchester: Manchester University Press.

Edwards, A. (1986) 'Male violence in feminist theory: An analysis of the changing conceptions of sex/gender violence and male dominance', in J. Hanmer and M. Maynard (eds), *Women, Violence and Social Control*. London: Macmillan.

Egan, J. (2003) 'Sobears: Finding Space, Seeking Community'. Paper presented at Queer Histories: Exploring Forms of Social Knowledge, first annual preconference of the Adult Education Research Conference, San Francisco, CA.

Eichelberger, K., Doll, K., Ekpo, G. and Zerden, M. (2016) 'Black lives matter: Claiming a space for evidence-based outrage in obstetrics and gynecology', *American Journal of Public Health*, 106 (10): 1771–72.

Elias, N. (1994 [1939]) *The Civilizing Process*. Oxford: Blackwell.

Engels, F. (1972 [1884]) *Origins of the Family, Private Property, and the State*. Oxnard, CA: Pathfinder.

Enke, A. (2012) *Transfeminist Perspectives in and beyond Transgender and Gender Studies*. Philadelphia: Temple University Press.

Epprecht, M. (2008) *Heterosexual Africa? The History of an Idea from the Age of Exploration to the Age of AIDS*. Athens: Ohio University Press.

Esterberg, K. (2002) 'The bisexual menace: or will the real bisexual please stand up?', in D. Richardson and S. Seidman (eds), *Handbook of Lesbian and Gay Studies*. London: Sage.

Evans, J. (1995) *Feminist Theory Today: An Introduction to Second-Wave Feminism*. London: Sage.

Faulkner, W. (1951) *Requiem for a Nun*. Harmondsworth: Penguin.

Fausto-Sterling, A. (2000) *Sexing The Body* (2nd edn). New York: Basic Books.

Featherstone, M. (2010) 'Body, image and affect in consumer culture', *Body & Society*, 16 (1): 193–221.

Feinberg, L. (1992) *Transgender Liberation: A Movement Whose Time Has Come*. New York: World View Forum.

Fellmeth, A. (2008) 'State regulation of sexuality in international human rights law and theory', *William and Mary Law Review*, 50 (3): 797–936.

Fenton, S. and Rickman, D. (2016) 'Ultra-orthodox rabbis ban women from going to university in case they get "dangerous" secular knowledge', *Independent*, 22 August. www.independent.co.uk/news/world/americas/ultra-orthodox-rabbis-ban-women-from-going-to-university-in-case-they-get-dangerous-secular-a7204171.html

Ferguson, M. (1983) *Forever Feminine: Women's Magazines and the Cult of Femininity*. London: Heinemann.

Fields, E., Morgan, A. and Arrignton Sanders, R. (2016) 'The intersection of sociocultural factors and health-related behavior in lesbian, gay, bisexual, and transgender youth: Experiences among young black gay males as an example', *Pediatric Clinics of North America*, 63 (6): 1091–106.

Fine, C. (2011) *Delusions of Gender: The Real Science Behind Sex Differences*. London: Icon.

Fine, C. (2017) *Testosterone Rex: Unmaking the Myths of Our Gendered Minds*. London: Icon.

Fineman, M. (1994) 'Preface', in M. Fineman and R. Myktiuk (eds), *The Public Nature of Private Violence: The Discovery of Domestic Abuse*. London: Routledge.

Finoh, M. and Sankofa, J. (2019) 'The Legal System Has Failed Black Girls, Women, and Non-Binary Survivors of Violence', www.aclu.org/blog/racial-justice/race-and-criminal-justice/legal-system-has-failed-black-girls-women-and-non

Firestone, S. (1970) *The Dialect of Sex*. London: Paladin.

Fish, J. (2008) 'Navigating queer street: researching intersections of lesbian, gay, bisexual and trans (LGBT) identities in health research', *Sociological Research Online*, 13 (1): 1–12 (www.socresonline.org.uk/13/1/12.html).

Fish, J. (2010) *Coming Out About Breast Cancer in Lesbian and Bisexual Women*. Leicester: Health Policy Research Unit, De Montfort University.

Fisher, L., Anderson, G., Chapagain, M., Montenegro, X., Smoot, J. and Takalkar, A. (2010) *Sex, Romance and Relationships: AARP Survey of Midlife and Older Adults*. Washington, DC: AARP.

Fiske, J. (1989) *Understanding Popular Culture*. London: Routledge.

Fixter, A. (2019) 'The Taboos Around Disability and Sex Put Limits on Everyone, Disabled or Not', *Guardian*, 18 March.

Fontanella, L., Maretti, M. and Sarra, A. (2014) 'Gender fluidity across the world: a multilevel item response theory approach', *Quality and Quantity*, 48: 2253–568.

Foster, L. (1984) *Religion and Sexuality: The Shakers, the Mormons, and the Oneida Community*. Chicago, IL: University of Illinois Press.

Foucault, M. (1973) *The Birth of the Clinic: An Archaeology of Medical Perception*. London: Routledge.

Foucault, M. (1979a) *The History of Sexuality. Vol. 1, An Introduction*. London: Allen Lane.

Foucault, M. (1979b) *Discipline and Punish: The Birth of the Prison*. New York: Vintage.

Foucault, M. (2000) 'Truth and power', in J.D. Faubion (ed.), *Power: Essential Works of Foucault, volume 3*. London: Penguin.

Fowler. D. (1995) *The First Teenagers: The Lifestyle of Young Wage-Earners in Interwar Britain*. London: Routledge.

Fox, R. (1983) *The Red Lamp of Incest: An Enquiry into the Origins of Mind and Society*. Notre Dame, IN: University of Notre Dame Press.

Frank, K. (2016) 'Observational methods in sexuality research', in J. DeLamater and R. Plante (eds), *Handbook of the Sociology of Sexualities*. New York: Springer, pp. 123–46.

Fredriksen-Goldsen, K. and Muraco, A. (2010) 'Aging and sexual orientation: A 25-year review of the literature', *Research on Aging*, 32: 372–413.

Fredriksen-Goldsen, K., Kim, H.J., Barkan, S.E., Muraco, A. and Hoy-Ellis, C.P. (2013) 'Health disparities among lesbian, gay, and bisexual older adults: results from a population-based study', *American Journal of Public Health*, 103 (10): 1802–9.

Freud, S. (1959 [1926]) *The Question of Lay Analysis*, Standard edition (Vol. 20). London: Hogarth.

Freud, S. (2011 [1905]) *On Sexuality: Three Essays on the Theory of Sexuality and Other Works*. Harmondsworth: Penguin.

Frosh, S., Phoenix, A. and Pattman, R. (2002) *Young Masculinities: Understanding Boys in Contemporary Society*. London: Palgrave.

Furedi, F. (2003) *Therapy Culture: Cultivating Vulnerability in an Uncertain Age*. London: Routledge.

Fuss, D. (1991) *Inside/Out: Lesbian Theories, Gay Theories*. New York: Routledge.

Gabb J. (2008) *Researching Intimacy in Families*. Basingstoke: Palgrave Macmillan.

Gagnon, J. (2004) *An Interpretation of Desire*. Chicago: University of Chicago Press.

Gagnon, J. and Simon, W. (1973) *Sexual Conduct: The Social Sources of Human Sexuality*. Chicago, IL: Aldine.

García, H., Soriano, E. and Arriaza, G. (2014) 'Friends with benefits and psychological wellbeing', *Procedia – Social and Behavioral Sciences* 132: 241–47.

Garrett, E. (1870) *An Enquiry into the Contagious Diseases Acts of 1866–1869*. London: (reprint from the *Pall Mall Gazette*).

Garton, S. (2004) *Histories of Sexuality: Antiquity to Sexual Revolution*. London: Equinox.

Gauntlett, D. (2008) *Media, Gender and Identity* (2nd edn). London: Routledge

Gay, P. (ed.) (1995) *The Freud Reader*. London: Vintage.

Gersen, J. (2019) 'Sex lex machina: Intimacy and artificial intelligence', *Columbia Law Review*, 119 (7): 1793–810.

Gewirtz-Meydan, A. and Ayalon, L. (2017) 'Physicians' response to sexual dysfunction presented by a younger vs. an older adult', *International Journal of Geriatric Psychiatry*, 32 (12): 1476–83.

Gibson, R. (2020) *Desire in the Age of Robots and AI: An Investigation in Science Fiction and Fact*. London: Palgrave Pivot.

Giddens, A. (1991) *Modernity and Self-Identity*. Cambridge: Polity.

Giddens, A. (1992) *The Transformation of Intimacy: Sexuality, Love and Eroticism in Modern Societies*. Cambridge: Polity.

Giddens, A. (1994) 'Living in a post-traditional society', in U. Beck, A. Giddens and S. Lasch (eds), *Reflexive Modernization: Politics, Tradition and Aesthetics in the Modern Social Order*. Cambridge: Polity.

Gillespie, B.J. (2016) 'Sexual synchronicity and communication among partnered older adults', *Journal of Sex & Marital Therapy*, 43 (5): 441–55.

Gillies, V. (2008) 'Childrearing, class and the new politics of parenting', *Sociology Compass* 2 (3): 1079–95.

Ginn, J. and Arber, S. (1995) '"Only connect": gender relations and ageing', in S. Arber and J. Ginn (eds), *Connecting Gender and Ageing: A Sociological Approach*. Buckingham: Open University Press.

Goffman, E. (1968) *Stigma: Notes on the Management of Spoiled Identity*. Harmondsworth: Penguin.

Goodyear, V.A. and Armour, K.M. (eds) (2019) *Young People, Social Media and Health*. London: Routledge.

Gordon, B. and Rosenblum, K. (2001) 'Bringing disability into the sociological frame: a comparison of disability with race, sex and sexual orientation statuses', *Disability & Society*, 16 (1): 5–19.

Gott, M. (2005) *Sexuality, Sexual Health and Ageing*. Milton Keynes: Open University Press.

Gott, M. and Hinchliffe, S. (2003) 'How important is sex in later life? The views of older people', *Social Science & Medicine*, 56 (8): 1617–28.

Gray, N.J., Klein, J.D., Noyce, P.R., Sesselberg, T.S. and Cantrill, J.A. (2005) 'Health information-seeking behaviour in adolescence: the place of the internet', *Social Science & Medicine*, 60 (7): 1467–78.

Greer, G. (1970) *The Female Eunuch*. London: Fourth Estate.

257

Greer, G. (1999) *The Whole Woman*. London: Random House.

Griebling, T.L. (2016) 'Sexuality and aging: a focus on lesbian, gay, bisexual, and transgender (LGBT) needs in palliative and end of life care', *Current Opinion in Supportive and Palliative Care*, 10 (1): 95–101.

Griffiths, M.D. (2012) 'The use of online methodologies in studying paraphilias – a review', *Journal of Behavioural Addictions*, 1 (4): 143–50.

Griffiths, M.D., Lewis, A.M., Ortiz de Gortari, A.B. and Kuss, D.J. (2013) 'Online forums and blogs: innovative methodologies for data collection', *Studia Psychologica*, 11 (1): 6–11.

Gross, L. (2003) 'The gay global village in cyberspace', in N. Couldry and J. Curran (eds), *Contesting Media Power: Alternative Media in a Networked World*. New York: Routledge.

Grosz, E. (1994) *Volatile Bodies: Toward a Corporeal Feminism*. Bloomington: Indiana University Press.

Group Sisterhood (1998) 'Prostitution, stigma and the law in Japan: a feminist roundtable discussion', in K. Kempadoo and J. Doezema (eds), *Global Sex Workers: Rights, Resistance and Redefinition*. New York: Routledge.

Hacker, H. (2007) 'Developmental desire and/or transnational jouissance: re-formulating sexual subjectivities in transcultural contact zones', in K. Browne, J. Lim and G. Brown (eds), *Geographies of Sexualities: Theory, Practices and Politics*. Aldershot: Ashgate.

Halberstam, J. (1998) *Female Masculinity*. Durham, NC: Duke University Press.

Halberstam, J. (2006) 'Boys will be ... bois? Or, transgender feminism and forgetful fish', in D. Richardson, J. McLaughlin and M. Casey (eds), *Intersections between Feminist and Queer Theory*. Basingstoke: Palgrave Macmillan.

Halberstam, J. (2010) 'The pregnant man', *The Velvet Light Trap*, 65: 77–8.

Hall, K. (1995) 'Lip service on the fantasy lines', in K. Hall and M. Bucholtz (eds), *Gender Articulated: Language and the Socially Constructed Self*. London: Routledge. pp 183–216.

Hall, S. (1977) 'Culture, the media, and the "ideological effect"', in J. Curran, M. Gurevitch and J. Woollacott (eds), *Mass Communication and Society*. London: Edward Arnold.

Hall, S. (1980) 'Encoding/decoding', in M.G. Durham and D.M. Kellner (eds), *Media and Cultural Studies: Keyworks*. Malden, MA: Blackwell, pp. 166–76.

Hall, S. (1996) 'Introduction: who needs "identity"?"', in S. Hall and P. du Gay (eds), *Questions of Cultural Identity*. London: Sage.

Halperin, D.M. (1995) *Saint Foucault: Towards a Gay Hagiography*. Oxford: Oxford University Press.

Hammond, N. (2018) 'Researching men who pay for sex: using online methods for recruiting and interviewing', *Methodological Innovations*, 11 (1). https://doi.org/10.1177%2F2059799118768408

Hammond, N. and Kingston, S. (2014) 'Experiencing stigma as sex work researchers in professional and personal lives', *Sexualities*, 17 (3): 329–47.

Han, E. and O'Mahoney, J. (2018) 'How Britain's Colonial Legacy Still Affects LGBT Politics Around the World', *The Conversation*, http://theconversa tion.com/how-britains-colonial-legacy-still-affects-lgbt-politics-around-the-world-95799

Haraway, D. (1985) 'A cyborg manifesto: science, technology, and socialist-feminism in the late twentieth century', *Socialist Review*, 80: 65–108.

Haraway, D. (1988) 'Situated knowledges: the science question in feminism and the partial perspective', *Feminist Studies*, 14 (3): 575–99.

Hart, M. and Barnard, G. (2003) '"Jump on top, get the job done": strategies employed by female prostitutes to reduce the risk of client violence', in E. Stanko (ed.), *The Meanings of Violence*. London: Routledge.

Hartley, L.P. (1958) *The Go-Between*. Harmondsworth: Penguin.

Hartnell, J. (2018) *Medieval Bodies: Life, Death and Art in the Middle Ages*. London: Profile.

Harvey, K.J., Brown, B., Crawford, P., Macfarlane, A. and McPherson, A. (2007) '"Am I normal?": teenagers, sexual health and the internet', *Social Science & Medicine*, 65 (4): 771–81.

Hausman, B. (1995) *Changing Sex Transsexualism, Technology, and the Idea of Gender*. Durham, NC: Duke University Press.

Hawkes, G. (1996) *A Sociology of Sex and Sexuality*. Buckingham: Open University Press.

Hawley, J. (1986) 'Fundamentalism', in C. Howland (ed.), *Religious Fundamentalisms and the Human Rights of Women*. New York: Palgrave Macmillan.

Heaphy, B. (2009) 'Choice and its limits in older lesbian and gay narratives of relational life', *Journal of GLBT Family Studies*, 5 (1–2): 119–38.

Heaphy, B., Yip, A. and Thompson, D. (2004) 'Ageing in a non-heterosexual context', *Ageing and Society*, 24: 881–902.

Heath, R. and Wynne, K. (2019) *A Guide to Transgender Health: State of the Art Information for Gender-Affirming People and their Supporters*. Westport, CT: Praeger.

Heffernan, K. (2013) 'From "It could happen to someone you love" to "Do you speak ass?": Women and discourses of sex education in erotic film and video', in T. Taormino, C. Penley, C. Shimizu and M. Miller-Young (eds), *The Feminist Porn Book: The Politics of Producing Pleasure*. New York: The Feminist Press.

Held, D. (2000) 'Regulating globalization', in D. Held and A. McGrew (eds), *The Global Transformations Reader: An Introduction to the Globalization Debate*. Cambridge: Polity.

Hemmings, C., Gedalof, I. and Bland, L. (2006) 'Sexual minorities', *Feminist Review*, 83:1–3.

Hemyng, B. (1862) 'Prostitution in London', in H. Mayhew, *London Labour and the London Poor: Volume IV – Those Who Will Not Work; Comprising Prostitutes, Thieves, Swindlers and Beggars*. New York: Dover.

Hennessy, R. (2000) *Profit and Pleasure: Sexual Identities in Late Capitalism*. New York: Routledge.

Herbenick, D., Bowling, J., Fu, T.C., Dodge, B., Guerra-Reyes, L. and Sanders, S. (2017) 'Sexual diversity in the United States: results from a nationally representative probability sample of adult women and men', *PLoS ONE*, 12 (7): e0181198. https://doi.org/10.1371/journal.pone.0181198

Herdt, G. (2007) 'Sexuality in times of war', in G. Herdt and C. Howe (eds), *21st Century Sexualities: Contemporary Issues in Health, Education and Rights*. Abingdon: Routledge.

Herdt, G. and Howe, C. (2007) *21st Century Sexualities: Contemporary Issues in Health, Education and Rights*. Abingdon: Routledge.

Hester, M. (2012) 'Portrayal of women as intimate partner domestic violence perpetrators', *Violence Against Women*, 18 (9): 1067–82.

Higate, P. (2007) 'Revealing the soldier: Peacekeeping and prostitution', in G. Herdt and C. Howe (eds), *21st Century Sexualities: Contemporary Issues in Health, Education and Rights*. Abingdon: Routledge.

Hillier, L. and Harrison, L. (2007) 'Building realities less limited than their own: young people practising same-sex attraction on the internet', *Sexualities*, 10 (1): 82–100.

Hinchliffe, S. and Gott, M. (2004) 'Intimacy, commitment and adaptation: sexual relationships within long-term marriages', *Journal of Social and Personal Relationships*, 21 (5): 595–609.

Hines S. (2006) 'What's the difference? Bringing particularity to queer studies of transgender', *Journal of Gender Studies*, 15 (1): 49–66.

Hines, S. (2009) 'A pathway to diversity? Human rights, citizenship and the politics of transgender', *Contemporary Politics*, 15 (1): 87–102.

Hines, S. (2010) 'Recognising diversity? Transgender citizenship and the Gender Recognition Act', in S. Hines and T. Sanger (eds), *Transgender Identities: Towards a Social Analysis of Gender Diversity*. London: Routledge.

Hinduja, S. and Patchin, J. (2010) 'Bullying, cyberbullying, and suicide', *Archives of Suicide Research: Official Journal of the International Academy for Suicide Research*, 14 (3): 206–21.

Hinrichs, K. and Vacha-Haase, T. (2010) 'Staff perceptions of same-gender sexual contacts in long-term care facilities', *Journal of Homosexuality*, 57 (6): 776–89.

Hinton, P. (2015) 'The perverse stereotype of the Japanese man in the British media', *ejcjs* 15 (2). www.japanesestudies.org.uk/ejcjs/vol15/iss2/hinton.html (accessed 4.3.20).

Hite, S. (1976) *The Hite Report on Female Sexuality*. New York: Dell.

Hochschild, A. (1979) 'Emotion work, feeling rules, and social structure', *American Journal of Sociology*, 85 (3): 551–75.

Hockey, J. and James, A. (1993) *Growing Up and Growing Old: Ageing and Dependency in the Life Course*. London: Sage.

Hockey, J. and James, A. (2003) *Social Identities Across the Life Course*. Basingstoke: Palgrave Macmillan.

Holsopple, K. (1998) 'Stripclubs according to strippers: exposing workplace violence', unpublished manuscript. www.uri.edu/artsci/wms/hughes/stripc1.htm

Home Office (2010) *The Sexualization of Young People Review*. London: Home Office. www.homeoffice.gov.uk/documents/Sexualisation-young-people

Hook, D. (2005) 'The racial stereotype, colonial discourse, fetishism, and racism', *Psychoanalytic Review*, 92 (5): 701–34.

Horvath, M., Hegarty, P., Tyler, S. and Mansfield, S. (2011) '"Lights on at the end of the party": are lads mags mainstreaming dangerous sexism?', *British Journal of Psychology*. http://onlinelibrary.wiley.com/doi/10.1111/j.2044-82 95.2011.02086.x/abstract

Howe, A. (2009) *Sex, Violence and Crime: Foucault and the 'Man' Question*. London: Routledge.

Hubbard, P. and Colosi, R. (2015) 'Respectability, morality and disgust in the night-time economy: exploring reactions to "lap dance" clubs in England and Wales', *The Sociological Review*, 63 (4). https://journals.sagepub.com/doi/full/10.1111/1467-954X.12278

Human Rights Watch (2001) 'Hatred in the Hallways Violence and Discrimination Against Lesbian, Gay, Bisexual, and Transgender Students in U.S. Schools', New York. www.hrw.org/report/2001/05/01/hatred-hallways/violence-and-discrimination-against-lesbian-gay-bisexual-and

Humm, M. (2014) *Feminisms: A Reader*. London: Routledge.

Hunt, R. and Fish J. (2008) *Prescription for Change, Lesbian and Bisexual Women's Health Check 2008*. London: Stonewall and De Montford University.

Hunt, S. (2005) *The Life Course: A Sociological Imagination*. Basingstoke: Palgrave Macmillan.

Hupperts, C. (2010) 'Homosexuality in Greece and Rome', in R. Aldrich (ed.), *Gay Life and Culture: A World History*. London: Thames and Hudson.

Hwang, S. and Nuttbrock, L. (2014) 'Adolescent gender-related abuse, androphilia, and HIV risk among transfeminine people of color in New York City', *Journal of Homosexuality*, 61 (5): 691–713.

Ingraham, C. (1994) 'The heterosexual imaginary: feminist sociology and theories of gender', *Sociological Theory*, 12 (2): 203–19.

Irvine, J. (2014) 'Is sexuality research "dirty work"? Institutionalized stigma in the production of sexual knowledge', *Sexualities*, 15 (5–6): 632–56.

Jackson, S. (1995) 'Gender and heterosexuality: a materialist feminist analysis', in M. Maynard and J. Purvis (eds), *(Hetero)sexual Politics*. London: Taylor & Francis.

Jackson, S. (1996) 'Heterosexuality and feminist theory', in D. Richardson (ed.), *Theorising Heterosexuality: Telling it Straight*. Buckingham: Open University Press.

Jackson, S. (2006) 'Heterosexuality, sexuality and gender: re-thinking the intersections', in D. Richardson, J. McLaughlin and M. Casey (eds), *Intersections between Feminist and Queer Theory*. London: Palgrave.

Jackson, S. and Scott, S. (2000) 'Sexuality' in G. Payne (ed.), *Social Divisions*. Basingstoke: Macmillan.

Jackson, S. and Scott, S. (2010) *Theorizing Sexuality*. Maidenhead: Open University Press.

Jacobs, R., Fernandez, I., Ownby, R., Bowen, S., Hardigan, P. and Kane, M. (2010) 'Factors associated with risk for unprotected receptive and insertive anal intercourse in men aged 40 and older who have sex with men', *AIDS Care*, 22 (10): 1204–11.

Jamieson, L. (2002) *Intimacy: Personal Relationships in Modern Societies*. Cambridge: Polity Press.

Javaid, A. (2018) *Male Rape, Masculinities, and Sexualities: Understanding, Policing, and Overcoming Male Sexual Victimisation*. London: Palgrave Macmillan.

Jeffreys, S. (1990) *Anticlimax: A Feminist Perspective on the Sexual Revolution*. London: The Women's Press.

Jeffreys, S. (2001) *The Sexuality Debates*. New York: Routledge.

Jeffreys, S. (2008) *The Industrial Vagina: The Political Economy of the Global Sex Trade*. London: Routledge.

Jewkes, Y. and Wykes, M. (2012) 'Reconstructing the sexual abuse of children: "cyber-paeds", panic and power', *Sexualities*, 15 (8): 934–52.

Johnson, J. (1973) *Lesbian Nation*. London: Simon and Schuster.

Jonason, P.K., Li, N.P. and Richardson, J. (2011) 'Positioning the booty-call relationship on the spectrum of relationships: Sexual but more emotional than one-night stands', *Journal of Sex Research*, 48 (5): 486–95.

Jones, E. (1955) *The Life and Work of Sigmund Freud* (Vol. 2). New York: Basic Books.

Jones, G. (2010) 'Changing marriage patterns in Asia', Asia Research Institute Working Paper No. 131. Available at SSRN: https://ssrn.com/abstract=1716533 or http://dx.doi.org/10.2139/ssrn.1716533

Jones, H.S. (2018) 'Lips of flame and heart of stone: the impact of prostitution in Victorian Britain and its global influence', in H.S. Hunter (ed.), *Sexuality and its Impact on History: The British Stripped Bare*. Barnsley: Pen and Sword.

Joppke, C. (2009) *Veil: Mirror of Identity*. Cambridge: Polity.

Katz, S. and Marshall, B.L. (2003) 'New sex for old: lifestyle, consumerism, and the ethics of aging well', *Journal of Aging Studies*, 17 (1): 3–16.

Keegan, P. (2014) *Graffiti in Antiquity*. Durham, NC: Acumen.

Kehily, M.J. (2011) 'Sexuality', in N. Lesko and S. Talbur, (eds), *Keywords in Youth Studies*. London: Routledge, pp. 223–7.

Kelly, L. (1987) 'The continuum of violence', in J. Hanmer and M. Maynard (eds), *Women, Violence and Social Control*. Basingstoke: Macmillan.

Kelly, L. (1988) *Surviving Sexual Violence*. Cambridge: Polity.

Kelly, L. (1996) 'Weasel words: paedophiles and the cycle of abuse', *Trouble & Strife*, 33: 44–9.

Kelly, L. (2016) 'The Conducive Context of Violence Against Women and Girls', *Discover Sociology*, 1 March. https://discoversociety.org/2016/03/01/theorising-violence-against-women-and-girls/

Kempadoo, K. and Doezema, J. (eds) (1998) *Global Sex Workers: Rights, Resistance and Redefinition*. New York: Routledge.

Kennedy, E. and Davis, M. (1993) *Boots of Leather, Slippers of Gold: The History of a Lesbian Community*. New York: Penguin.

Kennedy, H. (1993) *Eve was Framed: Women and British Justice*. London: Vintage.

Kennedy, H. (2005) *Just Law: The Changing Face of Justice and Why It Matters To Us All*. London: Vintage.

Khiabany, G. and Williamson, M. (2008) 'Veiled bodies – naked racism: culture, politics and race in the Sun', *Race & Class*, 50 (1): 69–88.

Kim, E. (2011) 'Asexuality in disability narratives', *Sexualities*, 14 (4): 479–93.

King, A., Santos, A. and Crowhurst, I. (eds) (2019) *Sexualities Research: Critical Interjections, Diverse Methodologies and Practical Applications*. London: Routledge.

King, M. and McKeowan, E. (2003) *Mental Health and Social Wellbeing of Gay Men, Lesbians and Bisexuals in England and Wales*. London: MIND.

Kinkaid, J. (1993) *Child-loving: Erotic Child in Victorian Culture*. London: Routledge.

Kollontai, A. (1920) 'Communism and the family', *Kommunistka*, no. 2.

Komesaroff, P., Rothfield, P. and Daly, J. (1997) *Reinterpreting Menopause: Cultural and Philosophical Issues*. London: Routledge.

Kosofsky Sedgwick, E. (1990) *Epistomology of the Closet*. Berkeley: University of California Press.

Krafft-Ebing, R. von (1998 [1886]) *Psychipathia Sexualis*. New York: Arcade, pp. 263–4.

Lacan, J. (1977) *Écrits: A Selection*. A. Sheridan (ed). New York and London: Norton.

Lambley, P. (1995) *The Middle-aged Rebel: Responding to the Challenges of Midlife: A Dynamic Approach*. New York: Element.

Larkin, P. (2010[1967]) 'Annus Mirabilis', in *High Windows*. London: Faber and Faber.

Larson, J. (2012) *Greek and Roman Sexualities: A Sourcebook*. London: Bloomsbury.

Lasch, C. (1979) *The Culture of Narcissism: American Life in an Age of Diminishing Expectations*. New York: Norton.

Laslett, P. (1996) *A Fresh Map of Life: The Emergence of the Third Age*. Basingstoke: Palgrave Macmillan.

Law, J. (2004) *After Method: Mess in Social Science Research*. London: Routledge.

Lawler, S. (2005) 'Disgusted subjects: the making of middle-class identities', *The Sociological Review*, 53 (3): 429–46, www.swetswise.com/eAccess/viewAbstract.do?articleID=24295121

Lees, S. (1993) *Sugar and Spice: Sexuality and Adolescent Girls*. London: Penguin.

Leigh, I. and O'Brien, C. (2019) *Deaf Identity: Exploring New Frontiers*. Oxford: Oxford University Press.

Level Up (2019) 'Sex and relationship education which is for everyone'. https://act.welevelup.org/campaigns/sre-lgbt?utm_campaign=2019-04-11.66

Lewis, L. (2007) 'Contesting the dangerous sexuality of Black male youth', in G. Herdt and C. Howe (eds), *21st Century Sexualities: Contemporary Issues in Health, Education, and Rights*. London: Routledge.

Lewis, R., Tanton, C., Mercer, C., Mitchell, K., Palmer, M., Macdowall, W. and Wellings, K. (2017) 'Heterosexual practices among young people in Britain: evidence from three national surveys of sexual attitudes and life-styles', *Journal of Adolescent Health*, 61 (6): 694–702.

Liepe-Levinson, K. (2002) *Strip Show: Performances of Gender and Desire*. New York: Routledge.

Livingstone, S. (2011) *Internet, Children and Youth: The Handbook of Internet Studies*. Oxford: Blackwell.

Livingstone, S., Mascheroni, G. and Staksrud, E. (2015) *Developing a Framework for Researching Children's Online Risks and Opportunities in Europe*. London: EU Kids Online.

Livingstone, S. and Sefton-Green, J. (2016) *The Class: Living and Learning in the Digital Age*. New York: NYU Press.

Lloyd, R. (2011) *Girls Like Us: Fighting for a World Where Girls Are Not for Sale: A Memoir*. New York: Harper.

Lock, M. and Farquhar, J. (2007) *Beyond the Body Proper: Reading the Anthropology of Material Life*. Durham, NC: Duke University Press.

Loe, M. (2004) 'Sex and the senior woman: Pleasure and danger in the Viagra era', *Sexualities*, 7 (3): 303–26.

Lowman, J. (2000) 'Violence and the outlaw status of (street) prostitution in Canada', *Violence Against Women*, 6: 987–1011.

Mac an Ghaill, M. (1994) *The Making of Men: Masculinities, Sexualities and Schooling*. Milton Keynes: Open University Press.

MacCulloch, D. (2009) *A History of Christianity: The First Three Thousand Years*. London: Penguin.

MacKinnon, C. (1982) 'Feminism, Marxism, method and the State: an agenda for theory', *Signs*, 7 (3): 515–44.

MacKinnon, C. (1987) *Feminism Unmodified: Discourses on Life and Law*. Cambridge, MA: Harvard University Press.

MacKinnon, C. (1992) *Women's Lives, Men's Laws*. Cambridge, MA: Harvard University Press.

MacKinnon, C. (1993) 'Prostitution and civil rights', *Michigan Journal of Gender and Law*, 1 (1): 13–31.

Madden, M., Lenhart, A., Cortesi, S., Gasser, U., Duggan, M., Smith, A. and Beaton, M. (2013) *Teens, Social Media, and Privacy*. Washington, DC: Pew Internet and American Life Project.

Maes, C.A. and Louis, M. (2011) 'Nurse practitioners' sexual history-taking practices with adults 50 and over', *Journal for Nurse Practitioners*, 7 (3): 216–22.

Maguire, K., Gleeson, K. & Holmes, N. (2019) 'Support workers' understanding of their role supporting the sexuality of people with learning disabilities', *British Journal of Learning Disabilities*, 47 (1): 59–65.

Makoni, B. (2016) 'Labeling black male genitalia and the "new racism": the discursive construction of sexual racism by a group of Southern African college students', *Gender and Language*, 10 (1): 48–72.

Marcuse, H. (1956) *Eros and Civilisation: A Philosophical Inquiry into Freud*. London: Routledge and Kegan Paul.

Marcuse, H. (1964) *One-Dimensional Man*. London: Routledge and Kegan Paul.

Marks, M. and Fraley, R. (2006) 'Confirmation bias and the sexual double standard', *Sex Roles*, 54 (1): 19–26.

Markwell, K. (2002) 'Mardi Gras, tourism and the construction of Sydney as an international lesbian and gay city', *GLQ: A Journal of Lesbian and Gay Studies*, 8 (1–2): 81–100.

Marshall, B.L. (2011) 'The graying of "sexual health": a critical research agenda', *Canadian Review of Sociology/Revue Canadienne de Sociologie*, 48 (4): 390–413.

Martin, K. (2009) 'Normalizing heterosexuality: mothers' assumptions, talk, and strategies with young children', *American Sociological Review*, 74 (2): 190–207.

Maxwell, C. (2007) '"Alternative" narratives of young people's heterosexual experiences in the UK', *Sexualities*, 10 (5): 539–58.

May, T. (2016) *Home Secretary's Police Federation Conference 2016 speech* www.gov.uk/government/speeches/home-secretarys-police-federation-2016-speech

McAlinden, A.M. (2014) 'Deconstructing victim and offender identities in discourses on child sexual abuse: hierarchies, blame and the good/evil dialectic', *British Journal of Criminology*, 54 (2): 180–98.

McAlister, H. (2003) 'In defence of ambiguity: understanding bisexuality's invisibility through cognitive psychology', *Journal of Bisexuality*, 3 (1): 23–32.

McArthur, N. and Twist, M. (2017) 'The rise of digisexuality: therapeutic challenges and possibilities', *Sexual and Relationship Therapy*, 32 (3–4): 334–44.

McIntosh, M. (1968) 'The homosexual role', *Social Problems*, 16 (2): 182–92.

McKee, A., Albury, K. and Lumby, C. (2008) *The Porn Report*. Melbourne: Melbourne University Press.

McKenney, S. and Bigler, R. (2016) 'Internalized sexualization and its relation to sexualized appearance, body surveillance, and body shame among early adolescent girls', *Journal of Early Adolescence*, 36 (2): 171–97.

McLaughlin, D. (2006) 'Homophobia Seeps Across New EU', *Observer*, 12 March, p. 40.

McLelland, M. (2000) *Male Homosexuality in Modern Japan: Cultural Myths and Social Realities*. London: Routledge.

McNulty, A. (2010) 'Great expectations: teenage pregnancy and intergenerational transmission', in S. Duncan, R. Edwards and C. Alexander (eds), *Teenage Parenthood: What's the Problem?* London: Tufnell. p.134.

McQueeney, K. (2009) '"We are all God's children, y'all": race, gender and sexuality in lesbian and gay affirming congregations', *Social Problems*, 56 (1): 151–73.

McRobbie, A. (1983) 'Jackie: an ideology of adolescent femininity', discussion paper, CCCS Stencilled Occasional Papers. Birmingham: University of Birmingham.

McRobbie, A. (2000) *Feminism and Youth Culture*. Basingstoke: Palgrave Macmillan.

McWilliams, S. and Barrett, A. (2014) 'Online dating in middle and later life: gendered expectations and experiences', *Journal of Family Issues*, 35 (3): 411–63.

Mead, G.H. (1934) *Mind, Self and Society*. Chicago: University of Chicago Press.

Meads, C. and Moore, D. (2013) 'Breast cancer in lesbians and bisexual women: systematic review of incidence, prevalence and risk studies', *BMC Public Health*, 13 (1): 1127.

Mearns, A. (1883) *The Bitter Cry of Outcast London: An Inquiry into the Conditions of the Abject Poor*. London: James Clarke & Co.

Mellor, P. and Shilling, C. (2010) 'Body pedagogics and the religious habitus: a new direction for the sociological study of religion', *Religion*, 40 (1): 27–38.

Miles, S. (1996) 'The cultural capital of consumption: understanding "postmodern" identities in a cultural context', *Culture & Psychology*, 2 (2): 139–58.

Miller, J. (2019) 'Manscaping and after: Power, parody and the hairy chest', *Fashion Theory*, 22 (60): 641–55.

Millett, K. (1970) *Sexual Politics*. London: Rupert Hart-Davis.

Millett, K. (1999) *Sexual Politics*. London: Virago.

Milligan, M. and Neufeldt, A. (2001) 'The myth of asexuality: a survey of social and empirical evidence', *Sexuality and Disability*, 19 (2): 91–101.

Mir-Hosseini, Z. (2004) 'Sexuality, rights and Islam: competing gender discourses in post-revolutionary Iran', in G. Neshat and L. Beck (eds), *Women in Iran from 1800 to the Islamic Republic*. Chicago, IL: University of Illinois Press.

Mitchell, J. (1971) *Women's Estate*. Harmondsworth: Penguin.

Moghadam, V. (2000) 'Transnational feminist networks: collective action in an era of globalization', *International Sociology*, 15 (1): 57–85.

Mohanty, C.T. (1997) 'Women workers and capitalist scripts: ideologies of domination, common interests and the politics of solidarity', in M.J Alexander and C.T. Mohanty (eds), *Feminist Genealogies, Colonial Legacies, Democratic Failures*. New York: Routledge.

Money, J. (1991) 'Sexology and/or sexosophy: The split between sexual researchers and reformers in history and practice', *SIECUS Report*, 19 (3): 1–4.

Monro, S. (2005) *Gender Politics: Citizenship, Activism and Sexual Diversity*. London: Pluto.

Monro, S., Hines, S. and Osborne, A. (2017) 'Is bisexuality invisible? A review of sexualities scholarship 1970–2015', *The Sociological Review*, 65 (4): DOI: 10.1177/0038026117695488

Montemurro, B. and Siefken, J. (2014) 'Cougars on the prowl? New perceptions of older women's sexuality', *Journal of Aging Studies*, 28: 35–43.

Montserrat, D. (1996) *Sex and Society in Graeco-Roman Egypt*. London: Routledge.

Moran, L., Skeggs, B., Tyrer, P. and Corteen, K. (2003) 'The formation of fear in gay space: the "straights" story', *Capital & Class*, 27 (2): 173–98.

Morgan, D. (1996) *Family Connections: An Introduction to Family Studies*. Cambridge: Polity Press.

Morrison, T. (2004) '"He was treating me like trash, and I was loving it...": Perspectives on gay male pornography', *Journal of Homosexuality*, 47 (3–4): 167–83.

Mottier, V. (2008) *Sexuality: A Very Short Introduction*. Oxford: Oxford University Press.

Mulholland, M. (2015) 'Walking a fine line: young people negotiate pornified heterosex', *Sexualities*, 18(5–6): 731–49.

Mulvey, L. (1975) 'Visual pleasure and narrative cinema', *Screen*, 16 (3): 6–18.

Murch, C. (2010) 'The sexualisation of young people: moral panic?', *Counterfire*. www.counterfire.org/index.php/features/38-opinion/4350-sex-sale-sand-morality-tales-the sexualisation-of-young-people

Murdoch, M., Polusny, M., Street, A., Noorbaloochi, S., Simon, A., Bangerter, A., Grill, J. and Voller, E. (2014) 'Sexual assault during the time of Gulf War I: A cross-sectional survey of U.S. service men who later applied for Department of Veterans Affairs PTSD disability benefits', *Military Medicine*, 179 (3): 285–93.

Murdock, G. (1949) *Social Structure*. Basingstoke: Macmillan.

Murray, A. (1998) 'Debt-bondage and trafficking: don't believe the hype', in K. Kempadoo and J. Doezema (eds), *Global Sex Workers: Rights, Resistance and Redefinition*. New York: Routledge.

Mustanski, B., Newcomb, M. and Garofalo, R. (2011) 'Mental health of lesbian, gay, and bisexual youth: a developmental resiliency perspective', *Journal of Gay and Lesbian Social Services*, 23 (2): 204–25.

Naezer, M. (2019) *Adventure, Intimacy, Identity and Knowledge: Exploring How Social Media are Shaping and Transforming Youth Sexuality*. Cambridge: Cambridge University Press.

National Fertility Survey (2015) *Marriage Process and Fertility of Married Couples' Attitudes toward Marriage and Family among Japanese Singles*. Tokyo: National Institute of Population and Social Security Research.

NATSAL (National Survey of Sexual Attitudes and Lifestyles) (2000) *National Survey of Sexual Attitudes and Lifestyles II*. London: National Centre for Social Research and London School of Hygiene & Tropical Medicine.

NHS Digital (2018) Mental Health of Children and Young People in England, 2017. https://digital.nhs.uk/data-and-information/publications/statistical/mental-health-of-children-and-young-people-in-england/2017/2017 (accessed 25.3.19).

Nussbaum, M. (1999) *Sex and Social Justice*. Oxford: Oxford University Press.

O'Connell Davidson, J. and Sanchez Taylor, J. (2005) 'Travel and taboo: heterosexual sex tourism to the Caribbean', in E. Bernstein and L. Schaffler (eds), *Regulating Sex: The Politics of Intimacy and Identity*. London: Routledge.

O'Neill, M. (2008) 'Sex, violence and work services to sex workers and public policy reform', in G. Letherby, P. Birch, M. Cain and K. Williams (eds), *Sex and Crime*. Cullompton: Willan.

O'Neill, M.G. (2014) 'Transgender youth and YouTube videos: self-representation and five identifiable trans youth narratives', in C. Pullen (ed.), *Queer Youth and Media Cultures*. London: Palgrave Macmillan, pp. 34–45.

O'Neill, R. (2018) *Seduction: Men, Masculinity and Mediated Intimacy*. Cambridge: Polity Press.

O'Toole, C.J. and Bregante, J.L. (1992) 'Lesbians with disabilities', *Journal of Sexuality and Disability*, 10 (3): 163–72.

O'Reilly, K. (2005) *Ethnographic Methods*. London: Routledge.

Oakley, A. (1972) *Sex, Gender and Society*. London: Temple Smith Gower.

Oakley, A. (1981) *Subject Women*. Oxford: Martin Robertson.

Oakley, A. (1998) 'Science, gender, and women's liberation: an argument against postmodernism', *Women's Studies International Forum*, 21 (2): 133–46.

Oakley, A. (2000) *Experiments in Knowing: Gender and Method in the Social Sciences*. Cambridge: Polity.

Offer, D. and Schonert-Reichl, K. (1992) 'Debunking the myths of adolescence: findings from recent research', *Journal of the American Academy of Child & Adolescent Psychiatry*, 31 (6): 1003–14.

ONS (Office for National Statistics) (2018) *Conceptions in England and Wales: 2016: Annual statistics on conceptions to residents of England and Wales; numbers and rates, by age group including women aged under 18 years.* www.ons.gov.uk/peoplepopulationandcommunity/birthsdeathsandmarriages/conceptionandfertilityrates/bulletins/conceptionstatistics/2016

ONS (2019) Domestic abuse in England and Wales overview: November 2019. www.ons.gov.uk/peoplepopulationandcommunity/crimeandjustice/bulletins/domesticabuseinenglandandwalesoverview/november2019

Optenet (2010) 'More than one third of web pages are pornographic', www.optenet.com/en-us/new.asp?id=270

Ortiz-Hernandez, L. and Granados-Cosme, J.A. (2006) 'Violence against bisexuals, gays and lesbians in Mexico City', *Journal of Homosexuality*, 50 (4): 113–40.

Osgarby, B. (1998) *Youth in Britain since 1945*. Oxford: Blackwell.

Ourahmoune, N. (2013) 'Gender, women and sexual experiences of tourism', in S. Botti and A. Labroo (eds) *NA – Advances in Consumer Research 41*. Duluth, MN: Association for Consumer Research.

Ovid (revised edition 1979) *Ars Amatoria, Volume IV*. Harvard: Harvard University Press.

Paasonen, S. (2016) 'Pornification and the mainstreaming of sex', in N. Rafter (ed.), *Oxford Encyclopedia of Criminology*. Oxford: Oxford University Press.

Page, J. (2006) 'Gay Pride Takes a Fall amid Fears and Threats', *The Times*, 27 May, p. 43.

Pagels, E. (1995) *The Origin of Satan*. London: Penguin.

Pahl, R. (2000) *On Friendship*. Cambridge: Polity Press.

Pahl, R. and Prevalin, D. (2005) 'Between family and friends: A longitudinal study of friendship choice', *British Journal of Sociology*, 56 (3): 433–50.

Pahl. R. and Spencer, E. (2004) 'Personal communities: Not simply families of "fate" or "choice"', *Current Sociology*, 52 (2): 199–221.

Papanastasiou, S. and Papatheodorou, C. (2018) 'Causal pathways of intergenerational poverty transmission in selected EU countries', *Social Cohesion and Development*, 12 (1): 5–19.

Parkinson, R.B. (2013) *A Little Gay History: Desire and Diversity Across the World*. London: The British Museum Press.

Parrenas, J. (2007) 'What kind of -sexual?', *Lesbian News Magazine*, 33: 20 March.

Parrinder, G. (1996) *Sexual Morality in the World's Religion*. Oxford: Oneworld.

Parsons, T. and Bales, R. (1955) *Family, Socialization and Interaction Process*. Chicago, IL: The Free Press.

Pascoe, C.J. (2011) *Dude, You're a Fag: Masculinity and Sexuality in High School*. Berkeley: University of California Press.

Paterson, K. and Hughes, B. (2000) 'Disabled bodies', in P. Hancock, B. Hughes, E. Jagger et al. (eds), *The Body, Culture and Society: An Introduction*. Milton Keynes: Open University Press.

Patiniotis, J. and Standing, K. (2012) 'License to cause harm? Sex entertainment venues and women's sense of safety in inner city centres', *Criminal Justice Matters*, 88 (1): 10–12.

Payne, D., Lonsway, K. and Fitzgerald, L. (1999) 'Rape myth acceptance: exploration of its structure and its measurement using the Illinois rape myth acceptance scale', *Journal of Research in Personality*, 33 (1): 27–68.

Penhollow, T., Young, M. and Denny, G. (2009) 'Predictors of quality of life, sexual intercourse, and sexual satisfaction among active older adults', *American Journal of Health Education*, 40 (1): 14–22.

Petchesky, R. (2000) 'Sexual rights: inventing a concept, mapping and international practice', in R. Parker, R.M. Barbosa and P. Aggleton (eds), *Framing the Sexual Subject: The Politics of Gender, Sexuality and Power*. Berkeley: University of California Press.

Pettett, C. (2007) 'Homophobia and harassment in school-age populations', in G. Herdt and C. Howe (eds), *21st Century Sexualities: Contemporary Issues in Health, Education and Rights*. Abingdon: Routledge.

Pew Research Center (2013) *A Survey of LGBT Americans' Attitudes, Experiences and Values in Changing Times*. New York: Pew Research Centre.

Pfeffer, C. (2014) 'Introduction: making space for trans sexualities', *Journal of Homosexuality*, 61 (5): 597–604.

Phillips, D. and Henderson, D. (1999) '"Patient was hit in the face by a fist …": a discourse analysis of male violence against women', *American Journal of Orthopsychiatry*, 69 (1):116–21.

Phillips, O. (2000) 'Constituting the global gay: issues of individual subjectivity and sexuality in Southern Africa', in C. Stychin and D. Herman (eds), *Sexuality in the Legal Arena*. London: Athlone.

Phillips, O. (2003) 'Zimbabwean law and the production of a white man's disease', in J. Weeks, J. Holland and M. Waites (eds), *Sexualities and Society: A Reader*. Cambridge: Polity.

Phipps, A. and Young, I. (2012) 'That's what she said: women students' experiences of "lad culture" in higher education', National Union of Students, University of Sussex.

Phipps, A. and Young, I. (2014) 'Neoliberalisation and "lad cultures" in higher education', *Sociology*. http://soc.sagepub.com/content/early/2014/08/19/0038038514542120

Phoenix, J. (2012) 'Sex work, sexual exploitations and consumerism', in K. Carrington, M. Ball, E. O'Brien and J. Tauri (eds), *Crime, Justice and Social Democracy: International Perspectives*. Basingstoke: Palgrave Macmillan.

Pilcher, J. and Whelehan, I. (2004) *50 Key Concepts in Gender Studies*. London: Sage.

Pilcher, K. (2008) 'Empowering, degrading or a "mutually exploitative" exchange for women? Characterising the power relations of the strip club', *Journal of International Women's Studies*, 10 (7): 73–83.

Plato (1951) *The Symposium*. W. Hamilton (translator). Harmondsworth: Penguin.

Plummer, K. (1975) *Sexual Stigma: An Interactionist Account*. London: Routledge and Kegan Paul.

Plummer, K. (1995) *Telling Sexual Stories: Power, Change and Social Worlds*. London: Routledge.

Plummer, K. (2003) *Intimate Citizenship: Private Decisions and Public Dialogues*. Seattle & London: University of Washington Press.

Plummer, K. (2005) 'Critical humanism and queer theory: living with the tensions', in N. Denzin and Y. Lincoln (eds), *The Landscape of Qualitative Research: Theories and Issues*. London: Sage, pp. 357–73.

Plummer, K. (2013) 'Editorial changeover: Farewell from Ken Plummer', *Sexualities*, 16 (7): 755–63.

Plummer, K. (2015) *Cosmopolitan Sexualities*. Cambridge: Polity.

Politt, K. (2013) 'Sexism and religion: can the knot be untied?', *Free Inquiry*, 34 (1): 27–31.

Postman, N. (1994) *The Disappearance of Childhood*. London: Vintage.

Poulin, R. (2003) 'Globalization and the sex trade: trafficking and the commodification of women and children', *Canadian Women Studies*, 22 (3): 38–43

Povey, D. (2005) 'Crime in England and Wales 2003/2004: Supplementary Volume 1: Homicide and Gun Crime', *Home Office Statistical Bulletin* No. 02/05. Home Office. London.

Power, N. (2009) *One Domensional Woman*. Winchester: 0 Books.

Price, L. (2005) *Feminist Frameworks: Building Theory on Violence Against Women*. Black Point, NS: Fernwood Publishing.

Puar, J.K. (2007) *Terrorist Assemblages: Homonationalism in Queer Times*. Durham, NC: Duke University Press.

Public Health England (2018) *Protect Against STIs*. London: Public Health England.

Pugh, S. (2005) 'Assessing the cultural needs of older lesbians and gay men: implication for practice', *Practice: A Journal of the British Association of Social Workers*, 17 (3): 207–18.

Pyle, J. and Ward, K. (2003) 'Recasting our understanding of gender and work during global restructuring', *International Sociology*, 18 (3): 461–89.

Qvortrup, J. (2004) 'The waiting child', *Childhood: A Global Journal of Child Research*, 11 (3): 267–73.

Radford, L., Corral, S., Bradley, C., Fisher, H., Bassett, C., Howat, N. and Collishaw, S. (2011) *Child abuse and neglect in the UK today*. London: NSPCC.

Rahmen, M. and Jackson, S. (2010) *Gender and Sexuality: Sociological Approaches*. Cambridge: Polity Press.

Ramazanoglu, C. (1992) 'On feminist methodology: male reason versus female empowerment', *Sociology*, 26 (2): 207–12.

Ramazanoglu, C. and Holland, J. (2002) *Feminist Methodology: Challenges and Choices*. London: Sage.

Ramone, M. and Kernes, M. (2003) 'AVN directors roundtable: old school/new school smackdown', *Adult Video News*. www.adultvideonews.com/cover/cover0103_01.html

Raymo, J.M., Park, H., Xie, Y. and Yeung, W.J. (2015) 'Marriage and family in East Asia: continuity and change', *Annual Review of Sociology*, 41: 471–92.

Raymond, J. (1979) *The Transsexual Empire: The Making of the She-Male*. Boston, MA: Beacon Press.

Reich, W. (1951) *The Sexual Revolution*. London: Vision.

Reicherzer, S. (2008) 'Evolving language and understanding in the historical development of the Gender Identity Disorder diagnosis', *Journal of LGBT Issues in Counselling*, 2 (4): 326–47.

Reeser, T.W. (2010) 'Theorizing masculinity', in T.W. Reeser (ed.), *Masculinities in Theory*, Hoboken: NJ: Wiley-Blackwell, pp. 1–54.

Renton, A. (2005) 'Learning the Thai sex trade', *Prospect*: 56–62; www.prospectmagazine.co.uk/magazine/learningthethaisextrade.

Reynolds, P. (2018) 'Sexual capitalism: Marxist reflections on sexual politics, culture and economy in the 21st century', *tripleC*, 16 (2): 696–706.

Ribbens McCarthy, J., Edwards, R. and Gillies, V. (2003) *Making Families: Moral Tales of Parenting and Step-Parenting*. York: Sociologypress.

Rich, A. (1980) 'Compulsory heterosexuality and lesbian existence', *Signs*, 5 (4): 631–60.

Richardson, D. (1992) 'Constructing lesbian sexualities', in K. Plummer (ed.), *Modern Homosexualities: Fragments of Lesbian and Gay Experience*. London: Routledge.

Richardson, D. (ed.) (1996) *Theorising Heterosexuality: Telling It Straight*. Buckingham: Open University Press.

Richardson, D. (1997) 'Sexuality and feminism', in D. Richardson and V. Robinson (eds), *Introducing Women's Studies: Feminist Theory and Practice*. London: Palgrave Macmillan.

Richardson, D. (2000) *Rethinking Sexualities*. London: Sage.

Richardson, D. (2007) 'Patterned fluidities: (re)imagining the relationship between gender and sexuality', *Sociology*, 41 (3): 457–74.

Richardson, D. (2010) 'Youth masculinities: compelling male heterosexuality', *The British Journal of Sociology*, 61 (4): 737–56.

Richardson, D. (2018) *Sexuality and Citizenship*. Cambridge: Polity.

Richardson, D. and May, H. (1999) 'Deserving victims? Sexual status and the social construction of violence', *Sociological Review*, 47 (2): 308–31.

Richardson, D. and Monro, S. (2012) *Sexuality, Equality and Diversity*. Basingstoke: Palgrave Macmillan.

Richardson, N., Smith, C. and Werndley, A. (2013) *Studying Sexualities: Theories, Representations, Cultures*. Basingstoke: Palgrave Macmillan.

Ringrose, J. (2012) *Post-Feminist Education? Girls and the Sexual Politics of Schooling*. London: Routledge.

Roberts, S. and Ravn, S. (2020) 'Towards a sociological understanding of sexting as a social practice: A case study of university undergraduate men', *Sociology* 54 (2): 258–74.

Robinson, K. (2017) 'Introduction to volume 1, part 1', in P. Aggleton (ed.), *Education and Sexualities: Major Themes in Education*. London: Routledge.

Robinson, V., Hall, A. and Hockey, J. (2011) 'Masculinities, sexualities, and the limits of subversion: being a man in hairdressing', *Men and Masculinities*, 14 (1): 31–50.

Rosenberger, J., Reece, M., Schick, V., Novak, D., Van Der Pol, B. and Fortenberry, J. (2011) 'Sexual behaviors and situational characteristics of most recent male-partnered sexual event among gay and bisexually identified men in the United States', *The Journal of Sexual Medicine*, 8 (11): 3040–50.

Roseneil, S. and Budgeon, S. (2004) 'Cultures of intimacy and care beyond the family: Personal life and social change in the early twenty-first century', *Current Sociology* 52: 135–59.

Rosewarne, L. (2019) 'The internet and research methods in the study of sex research: Investigating the good, the bad, and the (un)ethical'. in P. Liamputtong (ed) *Handbook of Research Methods in Health Social Sciences*. Singapore: Springer.

Rosser, B., Miner, M., Bockting, W., Ross, M., Konstan, J. and Gurak, L. (2008) 'HIV risk and the internet: Results of the men's INTernet (MINTS) study', *AIDS and Behavior* 13 (4): 746–56.

Royal Commission (1908) 'Report of the Royal Commission on the Care and Control of the Feeble-minded'. www.thelancet.com/journals/lancet/article/PIIS0140-6736(01)79965-5/fulltext

Rubin, G. (1984) *Thinking Sex: Notes for a Radical Theory of the Politics of Sexuality*. Durham, NC: Duke University Press.

Rubin, G. (1993) 'Misguided, dangerous and wrong: an analysis of anti-pornography politics', in A. Assiter and A. Carol (eds), *Bad Girls and Dirty Pictures: The Challenge to Reclaim Feminism*. London: Pluto.

Rush, E. and La Nauze, A. (2006) *Letting Children Be Children: Stopping the Sexualisation of Children in Australia*. Canberra: The Australia Institute.

Said, E. (1978) *Orientalism*. New York: Pantheon Books.

Sanchez Taylor, J. (2006) 'Female sex tourism: A contradiction in terms?', *Feminist Review*, 83 (1): 42–59.

Sanders, T. (2016) 'Inevitably violent? Dynamics of space, governance, and stigma in understanding violence against sex workers', *Special Issue: Problematizing Prostitution: Critical Research and Scholarship (Studies in Law, Politics, and Society)*, 71: 93–114.

Sanders, T. and Hardy, K. (2012) 'Devalued, deskilled and diversified: explaining the proliferation of the strip industry in the UK', *British Journal of Sociology*, 63 (3): 513–32.

Sanghera, J. (2007) *Shame*. London: Hodder & Stoughton.

Saraga, E. (1998) *Embodying the Social: Constructions of Difference*. London: Routledge.

Sarah, E. (1995) 'Judaism and lesbianism: a tale of life on the margins of the text', in J. Magonet (ed.), *Jewish Explorations of Sexuality*. Oxford: Berghahn.

Schilt, K. and Windsor, E. (2014) 'The sexual habitus of transgender men: negotiating sexuality through gender', *Journal of Homosexuality*, 61 (5): 732–48.

Schrager, A. (2019) *An Economist Walks into a Brothel: And Other Unexpected Places to Understand Risk*. New York: Penguin, Random House.

Schwartz, P. and Kempner, M. (2015) *Fifty Great Myths about Human Sexuality*. Chichester: Wiley.

Schwartz, P. and Velotta, N. (2018) 'The changing nature of intimate and sexual relationships in later life', *Journal of Aging Life Care*, 28 (1): 9–16. www.aginglifecarejournal.org/the-changing-nature-of-intimate-and-sexual-relationships-in-later-life/

Scott, S. and Dawson, M. (2015) 'Rethinking asexuality: A symbolic interactionist account', *Sexualities*, 18 (1–2): 3–19.

Scull, M. (2013) 'Reinforcing gender roles at the male strip show: a qualitative analysis of men who dance for women', *Deviant Behavior*, 34 (7): 557–78.

Seckinelgin, H. (2018) 'Same-sex lives between the language of international LGBT rights, international aid and anti-homosexuality', *Global Social Policy*, 18 (3): 284–303.

Segal, L. (1997) *Slow Motion: Changing Masculinities, Changing Men*. London: Virago.

Segran, E. (2013) 'The rise of the Islamic feminists', *The Nation*. www.thenation.com/article/archive/rise-islamic-feminists/

Seidman, S. (1997) *Difference Troubles: Queering Social Theory and Sexual Politics*. Cambridge: Cambridge University Press.

Seidman, S. (2010) *The Social Construction of Sexuality* (2nd edn). London: Norton.

Setty, E. (2020) '"Confident" and "hot" or "desperate" and "cowardly"? Meanings of young men's sexting practices in youth sexting culture', *Journal of Youth Studies*, 23 (5): 561–77.

Shackle, S. (2013) 'Can you be a Muslim and a feminist?', *NewStatesman*. www.newstatesman.com/religion/2013/11/can-you-be-muslim-and-feminist

Shakespeare, T. (1997) 'Researching disabled sexuality', in C. Barnes and G. Mercer (eds), *Doing Disability Research*. Leeds: The Disability Press, pp. 177–89.

Shakespeare, T. (2000) 'Disabled sexuality: towards rights and recognition', *Sexuality and Disability*, 18 (3): 159–66.

Shakespeare, T. (2006) *Disabilty Rights and Wrongs*. London: Rouledge.

Shakespeare, T. (2013) 'The social model of disability', in L. Davis (ed.), *The Disability Studies Reader*. London: Routledge, pp. 195–293.

Shakespeare, T., Gillespie-Sells, K. and Davies, D. (1996) *The Sexual Politics of Disability Untold Desires*. London: Cassell.

Shakespeare, W. (2014) *Hamlet*. Harmondsworth: Penguin.

Shakespeare, W. (2015) *As You Like It*. Harmondsworth: Penguin.

Shildrick, M. (2009) *Dangerous Discourse of Disability, Subjectivity and Sexuality*. New York: Palgrave Macmillan.

Shilling, C. and Mellor, P. (2014) 'Re-conceptualising the religious habitus: reflexivity and embodied subjectivity in global modernity', *Culture and Religion*, 15: 275–97.

Shrage, L. (1994) *Moral Dilemmas of Feminism: Prostitution, Adultery and Abortion*. New York: Routledge.

Shucksmith, M. (2004) 'A risk worth taking: sex, selfhood and adolescence', in E. Burtney and M. Duffy (eds), *Young People and Sexual Health*. Basingstoke: Palgrave Macmillan.

Shuttleworth, R. (2007) 'Critical research and policy debates in disability and sexuality studies', *Sexuality Research & Social Policy*, 4: 1–14.

Siddiqui, D. (2006) 'In the name of Islam? Gender, politics and women's rights in Bangladesh', *Harvard Asia Quarterly*, X (I): 1–13.

Sieghart, M.A. (2006) 'Can't Muslim Men Control Their Urges', *The Times*, T2, 2 Novemeber, p. 7.

Simpson, P., Almack, K. and Walthery, P. (2016) '"We treat them all the same": the attitudes, knowledge and practices of staff concerning old/er lesbian, gay, bisexual and trans residents in care homes', *Ageing and Society*, 29: 1–31.

Sinclair, J., Unruh, D., Lindstrom, L. and Scanlon, D. (2015) 'Barriers to sexuality for individuals with intellectual and developmental disabilities: a review', *Education and Training in Autism and Developmental Disabilities*, 50 (1): 3–16.

Sjöberg, J. (2008) 'Ethnofiction: drama as a creative research practice in ethnographic film', *Journal of Media Practice*, 9 (3): 229–42.

Skeggs, B. (1997) *Formations of Class & Gender: Becoming Respectable*. London: Sage.

Skeggs, B. (2004) 'Representing the working class', in B. Skeggs (ed.), *Class, Self, Culture*. London: Routledge.

Smart, C. (1989) *Feminism and the Power of Law*. London: Routledge.

Smart, C. (1995) *Law, Crime and Sexuality: Essays in Feminism*. London: Sage.

Smart, C. (1998) 'Collusion, collaboration, and confession: on moving beyond the heterosexuality debate', in D. Richardson (ed.), *Theorising Heterosexuality*. Buckingham: Open University Press.

Smart, C. (2008) *Personal Life: New Directions in Sociological Thinking*. Cambridge: Polity Press.

Smart, C. and Neale, B. (1999) *Family Fragments?* Cambridge: Polity Press.

Smith, A. (1994) *New Right Discourse on Race and Sexuality*. Cambridge: Cambridge University Press.

SmithBattle, L. (2013) 'Reducing the stigmatization of teen mothers', *American Journal of Maternal/Child Nursing*, 38 (4): 235–41.

Sontag, S. (1972) 'The double standard of aging', *Saturday Review of The Society*, 23 September, pp. 29–38.

Spencer, L. and Pahl, R. (2006) *Rethinking Friendship: Hidden Solidarities Today*. Princeton, NJ: Princeton University Press.

Spotose, T. (2013) 'Vulnerability of male commercial sex workers to HIV/AIDS', *HIV & AIDS Review*, 12: 1–3.

Stacey, J. (1996) *In the Name of the Family: Rethinking Family Values in the Postmodern Age*. Boston: Beacon Press.

Stanko, E. (1985) *Intimate Intrusions: Women's Experience of Male Violence*. London: Routledge.

Stanko, E. (1997) 'I second that emotion: reflections on feminism, emotionality and research on sexual violence', in M. Schwartz (ed.), *Researching Sexual Violence Against Women: Methodological and Personal Perspectives*. London: Sage, pp. 74–84.

Stanko, E. (2001) 'Murder and moral outrage: understanding violence', *Criminal Justice Matters*, 42 (1).

Stanko, E. and Hobdell, K. (1993) 'Assault on men: Masculinity and male victimization', *The British Journal of Criminology*, 33 (3): 400–15.

Stanley, L. (1995) *Sex Surveyed: From Mass-Observation's 'Little Kinsey' to the National Survey and the Hite Reports*. London: Taylor & Francis.

Stanley, L. and Wise, S. (1993) *Breaking Out Again: Feminist Ontology and Epistemology*. London: Routledge.

Starks, T., Payton G., Golub, S., Weinberger, C. and Parsons, J. (2013) 'Contextualizing condom use: Intimacy interference, stigma, and unprotected sex', *Journal of Health Psychology*, 19 (6): 711–20.

Staufenberg, J. (2015) 'Pansexual: What Is It – And When Did the Term Gain Popularity?', *Independent*, 31 August. www.independent.co.uk/life-style/love-sex/panseual-miley-cyrus-what-is-it-and-when-did-the-word-become-popular-104769640.html

Stein, D., Silvera, R., Hagerty, R. and Marmor, M. (2012) 'Viewing pornography depicting unprotected anal intercourse: Are there implications for HIV prevention among men who have sex with men?', *Archives of Sexual Behavior*, 41: 411–19.

Stone, S. (1991) 'The empire strikes back: Posttranssexual manifesto', in K. Straub and J. Epstein (eds), *Body Guards: The Cultural Politics of Gender Ambiguity*. New York: Routledge.

Stonewall (2018) *LGBT in Britain – Health Report*. www.stonewall.org.uk/system/files/lgbt_in_britain_health.pdf

Stryker, S. (1998) 'The transgender issue: an introduction', *GLQ: A Journal of Lesbian and Gay Issues*, 4 (2): 145–58.

Stryker, S. (2006) '(De)subjected knowledge: an introduction to transgender studies', in S. Stryker and S. Whittle (eds), *The Transgender Studies Reader*. London: Routledge.

Stryker, S. (2008) *Transgender History*. Berkeley, CA: Seal.

Suarez, E. and Gadalla, T. (2010) 'Stop blaming the victim: a meta-analysis on rape myths', *Journal of Interpersonal Violence*, 25 (11): 2010–35.

Sumpter, K. (2015) 'Masculinity and meat consumption: An analysis through the theoretical lens of hegemonic masculinity and alternative masculinity theories', *Sociology Compass*, 9 (2): 104–14.

Sun, Y., Mensah, F.K., Azzopardi, P., Patton, G. and Wake, M. (2017) 'Childhood social disadvantage and pubertal timing: a national birth cohort from Australia', *Pediatrics*, DOI: https://doi.org/10.1542/peds.2016-409

Tamer, C. (2011) 'Toddlers, tiaras, and pedophilia? The "borderline child pornography" embraced by the American public', *Texas Review of Entertainment & Sports Law*, 13 (1): 85–101.

Taylor, Y. (2009) 'Complexities and complications: intersections of class and sexuality', *Journal of Lesbian Studies*, 13 (2): 189–203.

Temkin, J. and Krahe, B. (2008) *Sexual Assault and the Justice Gap*. Oxford: Hart.

Thomson, R. (1994) 'Moral rhetoric and public health pragmatism: the recent politics of sex education', *Feminist Review*, 48: 40–60.

Thomson, R. (2004) 'Sexuality and young people', in J. Carabine (ed.), *Sexualities: Personal Lives and Social Policy*. Milton Keynes: The Open University Press.

Thomson, R. (2009) 'Transitions to adulthood', in W. Taylor, R. Earle and R. Hester (eds), *Youth Justice Handbook: Theory, Policy and Practice*. Cullompton: Willan.

Thompson, S. (2005) *Age Discrimination: Theory into Practice*. Lyme Regis: Russell House.

Thornhill, R. and Palmer, C. (2000) *A Natural History of Rape: Biological Base of Sexual Coercion*. Cambridge, MA: MIT Press.

Threlfal, M. (1996) *Mapping the Women's Movement*. London: Verso.

Tiefer, L. (2001) 'Arriving at a "new view" of women's sexual problems: background, theory, and activism', in E. Kaschak and L. Tiefer (eds), *A New View of Women's Sexual Problems*. Binghamton, NY: Haworth.

Tilley, C. (1996) 'Sexuality in women with physical disabilities: a social justice or health issue?', *Sexuality and Disability*, 14 (2): 139–51.

Todd, M. (2011) 'Sexuality and health', in A. Barry and C. Yuill (eds), *Understanding the Sociology of Health*. London: Sage.

Todd, M. (2013) 'Blue rinse blues? Older lesbians' experiences of domestic violence', in T. Sanger and Y. Taylor (eds), *Mapping Intimacies: Relations, Exchanges, Affects*. London: Palgrave Macmillan.

Todd, M. (2017) 'Virtual violence: cyberspace, misogyny and online abuse', in T. Owen, W. Noble and F. Speed (eds), *New Perspectives on Cybercrime*. London: Palgrave Macmillan.

Tolman, D. (2002) *Dilemmas of Desire: Teenage Girls Talk About Sexuality*. Cambridge, MA: Harvard University Press.

Tolman, D. and McLelland, S. (2011) 'Normative sexuality development in adolescence: a decade in review, 2000–2009', *Journal of Research on Adolescence*, 21 (1): 242–55.

Tong, R. (2009) *Feminist Thought: A More Comprehensive Introduction*. Boulder, CO: Westview.

Tucker, A. (2009) *Queer Visibilities: Space, Identity and Interaction in Cape Town*. Oxford: Wiley-Blackwell.

Turner, B. (1991) *Religion and Social Theory*. Thousand Oaks, CA: Sage.

Tutu, D. (2004) 'Foreword', in V. Baird (ed.), *Sex, Love and Homophobia: Lesbian, Gay, Bisexual and Transgender Lives*. London: Amnesty International.

Twenge, J.M., Sherman, R.A. and Wells, B.E. (2017) 'Declines in sexual frequency among American adults, 1989–2014', *Archives of Sexual Behavior*, 46 (8): 2389–401.

Tyler, I. (2008) 'Chav mum, chav scum: class disgust in contemporary Britain', *Feminist Media Studies*, 8 (1): 17–34.

Tyler, M. (2010) 'Now that's pornography! Violence and domination in adult video news', in K. Boyle (ed.), *Everyday Pornography*. London: Routledge.

Valentine, G. and Waite, M. (2012) 'Negotiating difference through everyday encounters: the case of sexual orientation and religion and belief', *Antipode: A Radical Journal of Geography*, 44 (2): 474–92.

Valocchi, S. (2005) 'Not yet queer enough: the lessons of queer theory for the sociology of gender and sexuality', *Gender and Society*, 19 (6): 750–70.

Vance, C. (1989) 'Social construction theory: Problems in the history of sexuality', in D. Altman et al. (eds), *Homosexuality, Which Homosexuality?* London: GMP Publishers.

Vanita, R. and Kidwai, S. (2001) *Same-sex Love in India: Readings from Literature and History*. New York: Palgrave.

Vares, T. (2009) 'Reading the 'sexy oldie': gender, age(ing) and embodiment', *Sexualities*, 12 (4): 503–24.

Wada, M., Hurd-Clarke, L. and Rozanova, J. (2015) 'Constructions of sexuality in later life: analyses of Canadian magazine and newspaper portrayals of online dating', *Journal of Aging Studies*, 32: 40–9.

Walby, S. (1989) 'Theorizing patriarchy', *Sociology*, 23 (2): 213–34.

Walby, S. (1990) *Theorizing Patriarchy*. Oxford: Blackwell.

Walby, S. (2005) 'Gender mainstreaming: productive tensions in theory and practice', *Social Politics: International Studies in Gender, State & Society*, 12 (3): 321–43.

Walby, S. and Allen, J. (2004) *Domestic Violence, Sexual Assault and Stalking: Findings from the British Crime Survey*, Home Office Research No. 276. London: Home Office.

Waldeck, S. (2003) 'Using male circumcision to understand social norms as multipliers', *University of Cincinnati Law Review*, 72 (3): 455–526.

Waling, A. and Pym, T. (2019) '"C'mon, no one wants a dick pic": Exploring the cultural framings of the "dick pic" in contemporary online publics', *Journal of Gender Studies* 28 (1): 70–85.

Walker, S., Temple-Smith, M., Higgs, P. and Sanci, L. (2015) '"It's always just there in your face": young people's views on porn', *Sexual Health*, 12 (3): 200–6.

Walkerdine, V. and Lucey, H. (1989) *Democracy in the Kitchen*. London: Virago Press.

Wallace, S., Wallace, C., Kenkre, J. and Brayford, J. (2018) 'Men who experience domestic abuse: a service perspective', *Journal of Aggression*. DOI: 10.1108/JACPR-03-2018-0353

Walter, N. (2010) *Living Dolls: The Return of Sexism*. London: Virago.

Wang, Y., Hunt, K., Nazareth, I., Freemantle, N. and Peterson, I. (2013) 'Do men consult less than women? An analysis of routinely collected UK general practice data', *BMJ Open*, 3 (8) doi:10.1136/bmjopen-2013-003320

Ward, R., Rivers, I. and Sutherland, M. (2012) *Lesbian, Gay, Bisexual and Transgender Ageing: Biographical Approaches for Inclusive Care and Support*. London: JKP.

Wardere, H. (2016) *Cut: FGM in Britain Today*. London: Simon & Schuster.

Warner (1999) *The Trouble with Normal: Sex, Politics and the Ethics of Queer Life*. New York: Free Press.

Webster, A. (2012) 'Living in a sexualised society: the effects on young girls', University of Essex, Department of Sociology, p. 8. https://schools. oxfordshire.gov.uk/cms/sites/schools/files/folders/folders/documents/ healthyschools/SRE%20-%20Sexualisation%20-%20The%20 effects%20on%20young%20girls.pdf

Wedow, R., Schnabel, L., Wedow, L. and Konieczny, M. (2017) "'I'm gay and I'm catholic": Negotiating two complex identities at a catholic university', *Sociology of Religion*, 78 (3): 289–317.

Weeks, J. (1985) *Sexuality and Its Discontents: Meanings, Myths, and Modern Sexualities*. London: Routledge.

Weeks, J. (1986) *Sexuality*. London: Tavistock.

Weeks, J. (1989) *Sex, Politics and Society: The Regulation of Sexuality Since 1800*. London: Longman.

Weeks, J. (1990) 'Sexuality and history revisited', in L. Jamieson and H. Corr (eds), *State, Private Life and Political Change: Explorations in Sociology*. London: Palgrave Macmillan.

Weeks, J. (2004) *Sexuality*. London: Routledge.

Weeks, J. (2007) *The World We Have Won: The Remaking of Erotic and Intimate Life*. London: Routledge.

Weeks, J. (2011) *The Languages of Sexuality*. London: Routledge.

Weeks, J., Heaphy, B. and Donovan, C. (2001) *Same Sex Intimacies: Families of Choice and Other Life Experiments*. London: Routledge.

Westmarland, N. (2001) 'The quantitative/qualitative debate and feminist research: a subjective view of objectivity', *Forum: Qualitative Social Research*, 2 (1): 223–35.

Whiting, J.W., Burbank, V. and Ratner, M. (1986) 'The duration of maidenhood', in J.B. Lancaster and B.A. Hamburg (eds), *School-age Pregnancy and Parenthood*. New York: Aldine.

WHO (2006) *Defining Sexual Health: Report of a Technical Consultation on Sexual Health, 28–31 January 2002*. Geneva: World Health Organization.

WHO (2008) *Eliminating Female Genital Mutilation: An Interagency Statement* Geneva: World Health Organization.

WHO (2014) 'The men's health gap: men must be included in the global health equity agenda', *Bulletin of the World Health Organization* doi: http://dx.doi.org/10.2471/BLT.13.132795

Willey, A. (2016) *Undoing Monogamy: The Politics of Science and the Possibilities of Biology*. Durham, NC: Duke University Press.

Williams, L. (2007) 'The pornography of consumption/the consumption of pornography', in G. Herdt and C. Howe (eds), *21st Century Sexualities: Contemporary Issues in Health, Education and Rights*. London: Routledge.

Willis, P. (1990) *Common Culture: Symbolic Work at Play in the Everyday Cultures of the Young*. Boulder, CO: Westview.

Wilson, A. (2006) 'Queering Asia. Intersections: gender, history and culture in the Asian context', *Intersections*, 14. http://intersections.anu.edu.au/issue14/wilson.html

Wilson, G. (2000) *Understanding Old Age: Critical and Global Perspectives*. London: Sage.

Wilton, T. (2000) *Sexualities in Health and Social Care: A Textbook*. Buckingham: Open University Press.

Wintermute, R. (2005) 'From "sex rights" to "love rights": partnership rights as human rights', in N. Bamforth (ed.), *Sex Rights: The Oxford Amnesty Lectures*. Oxford: Oxford University Press.

Witten, T. (2015) 'Elder transgender lesbians: exploring the intersection of age, lesbian sexual identity and transgender identity', *Journal of Lesbian Studies*, 19 (1): 73–89.

Witten, T. (2016) 'Aging and transgender bisexuals: exploring the intersection of age, bisexual sexual identity, and transgender identity', *Journal of Bisexuality*, 16 (1): 58–80.

Wonders, N. and Michalowski, R. (2001) 'Bodies, borders, and sex tourism in a globalized world: A tale of two cities – Amsterdam and Havana', *Social Problems*, 48 (4): 545–71.

Woodward, K. (1997) 'Motherhood: meanings and myths', in K. Woodward (ed.), *Identity and Difference*. London: Sage.

Woodward, K. (2016) 'Gender, sex and sexuality grand challenge', *Frontiers in Sociology*. https://doi.org/10.3389/fsoc.2016.00004

Wriggins, J. (1983) 'Rape, racism, and the law', *Harvard Women's Law Journal*, 6: 103–41.

Wright, L. (1997) 'Theoretical bears', in L. Wright (ed.), *The Bear Book*. Binghamton, NY: Haworth.

Wykes, M. and Gunter, B. (2005) *The Media and Body Image: If Looks Could Kill*. London: Sage.

Yamada, M. (2007) *The Age of Marriage Hunting*. Tokyo: Discover Twentyone.

Ybarra, M., Mitchell, K., Hamburger, M., Diener-West, M. and Leaf, J. (2011) 'X-rated material and perpetration of sexually aggressive behaviour among children and adolescents: is there a link?', *Aggressive Behaviour*, 37: 1–18.

Yip, A. (2009) 'Islam and sexuality: orthodoxy and contestations', *Contemporary Islam*, 3 (1): 1–5.

Yllo, K. and Bograd, M. (eds) (1988) *Feminist Perspectives on Wife Abuse*. London: Sage.

Yoshino, K. (2000) 'The epistemic contract of bisexual erasure', *Stanford Law Review* 52: 353–461.

281

Young, J. (1999) *The Exclusive Society: Social Exclusion, Crime and Difference in Late Modernity*. London: Sage.

YRBSS (Youth Risk Behavior Surveillance System) (2017) *Data Summary and Trends Report 2007–2017*. Division of Adolescent and School Health, National Center for HIV/AIDS, Viral Hepatitis, STD, and TB Prevention. www.cdc.gov/healthyyouth

Zaretsky, E. (1976) *Capitalism, the family and personal life*. New York: Harper & Row.

Zarzycka, M. (1997) 'Fashion photography', in R. Buikema and I. van der Tuin (eds), *Doing Gender in Media, Art and Culture*. London: Routledge.

Zuckerman, P. (2003) *Invitation to the Sociology of Religion*. New York: Routledge.

INDEX

CPSIA information can be obtained
at www.ICGtesting.com
Printed in the USA
FSHW021554190121
77679FS